Child Custody Made Simple

Understanding the Laws of Child Custody and Child Support

Webster Watnik

Cover design and illustration by Lightbourne Images copyright (c) 1997

Grateful acknowledgment is made for permission to reprint excerpts from CALIFORNIA DIVORCE HANDBOOK: HOW TO DISSOLVE YOUR MARRIAGE WITHOUT FINANCIAL DISASTER, by Judge James W. Stewart. Copyright (c) 1990 by Judge James W. Stewart. Reprinted by permission of Prima Publishing, Rocklin, CA.

Grateful acknowledgment is made for permission to reprint excerpts from DIVIDING THE CHILD: SOCIAL AND LEGAL DILEMMAS OF CUSTODY, by Eleanor E. Maccoby and Robert H. Mnookin. Copyright (c) 1992 by the President and Fellows of Harvard College. Reprinted by permission of Harvard University Press.

Library of Congress Catalog Card Number: 95-92580

Publisher's Cataloging in Publication

Watnik, Webster.
Child custody made simple: understanding the laws of child custody and child support / Webster Watnik.
p. cm.
Includes appendix, index, glossary.
ISBN 0-9649404-0-X
1. Custody of children--popular works. 2. Child support--popular works. I. Title KF547.Z9W38   1997
346.73017   QBI95-20814

Single Parent Press
P.O. Box 1298
Claremont, CA 91711
(909) 624-6058 phone
(909) 624-2208 fax

This book is dedicated to Wyeth

Table of Contents

Creating a Parenting Plan

Hiring a Lawyer

Going to Court

Alternatives to Courts and Lawyers

Legal Problems

Child Support

Acknowledgments

One of the benefits of writing a book is being able to thank my friends and others who were kind enough to help.

Towards that end, I want to thank my good friends Brad and Jeanne. We've spent way, way too much time on the phone, but I've enjoyed every second of those conversations.

Also, a very special thanks to Stephanie Sharf, a careful editor and a fantastic editorial find. Steph was brilliant at spotting disagreement in person (editorially speaking, that is). It's because of her willingness to believe in and work with a new publisher that this book came about. I can't thank her enough.

And a heartfelt thanks to my readers: Harry, a good man and a good father; Candace, a very nice mom; Neil, an incredible juggler; and Sue, a friend who was encouraging early on. I truly know how hard it is take on something else when your life is already too full.

Thanks to Shannon Bodie, a highly talented designer I was lucky to find, and Gaylene Hatch, who did a great job under a tight deadline.

Much thanks to Jacqueline Jacobsen, a special woman who truly cares about children.

And finally, thanks to my mother, Bette Watnik, who is a wonderful mother.

In memory of my father, Bud Watnik, who died June 12, 1988.

Preface

I really wrote this book for myself. When I first separated, I didn't know anything about the laws of child custody and child support. Oh, sure, I had read an article or two, but basically, I was pretty clueless.

That all changed, of course, as my own custody battle dragged on, and on, and on. Somewhere in the middle of the book, I've included a quote about how litigation can be a black hole right here on earth, consuming most of your time and money. Boy, is that the truth.

Being a writer, I tried to cope with the situation by doing what comes naturally to me—buying a good book on the subject. Unfortunately, I couldn't find one. After a lot of digging around, I found bits and pieces in various books, but no one had pulled it all together. So I did.

I tried to put in as much useful information as I could. In fact, I've made it so dense that the book turned out a bit "dry" and "legalese"-sounding.

That's why at the end of each section I've added a short story. The Story of Jessica and James is fiction. It's about a couple who must resolve custody of their only child. I included it strictly to liven up the book a bit. It's not my story or that of anyone I know.

I hope you enjoy the book.

Introduction

At first, child custody can seem complex—so many new rules, so many new obligations, so many new problems. But custody is not rocket science; it can be broken down into discrete areas and understood.

The laws of child custody describe what you are allowed to do with your children. These laws derive from more than just statutes—they are also created by court decisions that have happened in the past. While few parents have custody of their children decided by a judge, when it does happen, the judge is guided by many factors, including recommendations made by a custody evaluator.

You can avoid court by making a parenting plan, which gives you the ability to account for the uniqueness of your particular situation.

Lawyers are almost always involved in child custody, because they are your main source of legal information. It's almost inevitable that you will have to hire one.

Even though you may not fight over custody, the court retains the final authority over the children, and any arrangements you make must be approved or rejected by a judge.

When you disagree over custody but want to avoid litigation, you can choose a form of alternative dispute resolution (ADR). Even if you don't voluntarily choose ADR, in some states, you may be ordered to attend mediation.

And finally, with child custody comes child support. Dividing the children also means splitting the costs to raise them, and you are more likely to return to court to modify child support than you are to modify child custody.

This book covers the main areas of child custody.

Child Custody
and
Visitation

Chapter 1
Where Laws Come From

For all practical purposes, when you separate or divorce and you have children, you lose control.

When you were married or living together, you were in charge. You decided where to live, you decided what the children would do, and you decided how much time you spent with them.

But when you separated or divorced, you lost that authority. Now, you no longer decide where the children will live. You no longer decide how much time you'll spend with them or how much you'll buy them. Those decisions are no longer yours to make.

That's because the moment you separated, the government took over the job of deciding what is best for your children. The state—usually in the form of a family court judge—will decide what your children will do. And you will not.

That means you'll have to learn a whole new set of rules. As a separated or divorced parent, you'll have to navigate the rocky road of courts, laws, and lawyers. And you'll have to do it without a clear map of where you're going.

This book is your guide through your new world.

Where Laws Come From

When you were married or living together, you decided how to raise your children. You chose their bedtimes, you selected their activities, and you picked their school. That's what a parent does, and unless you were harming your children, you could do as you wanted.

But once you separated or divorced, your life immediately changed. The moment you were apart, you were subject to a whole new set of laws. These are the laws of *child custody.*

Child custody is composed of *laws*—formal, written-down rules that tell you what you can and cannot do—and *policies*—informal, subjective rules that spring from the personality of the judge who hears your case.

Here's a diagram:

Where Laws Come From

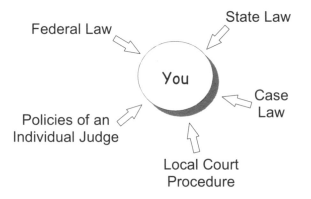

When it comes to custody, some of the rules, such as *federal statutes,* may never apply to you, while others, such as *local court procedure,* may only affect you if you actually go to court. Nevertheless, as a separated or divorced parent, you must learn the new rules.

Since there are many sources of rules and laws, it can be confusing to decide what's important and what's not. But the best place to start—and the source of most rules—are *federal and state laws.*

Federal and State Laws

When thinking about the laws in the United States, it's useful to remember that the United States is just that—a group of united states. That is, America is really a collection of individual states banded together by a common constitution, called the *United States Constitution.*

This means there is one unifying federal government and 50 individual state governments. In each government, a body of lawmakers—called a legislature—creates laws. The U.S. Congress creates federal statutes, and state legislatures create state statutes.

You need to know this because wherever you go, there are two sets of laws that apply to you—the laws of the state you are in, and the laws of the federal government. The laws of the state only apply to people who live or work in that state, while federal laws apply to everyone in the entire country.

There are other types of law—such as *ordinances* and *regulations*—but they normally don't affect you any differently because you're a separated or divorced parent.

Federal Statutes
Federal statutes cover many issues, but are usually limited to topics specifically mentioned in the U.S. Constitution—crimes, bankruptcy, immigration, interstate commerce, and so on.

When child custody is involved, there are only a few federal laws you need to know (such as the *Parental Kidnapping Prevention Act*). Most of the laws that influence your case are state laws.

State Statutes
State statutes, on the other hand, are where you'll find many of the laws that affect you. State laws, or codes, cover many issues, such as: tort law, which concerns personal injury, probate law, which covers wills, trusts, and probate proceedings, and much more.

State law also includes family law, which—among other things—describes divorce, child custody, child support, and guardianship.

As you begin to understand the laws that affect you, you'll discover that child custody and child support are always determined by the state. Because each state can—and does—create its own laws, this creates endless complications.

For example, on a simple level, the very words used to decide the issues may change. In New York, money paid to an ex-spouse for their benefit is called *alimony*. In California, that same payment is called *spousal support*.

On a more substantial level, when custody is determined by a court in one state, and a parent moves to a different state and tries to have the custody changed, this creates endless problems. The courts in both states have to determine exactly who has the authority to make the decision.

Federal and state statutes are organized by subject and published in books. Federal laws can be found in a series of books called the *United States Code,* and state laws can be found in state code books. You can find both types of books in a law library.

How Law Is Organized

To create some order out of a diverse collection of laws, lawmakers have devised a system. This system groups together laws that are similar.

The type of law can be *criminal* or *civil, substantive* or *procedural.*

Criminal Law
Criminal law concerns offenses against society. When a person commits a crime, the state charges them. In order to prove the defendant guilty, the prosecution must convince a jury beyond a reasonable doubt. If the accused person is convicted, the punishment is usually imprisonment.

Criminal defendants have many rights, including the right to a jury trial if the crime carries a punishment of six months or more in jail or prison. Also, the jury must reach a unanimous verdict for the person to be found guilty. Additionally, a criminal defendant has the right to have an attorney appointed to represent them if they cannot afford one.

Civil Law

Civil law, on the other hand, concerns private disputes between two individuals or businesses. When someone violates a civil law, they are sued by another person—the plaintiff. To prove the defendant is liable, the plaintiff must convince a judge or jury by a preponderance of the evidence. If found liable, usually that person has to pay the other.

Civil defendants don't automatically have the right to a jury trial, and if they do, only three-fourths of the jurors must agree. Also, civil defendants do not automatically have the right to have an attorney appointed to represent them if they can not afford one.

The laws of child custody and child support are civil law, and are often called family law.

Substantive Law

Substantive law governs the behavior of people. Substantive laws describe the rights we enjoy and the responsibilities we have to each other.

Substantive criminal law includes murder, kidnapping, assault, battery, etc. Substantive civil law includes—among other areas—family law, tort law, worker's compensation, and so on.

Procedural Law

Procedural law governs the process of law. Procedural laws describe how a crime or a dispute will be resolved.

Procedural criminal law involves the way people are accused and tried for crimes, and includes indictments, bail, jury trials, etc. Procedural civil law, or civil procedure, includes determining which court has authority to try your case, how much time you have to respond to a complaint, and so on.

While federal courts must follow the *Federal Rules of Civil Procedure*, state courts are free to make up their own procedures, and there are differences in procedural laws from one state to the next.

Uniform Laws

One of the problems created when each state makes its own laws is that some people may try to shop around, looking for a court in a state that will give them a favorable decision.

That's why the National Conference of Commissioners on Uniform State Laws—a group of judges, lawyers, and law professors—has created *uniform laws.* Uniform laws are drafts of laws that each state may adopt in whole, in part, or not at all.

By adopting uniform laws, states remove some of the inconsistencies, and make it more likely a case will be decided the same across state lines. Unfortunately, not all states have adopted the laws, and when they have, they may have changed them. This, of course, makes uniform laws no longer uniform.

Here are some uniform laws that may have been adopted by your state:

- *Uniform Child Custody Jurisdiction Act.* This act creates a structure for resolving interstate child custody disputes. Put simply, the state in which the child had resided in the last six months usually has jurisdiction.

- *Parental Kidnapping Prevention Act.* This act requires existing custody orders to be enforced when a child is abducted. It also authorizes use of the Parental Locator Service for tracking down kidnappers.

- *International Child Abduction Remedies Act.* This act establishes the procedures for returning abducted children to another country.

- *Family Support Act.* Among other things, this act requires new or modified child support orders to include and automatic wage assignment.

- *Uniform Interstate Family Support Act.* This act supersedes the Revised Uniform Reciprocal Enforcement of Support Act (RURESA). It is concerned with how states establish, enforce, and modify child and spousal support.

If you want to read about a uniform law that was adopted
by your state, try the *Uniform Laws Annotated (U.L.A.)*
series. These books contain the laws, a list of states that
adopted the laws, and summaries of cases that interpreted
the laws. You'll find these law books in—where else—a law library.

Case Law

Another source of rules that affect you are *case laws*.

When a court decides a case, the decision may influence future cases
with similar circumstances. That's because each judge tries to be
consistent and decide similar cases in similar ways. This history of
decisions is called case law.

A judge may follow previous decisions for three reasons:

Persuasive Authority
Sometimes a previous case has no formal authority over cases that follow
it, but the decision by the court was so clearly written, thorough, and
well-reasoned, that other judges voluntarily choose to follow it. This is
called persuasive authority.

Interpreted Statute
When lawmakers write laws, they frequently create text that is difficult to
understand or full of words that have specialized meaning. Eventually, a
judge has to apply the law, and he or she must interpret what those words
mean. When a judge decides a case by interpreting a statute, he or she
guides the decisions of future judges.

Established Precedent
When someone doesn't agree with the decision of a trial judge, they can
appeal that decision to the next higher court—called an appellate court.
When the justices in the appellate court reach a decision, their decision
creates a precedent. A precedent is a decision that judges must follow
when deciding future similar cases.

Because the court system is organized in a hierarchy, decisions made by
higher courts are formally binding on lower courts—but not the other way

around. Also, decisions made by courts in one state are only binding on lower courts in that same state. Only the very top court in the nation—the U.S. Supreme Court—makes decisions that every other court must follow.

Precedent is an important part of the law, and judges strive to make decisions consistent with earlier cases. However, when a judge decides a case, he or she is only resolving a given set of facts and a specific legal issue. Because—like snowflakes—virtually no two cases are exactly the same, judges in future cases can deviate from the decision by differentiating the case based on some inconsequential point. Also, a judge can decide a case differently by reasoning that the times have changed, and the precedent no longer holds.

When appellate or supreme courts decide a case, they publish their opinions in books called case reporters. Case reporters are organized by court and region, and can be found in—that's right—a law library.

"The court does not accept as legal precedent legal decisions in cases on 'LA Law'."

Where to Find the Law

If you want to examine your state's statutes, your public library may have them in the legal section. If you want to do more involved research—such as review cases—you'll need a law library.

Law Libraries
To find a law library open to the public, ask a reference librarian, court clerk, or a lawyer. They may steer you towards:
- The county courthouse.
- A public law school library.
- The state capital building.

Online Information
Virtually all the information published in books and stored in law libraries is available online. However, the two major legal databases, *LEXIS* and *Westlaw,* charge by the minute, and they are very expensive. Here are some others:

Cornell Law School Legal Information Institute
www.law.cornell.edu
There are many law schools on the web, and Cornell is one of the best. The resources are very well organized.

Family Law Advisor
www.divorcenet.com/law/fla.html
This site contains dozens of articles on custody, support, court procedure, grandparent's rights, mediation, visitation, and much more.

Family Law, An Overview
www.legal.net/family.htm
The Legal.Net web site includes divorce forms and much more.

Legal dot Net
www.legal.net
A site where attorneys, non-attorneys, and law students can "meet to discuss law related issues." Maintains a variety of interesting articles, as well as a list of answers to questions asked by pro pers.

Local Court Procedure

The next set of rules that affect you are known as *local court rules.* These are the rules specific to each of the thousands of family courts across the nation.

Courts make local rules to manage caseflow. For example, on a typical day, many dozens of people may be ordered to appear, a sizable number of attorneys may represent them, all the proper forms must have been filled out, copies of the forms will have to have been given to both the judge and the other party, and so on. Ensuring that all this gets done is a complex logistical undertaking, and it must occur every day the court is open.

Court rules are designed to process people and paperwork through the system. The rules help move people through the court, yet give everyone a chance to tell their story.

Court rules come from two places:

State Rules of Court

State rules usually apply to all courts within the state. A typical example is when a statute requires that certain information be given to the court— the state rule will specify the exact document that is to be used. State rules often come from the state's supreme court. They may be tailored for different counties or for different types of courts, such as municipal courts, superior courts, appellate courts, and so on.

Local Rules of Court

Local rules apply only to a particular courthouse. These rules can be quite detailed, and may include everything from the size of the paper used, to how many holes must be punched and on what edge. Local rules are created by the personnel in the local court.

When you have a dispute, you must not only understand the laws that apply, but also the rules that dictate how the dispute will be resolved. You may have a good case, but if you don't follow the rules, it will not proceed.

If you hire a local attorney, you can assume that he or she will know the local court rules. If you represent yourself, you'll need to learn the rules.

Local court rules are often published in a book that is used by paralegals and legal secretaries. Ask the court clerk where you can get a copy.

Policies of an Individual Judge

The final rules that affect you are the *policies of the individual judge.*

This one person will be making the major decisions in your life. The trial judge will decide who gets custody of the children and who pays support.

Judges play such a significant role due to two reasons: the laws allow for individual discretion by the trial judge, and each judge will interpret a situation differently.

Judge's Discretion

Though the laws in each state specify how to decide a dispute, they are—by necessity—somewhat vague. If the laws were written with exacting precision, there would be times when a strict application of those laws would be unfair. Thus, judges are given the authority to tailor the broad intent of the law to the special circumstances of your case.

This makes the individual trial judge very important. In family law, the judge must listen to all the evidence, decide what is relevant, and then apply the correct laws to reach a decision. And he or she must decide based on a preponderance of the evidence.

Judge's Interpretation

When evaluating evidence, a judge must interpret the facts to arrive at a solution. How the judge interprets those facts reflects his or her opinions and prejudices.

A judge is not a computer, and he or she will have a certain outlook, beliefs, and attitudes. When a judge evaluates a set of facts, he or she will attempt to categorize those facts and make a decision. Over time, the accumulated history of those decisions reveals the individual thinking of the judge.

The policies of an individual judge may include whether to:
- Favor mothers or fathers in awarding custody of the children.
- Accept or decline the recommendation made by a custody evaluator.
- Encourage or discourage joint custody awards.
- Consider or dismiss the child's custody preference.
- Accept or deviate from the guideline amount of child support.
- Award attorney's fees to one parent.

Lawyers know how important the personality of the judge is, and that's why they have a saying:

"Don't tell me the law, tell me who the judge is."

 How important is the judge? Here's what Lynne Gold-Bikin, former head of the American Bar Association's family law section, had to say, "Judges have enormous discretion. You can take the same set of facts and put them in front of five different judges and get five different results."

Chapter 2
The Laws of Child Custody and Visitation

Custody is the right to raise your children. Parents share custody of their children when they stay together, but when they separate or divorce, they must divide up custody.

Depending on the laws in your state, custody may be divided between legal custody, which is the right to make major decisions about the children, and physical custody, which is the right to raise the children day-to-day.

Also, many states allow each custody component to be divided between sole and joint. Sole gives one parent full and exclusive rights, while joint shares those rights between both parents.

If one parent is awarded sole custody, the other parent is almost always allowed visitation. Visitation is when the noncustodial parent may see their children.

This chapter discusses custody and visitation arrangements.

Custody Orders

When you first separate, you must decide how to share your children. If you can agree on your own, you do not need to go to court. You can simply begin living the new arrangement. But if you do not agree—or if you do agree but you want a court order that spells out what you've decided—then you have to go to court for *custody and visitation orders.*

Temporary Custody

When you go to court for the first time, the judge will create a *temporary* custody order. The purpose of this order is to say who will care for the children during the divorce.

If you agree on most issues, it may simply restate what you've told the judge. But if you do not agree, the judge will decide after a brief *hearing.*

To the judge, the most important factor in deciding temporary custody is to maintain the *status quo* of the children's living arrangements. That is, the judge seeks to assist the divorce of the parents but not disrupt the lives of the children any more than is necessary.

So, if the children were living with one parent prior to the divorce being filed, it's common for the judge to keep them in the same home during the divorce. And once the divorce is over, the judge will still be reluctant to disrupt the children's lives. That's why temporary custody is very important, and will have a dramatic effect on the final custody order.

Permanent Custody

When the divorce is over, you will be given a *permanent* custody order. This order is intended to remain in place until the children reach the *age of majority* or are *emancipated.*

If you reached an agreement on custody during the divorce, you can simply submit your agreement and the judge will likely approve it. Judges are very busy, and when you work out custody on your own, it's rare for a judge to interfere unless the children are seriously endangered.

But if you have not reached an agreement, you will have to present your arguments to the judge, and then he or she will decide where the children will live. Depending on your court, you may be able to accomplish this with another custody hearing, or you may have to go to a custody *trial.*

However you create your permanent order, it's likely the arrangement will change before the children become adults. You can agree to change the order at any time, but if you do not agree, you can return to court to change the order due to a *significant change of circumstances.*

Types of Custody

When parents divorce and children must be shared, the responsibilities for the children are usually divided two categories: *legal custody* and *physical custody.*

Legal custody is the right to make major decisions about the children, and *physical custody* is the right to have the children live with you.

In addition, legal and physical custody are each divided into two more categories: sole and joint. Sole assigns the right to one parent exclusively, while joint shares the right between the parents.

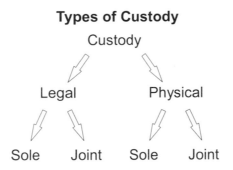

Types of Custody

Custody

Legal   Physical

Sole   Joint   Sole   Joint

Legal Custody

Legal custody is the right to make major decisions about the child. The parent granted legal custody is the guardian of the child and will make the important decisions about the child's health, education, and welfare.

The rights of legal custody can include making decisions about:
- What schools the children will attend.
- What medical and dental care they will receive.
- What religion they will be raised in.

The right to makes these decisions can be assigned to one parent exclusively, or shared between the parents.

Sole Legal Custody
Sole legal custody entitles one parent—and one parent alone—to make all major decisions in a child's life. The parent becomes the sole legal guardian, with the exclusive right to decide what is best for the child.

The advantage of sole legal custody is that it may reduce parental conflict by clearly establishing who has authority to make decisions. The disadvantage is that by making one parent solely responsible for the child, the other parent is reduced to being a visitor, prevented from having a meaningful say in the child's life.

Sole legal custody may be appropriate when one parent prefers to relinquish his or her involvement with the children, or when a parent is too unstable to make basic decisions for the children.

Joint Legal Custody
Joint legal custody shares the authority to make child-raising decisions between the two parents.

Under joint legal custody, the parents must share information with each other and must consult and agree on issues regarding the children's health, education, and welfare. The scope of issues may be stated in the custody order, or may be left undetermined.

Typically, joint custodians are required to consult each other on:
- Education.
- Religion.
- Nonemergency medical care.

Joint legal custody requires the parents to cooperate, and may create conflict when they cannot resolve even the simplest child-rearing issues. However, if a conflict arises under this arrangement, the parents may agree to consult a friend, attempt mediation, or take the issue to court.

 If you want custody of your children, do not move out of the family home. If you leave, you abandon the care of the children to the other parent, who may be granted temporary custody.

Physical Custody

Physical custody is the right to care for the children on a daily basis. The parent granted physical custody is the caretaker who provides day-to-day nurturance for the child

The rights of physical custody can include:
- In whose home the children will live.
- Who will make day-to-day child care decisions.

As with legal custody, physical custody can also be assigned solely to one parent, or shared between them.

Sole Physical Custody
Sole physical custody—also known as *primary physical custody*—assigns the day-to-day child care responsibilities to one parent. Sole physical custody usually means the children live primarily with one parent, and that parent is solely responsible for supervising their daily activities.

 In *California Divorce Handbook,* Judge Stewart offers one reason why many judges resolve custody disputes by awarding sole custody to one parent: "Designing a structured custody order requires compulsive attention to details—judges are often mind-boggled by such potential work and may unfortunately give in to a misbelief that if they order sole custody and traditional visitation, such structure and detail is less necessary."

Joint Physical Custody
Joint physical custody, also called *joint parenting,* or *shared parenting,* shares the day-to-day child care decisions between the parents. Under joint physical custody, both parents typically spend a more equal amount of time with their children than under sole custody arrangements.

An order of joint physical custody does not automatically determine how much time the children will spend with each parent. Some joint physical custody awards divide the children's time evenly, while others do not. For example, one joint arrangement might require the children to live with one parent during one week, and the other parent during the next. Or, the children might spend one-half of all non-school days with one parent, and the remainder with the other.

The advantages to joint physical custody are that because one parent is no longer burdened with the entire obligation to raise the children—each has more time to go back to school, pursue a more demanding job, build a new family, and so on. Also, because joint physical custody assures that the parents will have frequent and continuing contact with their children, it more closely approximates the relationship the children had with their parents when everyone was together. And finally, this arrangement allows the children to grow up with both male and female role models.

The disadvantage to joint physical custody is that since each parent is assured of regular contact with their children, they will also have regular contact with each other. While some parents may be able to resolve differences peacefully, others may not. Also, joint physical custody may cost more money, since each parent will have to maintain a complete family household.

Many states have statutes referring to joint custody. Some states make joint custody a *presumption* or *preference,* which means that it will be ordered unless someone proves that it would not be best for the child. Other states make it an option the parents can ask for or the judge can order. Some states allow the judge to award joint custody even over the objection of one of the parents.

Joint physical custody is appropriate when the parents can afford two family homes, and when they live close enough so that the children can maintain consistency in their school and friends.

 Joint physical custody may influence the amount of child support ordered. Under joint physical custody, parents are supposed to share the daily child-rearing responsibilities and costs more evenly, which may result in each parent paying his or her expenses directly.

Other Forms of Custody

Because individual circumstances vary, a variety of custodial arrangements have evolved. Here are some common ones:

Bird's Nest Custody
In *bird's nest custody,* the children do not go back and forth from one parent's house to the other, but instead, the parents move in and out. This schedule minimizes the disruption to the children's lives, and forces the parents to cope with the upheaval of regular moves. A common arrangement calls for the children to stay in the family home, and the parents to move in and out from a separate apartment.

Alternating Custody
Also known as *serial custody,* this arrangement calls for the children to live for a long time with one parent, and then switch and live for a long time with the other parent. While the amount of time can vary, one example would be if the children lived with one parent for a year, and then moved in with the other parent for a year. This differs from joint custody in that each parent assumes sole authority over the children while they are with them. Generally, parents choose this custody when they live too far apart—such as in different states or countries—to make other arrangements practical.

> If the custodial parent dies, custody of the children will go to the noncustodial parent. If the noncustodial parent cannot care for the children, a third party—such as a grandparent—may be appointed guardian. If no third party is available, another adult will be appointed guardian.

Split Custody

Custodial terms can be confusing, but generally *split custody* refers to the decision to split up the children by having one or more live with one parent while one or more of the children lives with the other parent. Split custody has the appearance of fairness, since each parent is granted custody of a child.

Parents who choose split custody do so because it eliminates the need for the children to routinely move back and forth. Also, it is a way to separate siblings who don't get along with each other or with a new mate.

Split custody has been criticized because it is believed that when siblings are separated from one another, they are also severed from the emotional support they gain by having brothers or sisters. This forced separation may only compound the distress they are experiencing from the divorce.

In some cases, however, the damage to the children from split custody can be reduced by arranging visitation so that the children are together at least every other weekend.

> "Often, parents not living with their children question where they should take the children and what they should plan in the way of amusement for them, particularly if the children are young. Activities may add to the pleasure of the time together, but most important is the parent's involvement with the children. A giving of self is more important than whatever material things they may get."
> *Parents Are Forever,* Association of Family and Conciliation Courts

Third-Party Custody

In some families, the children do not remain with either natural parent, but instead, are awarded to a third person. This is known as *third-party custody.* Third-party custody occurs when the biological parents either do not want the children, or are incapable of caring for them. Third parties can include grandparents, stepparents, family friends, or government sponsored foster homes.

Third-party custody disputes typically arise when the parents have voluntarily relinquished their children, or when a judge deems both parents unfit. While there is no absolute rule regarding third-party disputes, case law has established that biological parents have a "natural" right to their children superior to the claims of third parties.

Voluntary Relinquishment. Sometimes, the parents agree to let another adult raise the children. If either parent later changes his or her mind, that parent has a right to seek custody.

Unfit Parents. Because the court retains authority over the children, it can award custody to another adult if the biological parents appear unfit. Reasons that could cause a parent to be declared unfit include:

- Child abuse or neglect.
- Substance abuse.
- Deliberate abandonment of the children.
- Inability to provide the minimum income necessary to raise the children.

In the *Matter of Marriage of Hruby,* an Oregon court granted custody to the father even though he had given the child to his sister four years earlier. In that case, when a couple divorced, they gave their child to the father's sister. Four years later, the father sought custody. The court granted it, declaring, "A natural parent has the right to the custody of his or her children, absent a compelling reason for placing the children in the custody of another. The 'best interests of the child' standard applicable to custody disputes between natural parents in a marriage dissolution proceeding is not applicable to custody disputes between natural parents and other persons."

Social Theories about Child Custody

There is no consensus regarding which custody arrangement is best. Various psychologists and social theorists have speculated about how to share the children, but they do not agree. Here are some common beliefs:

Sole Custody

	Parent A	Parent B
Legal	X	
Physical	X	

Proponents of sole custody argue that children need to belong to one family unit. Firm boundaries need to be drawn around the custodial parent and the child, and the noncustodial parent should be relegated to the role of an "outside" visitor. They believe that continuing contact with conflicting parents is more harmful to the children than would be the loss of one parent.

Opponents of sole custody acknowledge that parental conflict hurts the children, but point out that few families are that high-conflict. Also, they believe that the loss of the noncustodial parent is much more harmful to the children, noting the grief and sense of abandonment children experience when they lose a parent. Additionally, they argue that a source of conflict in sole custody situations comes from the custodial parent's having power to control or deny visitation by the noncustodial parent. And finally, they point out that relegating one parent to "visitor" status is the main reason why so many noncustodial parents fail to either visit their children or pay child support.

Joint Legal and Sole Physical Custody

	Parent A	Parent B
Legal	X	X
Physical	X	

Proponents of joint legal and sole physical custody believe that this arrangement eliminates many of the problems of sole custody. They argue that it does not isolate the visiting parent as much as sole custody does, primarily because he or she still retains legal authority over the child. Also, if the parents do not cooperate, the judge can add highly detailed schedules that resolve most day-to-day disputes. This arrangement also gives the child the stability of having one primary home.

Opponents agree that this custody offers certain advantages, but state that it does not go far enough. For all practical purposes, the noncustodial parent is still cut off from having a meaningful say in the children's lives. And if the parents are truly high-conflict, the arrangement still exposes the children to parental disputes.

Joint Custody

	Parent A	Parent B
Legal	X	X
Physical	X	X

Those who argue for joint legal and physical custody point out that the children are the ones who suffer the most when parents divorce. By sharing child care responsibilities more evenly, joint custody reduces the day-to-day stress put on sole custodial parents—which helps the children. Also, joint custody protects the children by preventing either parent from controlling the other's access to them. And finally, they point to studies that show that parents with joint custody are much more likely to spend time with their children and pay child support. Put simply, they say, two parents are better than one.

Opponents of joint custody believe that it harms the children. They believe that joint custody forces the children to remain in the middle of the conflict, which can only inflict more emotional damage. They also argue that children who bounce back and forth from one home to another cannot develop a stable home life.

 Fatherless America, by David Blankenhorn, eloquently expresses the noncustodial parent's experience, "A great many visiting fathers, angered and ultimately defeated by the realization that they are reduced to becoming visitors in their children's lives, simply give up the effort and withdraw completely from their children's lives."

Visitation

Even if one parent is awarded physical custody of the children, the other parent still has a legal right to see them. The time the noncustodial parent is allowed to spend with their children is called *visitation.*

Visitation lets the parents share the children, but still protects the authority of the custodial parent to make child care decisions. For all practical purposes, *visitation time is the parenting time for the noncustodial parent.*

Types of Visitation

There are several kinds of visitation orders:

Reasonable Visitation
Reasonable visitation is a court order that allows the parents to create their own visitation schedule. It does not specify days and times, but rather, gives the parents the flexibility to work out their own schedule. The noncustodial parent is allowed to see the children upon "reasonable notice" to the custodial parent.

Because reasonable is vague and undefined, it gives the custodial parent the authority to approve or deny visitation. Reasonable visitation is best suited when the parents cooperate and communicate frequently. Reasonable visitation is not appropriate when the parents disagree about how to raise their children.

Fixed-Schedule Visitation
Fixed-schedule or *court-scheduled* visitation specifies exactly which days and times the parents will have the children. The orders are very detailed, and can include which parent will transport the children, where the exchange will take place, etc.

A fixed schedule minimizes the need for negotiation between the parents, which makes it appropriate when the parents argue and their continued contact puts the children at risk.

A fixed schedule is also useful if the noncustodial parent anticipates that the custodial parent will interfere with his or her visitation. The detailed schedule allows the judge to determine fault in the event of a disagreement.

Custodial parents must do more than simply let visitation happen—they must facilitate it. In *Smith v. Smith,* an Ohio court decided that "The plaintiff must do more than merely encourage the minor children to visit the defendant. Until the children can affirmatively and independently decide not to have any visitation with the defendant, the plaintiff must follow the court order that she deliver the children to the defendant for purposes of visitation."

Supervised Visitation

Another type of visitation is *supervised visitation.* Supervised visitation is when a neutral third party remains present during the visit in order to protect the children from dangerous behavior by the noncustodial parent. The court must approve the adult who supervises, and if the parents don't agree on who this should be, the court will appoint someone.

A judge may order supervised visitation when he wants to allow visitation, but is convinced the behavior of the noncustodial parent poses a threat to the child.

For example, supervised visitation may be ordered if the parent:
- Has been convicted of child abuse or drunk driving.
- Abuses alcohol or drugs.
- Has attempted suicide.
- Has a history of violence or domestic abuse.

Additionally, if the noncustodial parent has not seen the children for a long time, that parent may be awarded supervised visitation until he or she demonstrates ability to care for the children.

Third-Party Visitation

After divorce, other family members have the right to continue their relationship with the child. Thus, most states have enacted statutes that specifically grant visitation rights to third parties, including:
- Grandparents.
- Great-grandparents.
- Stepparents.
- Foster parents.
- Siblings.

Also, some states expand the definition of third parties beyond family members to allow visitation by "any other person having an interest in the welfare of the child."

Third-party suits typically occur when parents have divorced, and the parents of the noncustodial parent are prevented from seeing the children. Grandparents have also sued to see their grandchildren even when the parents are not divorced or separated.

Third parties can join in any lawsuit filed by the parents, or can initiate their own. They do not need the approval of the parents. If a third party seeks visitation over the objections of the parents, there is no guarantee the parents will be able to prevent it.

Third-party visitation rights may be enforced even when both parents object.

 If a third party is awarded visitation, it may affect the child support calculations. That's because a third-party may reduce the time each parent has with the children.

When Child Custody Ends

Generally, the authority of the court to decide custody ends when the child reaches the age of majority or is *emancipated.*

Emancipation occurs when a child demonstrates freedom from parental control. For a child to become emancipated, the court must order it, or a significant act must occur, such as when the child:
- Gets married.
- Joins the military.
- Moves out and becomes self-supporting.

Parents cannot simply declare a child emancipated, but must bring a special proceeding to have the child declared emancipated. The child can also seek to be emancipated. One exception occurs when a child reaches adulthood, but is incapable of managing his or her own affairs. In that situation, the parent or a third party may be appointed guardian.

Read About Divorce

The Complete Idiot's Guide to Surviving Divorce, Pamela Weintraub, Terry Hillman, Elayne Kesselman, Alpha Books, $16.95. This easy-to-read book covers everything you need to know about divorce.

Crazy Time, Abigail Trafford, HarperPerennial, $13.00. Trafford weaves her own life experiences with well-written insights and observations about the "process" of divorce.

Divorce Busting, Michele Weiner-Davis, Simon and Schuster, $12.00. Weiner-Davis offers straightforward advice on how couples can work together to save a troubled marriage.

The Divorce Decisions Workbook, Margorie L. Engle, Diana Gould, McGraw-Hill, $27.95. Filled with tear-out forms, this is a great book to get your life organized.

Divorce for Dummies, John Ventura, Mary Reed, IDG Books Worldwide, $19.99. This very readable and comprehensive book covers most of the issues you'll need to know

Divorcing, Melvin Belli, Mel Krantzler, St. Martins, $6.99. Co-written by Belli, a legendary trial attorney, this book offers excellent legal advice, as well as coping with the emotional side of divorce.

Getting Divorced Without Ruining Your Life, Sam Margulies, $9.00. Written by a divorce lawyer, here's a friendly and sensible book on getting divorced without being chewed up by the legal system.

Joint Custody With a Jerk, Julia A. Ross, Judy Corcoran (Contributor), St. Martin's Press, $13.95. A straight-from-the-hip, dead-on discussion of sharing custody with an "immature" ex-spouse.

The New Creative Divorce, Mel Krantzler, Patricia B. Krantzler, Adams Media Corporation, $22.95. An update of the long time best-seller, it takes into account recent changes in American society.

Divorce Web Sites

Divorce Care
www.divorcecare.com
A web site for joining or creating a Christian-centered support group.

Divorce Info
www.divorceinfo.com
This site has more than 190,000 articles about divorce. It includes everything from property division to parental abduction.

Divorce Net
www.divorcenet.com
A well-established site with state-by-state resources, bulletin boards, reading room, etc.

Divorce Online
www.divorceonline.com
Free articles and information on all aspects of divorce.

Divorce Source
www.divorcesource.com
A great site with helpful links, a message center, chat rooms, a bookstore, and much more.

Divorce Support
www.divorcesupport.com
How to find a divorce professional, calculate child support, etc.

Divorce Wizards
www.divorcewizards.com
Fill-in guides that take you through divorce at your own pace.

Divorce+
pages.prodigy.com/divorceplus/div00.htm
Resources, articles, "coping essays," a chat schedule, and more.

Divorcing.Com
www.divorcing.com
Lots of free information about all aspects of divorce.

Chapter 3
The Reality of Child Custody

When it comes to child custody, there's a big difference between what the law says will happen and what really happens. Here's what really happens.

First, don't be surprised if you feel differently about the children. The fact is, most mothers want custody and most fathers don't.

Second, even though you may not agree on custody, you probably won't fight. About 80% of all parents decide custody on their own.

Third, even if you disagree, you'll settle long before trial. Less than 2% of all custody decisions are made by a judge.

Fourth, if a judge does make the decision, there's a good chance it will be in favor of joint custody. At the end of a trial, joint custody is ordered 40% of the time.

And finally, divorce often means the children stop seeing one of their parents. After parents separate or divorce, more than 20% of all children have no visitation with the other parent.

This chapter discusses the reality of child custody.

Who Wants the Children

The best study for illustrating custody negotiations is *The Stanford Custody Project,* a survey of 1,123 divorcing California families conducted by Eleanor Maccoby and Robert Mnookin.[1]

When Maccoby and Mnookin asked divorcing parents what custodial arrangement they wanted, here's what they found:

What Mothers Want[2]

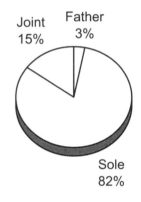

Among the separated or divorcing mothers, 82% wanted sole custody, 15% wanted joint, and 3% wanted another arrangement.

What Fathers Want[3]

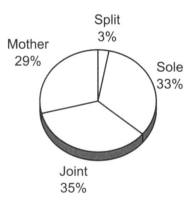

Fathers, on the other hand, only wanted sole custody 33% of the time, 35% wanted joint, and 29% wanted the mother to have custody.

To explain the difference, Maccoby and Mnookin offered several reasons. First, many parents may have felt that the mother was more experienced in the care of the children, and decided it was impractical for the father to suddenly assume the extra burdens. Still others may have believed the mother was naturally better suited to raising the children. And a third group may have disagreed, but the father deferred to the mother in the face of her strong desire for custody.

Since most mothers wanted the children, and most fathers were flexible, the parents should have been able to agree much of the time... and that's just what they did.

How Custody Is Decided

When Maccoby and Mnookin tracked how the parents decided custody, here's what they found:

How Custody is Decided[4]

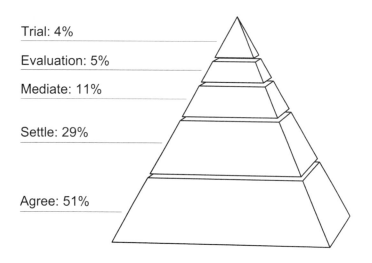

Trial: 4%

Evaluation: 5%

Mediate: 11%

Settle: 29%

Agree: 51%

In their study, 51% of the parents completely agreed on custody, 29% settled their differences without any third-party involvement, 11% decided custody during mediation, 5% resolved their differences after a custody evaluation, and only a small portion—4% of all parents who disputed custody of the children—made it to trial.

As they reported in *Dividing the Child,* "The common perception of
widespread conflict is a myth: most parents resolve the custody and
money issues without substantial conflict, and it is extremely uncommon
for disputes to require resolution by a judge."

When Parents Agree

When parents agreed on custody, they overwhelmingly decided to give
custody to Mom. Here's what they did:

Who Gets Custody When Parents Agree[5]

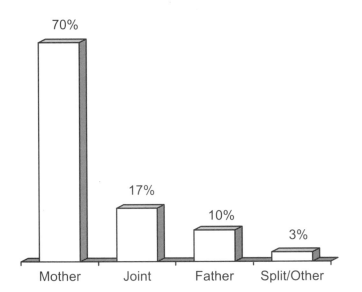

Parents agreed to give custody to the mother 70% of the time, custody to
the father 10%, and they settled on joint custody of their children 17% of
the time.

In explaining these results, Maccoby and Mnookin hypothesized that
many parents held a traditional view of parenting—meaning that mothers
should be the primary caretakers. Also, when the parents first separated,
the children remained with the mother 67% of the time.[6] This *initial
residence of the children* was important to parents who wanted to avoid
disturbing the status quo of the living arrangements.

Not all parents agreed on custody, however, and when they didn't, things changed.

When Parents Settle

Of the total number of parents who faced a custody decision, about half disagreed. Of those, many managed to settle their differences on their own. Here's what they decided:

Who Gets Custody When Parents Settle[7]

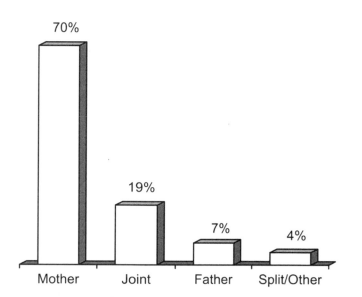

When parents settled on their own, they gave custody to Mom about 70% of the time, custody to Dad about 7% of the time, and decided on joint custody 19% of the time. These results were not very different from those of the parents who agreed on custody.

Among the many reasons why these parents settled, some may have been bargaining in the *shadow of the law.* That meant they wanted to decide custody as closely as possible to what they believed would happen in court—without actually going to court. They chose to resolve their dispute without consuming the time and money involved in litigation.

Of course, many parents could not resolve their incompatible custody desires, and they entered the legal system.

When Parents Mediate

The remaining 20% of the parents in the study could not resolve custody on their own. They were "assisted" by a third party—often a court-appointed mediator. Here's what happened:

Who Gets Custody When Parents Mediate[8]

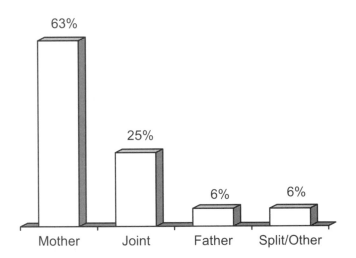

When parents took their first step into the legal system—court-assisted mediation—they ended up agreeing to give custody to Mom 63% of the time, custody to Dad 6% of the time, and settled on joint custody 25% of the time.

In the California counties where the study took place, mediation is court-ordered, and parents face a mediator who can make a custody recommendation to the judge. Because judges often adopt the mediator's recommendation, this authority is a powerful deterrent to parents who cannot resolve their custody dispute, and many parents settled at this point.

But some did not.

When Parents Go to Evaluation or Trial

The final two groups doggedly pursued their dispute to the very end of the line. These two groups—parents who settled after a custody evaluation and parents who actually went to trial—were so small that Maccoby and Mnookin combined their custody results into one table.

Here's what happened:

Who Gets Custody When Parents Go To Evaluation or Trial[9]

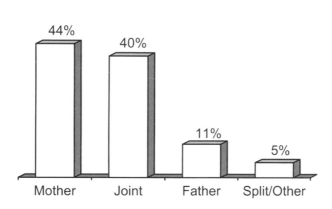

As the study revealed, something interesting happened when the parents pursued their custody dispute.

At this stage, Mom got custody 44% of the time, Dad got custody 11% of the time, and the parents ended up with joint custody 40% of the time.

In other words, when the conflict reached the end of the legal system, the odds of a mother getting custody dropped to 44%, and the odds of joint custody being awarded increased to 40%.

Maccoby and Mnookin found that—despite what happens in the movies—very few parents actually finished a trial. Of the 4% that made it to trial, only 1.5% completed it. A number of parents decided to settle "either on the courthouse steps or during the trial itself."

This means that only a tiny fraction of all divorcing parents actually have the custody of their children decided by a judge.

The Stanford Custody Project also illustrated who "wins" a custody dispute by measuring which parent achieved what they sought.

Mothers "won" more than twice as often as fathers.

In custody disputes, mothers prevailed 59% of the time, fathers prevailed 26% of the time, and neither side prevailed 15% of the time. When neither side prevailed, typically each parent sought sole custody, and the result was joint custody.

Final Custody Arrangements

When Maccoby and Mnookin added up all the custody decisions from the families in their study, here's what they found:

Final Custody Arrangements[10]

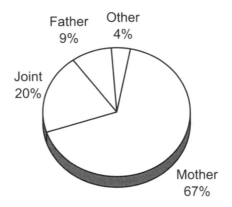

In the custody orders, mothers got custody of the children about 67% of the time, fathers got custody about 9% of the time, the parents ended up with joint custody 20% of the time, and the remaining 4% of the families reached a different arrangement.

The results of the Stanford Custody Project were very similar to those in a national study. The *National Center for Health Statistics* reported that 71% of children of divorce were living with their mothers, 15.5% were shared by their parents, 8.5% were living with their fathers, and 5% were living with other relatives. *"Advance Report of Final Divorce Statistics,"* National Center for Health Statistics.

Visitation

After custody is decided, the amount of visitation must be determined. Here's what the families in the Stanford study did:

How the Children's Time Was Divided[11]

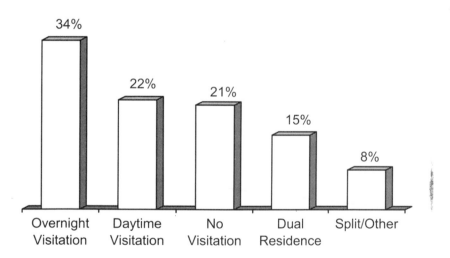

34%	22%	21%	15%	8%
Overnight Visitation	Daytime Visitation	No Visitation	Dual Residence	Split/Other

When the children lived primarily with one parent, about 34% had overnight visitation and 22% had daytime visitation with the other parent. In the study, visitation was defined as less than 4 overnight visits in a two-week period. Typically, this meant the children lived with one parent and visited the other on alternate weekends.

Another 21% of the children had no visitation with the other parent at all, while 15% of the children had just the opposite experience—they had two homes. Dual residence meant that the children spent as few as four, but as many as 10, overnights in a two-week period with the other parent.

The last group of children either lived in a split situation or were in some other arrangement. Interestingly, for many of these children, the parents were divorcing but still lived together.

The Facts of Child Custody

Dividing the Child: Social and Legal Dilemmas of Custody, Eleanor Maccoby and Robert Mnookin, Harvard University Press, $12.95.

Results from a survey of over 1,100 California families. A terrific work that contains fascinating insights into the unique problems of child custody. Be forewarned, though, some sections will make you wish you had stayed awake in statistics class.

---

1 *Dividing the Child,* Eleanor Maccoby and Robert Mnookin, Harvard University Press, 1992.
2 Ibid. Custody requested in divorce petition (table 5.1, page 99).
3 Ibid.
4 Ibid. Conflict pyramid for custody and visitation issues (figure 7.2, page 137).
5 Ibid. Physical custody outcomes by mode of resolution (figure 7.6, page 151).
6 Ibid. De facto residence of children and visitation patterns at time 1 (table 4.1, page 74).
7 Ibid. Physical custody outcomes by mode of resolution (figure 7.6, page 151).
8 Ibid.
9 Ibid.
10 Ibid. Distribution of custodial decrees (table 5.3, page 113).
11 Ibid. De facto residence of children and visitation patterns at Time 1 (table 4.1, page 74).

Chapter 4
Deciding Child Custody

Who gets the kids? That's the decision a judge must make when parents do not agree.

In the last century, fathers held the upper hand when custody of the children was in dispute. But during the 1900s, mothers gained the advantage when battling for custody.

Presently, however, every state has a formalized standard for deciding child custody. This standard is known as the *best interests of the child.*

When deciding what is best for the child, the judge considers a long list of factors. Some factors are quite specific—such as denying custody to a parent convicted of child molestation—while others are quite vague—such as determining which parent has the closer emotional bond to the child. And if the children are old enough, the judge may interview them to determine their preferences. The desires of the children, however, are usually given weight only when they are older.

After listening to both sides and reviewing the evidence, the judge then decides where the children will live and how much time they will spend with each parent.

This chapter discusses the custody decision.

Best Interests of the Child

When deciding custody, the judge must follow a legal standard to make the decision. This standard is called *the best interests of the child.*

Because parents are more than parents, and custody disputes often involve charges and counter-charges that have little to do with actual parenting skills, the judge must find a way to sift through the debris of the failed relationship and reach a practical decision.

That's why the custody decision is based on the best interests of the child. By doing what is best for the child—and not what is best for either parent—the judge focuses on the important issues and eliminates the unimportant ones.

The judge evaluates the adults in their role as parents.

 Up until the mid-1800s, children were considered property of the father, who was usually awarded custody following a divorce. Then, the *Talfourd Act* instructed judges to award custody of children of tender years to the mother. Today, the laws in all states require judges to consider what is in the best interests of the child when making a custody decision.

Deciding what is best for the child sounds good, but it's actually quite vague and open-ended. Some critics have argued that it creates *judicial bias*—custody decisions that vary from one judge to the next.

Proponents of the standard, however, insist that it cannot be any other way. If the qualifications for custody were more definite—say, a series of tests a parent must pass to get their children—then the government would be intruding into people's lives and dictating the "perfect" family.

Regardless of its flaws, the best-interests standard is one that will be followed when a judge decides custody.

Factors That Influence Custody

When deciding what is best for the child, the judge must consider a long list of factors.

Some factors are negative, such as things that might harm the child, while others are positive, such as things that will help. Some are based on past behaviors, while others are predictive of the future. No one factor is more important than the others.

Primary Caretaker

When judges decide custody, they try to determine which parent has been the child's *primary caretaker.* The primary caretaker is the parent who cared for the child day-to-day. This includes such activities as making the child's meals, taking the child to and from school, bringing the child to the doctor, helping with homework, and so on.

Generally, the parent who has been the primary caretaker is favored for custody. This reflects the belief that whoever has been raising the child may not only be more committed, but is more experienced.

Established Residence

Normally, judges want to maintain the *status quo*—or established living pattern—in a child's life. This means keeping the child in the same home, the same school, the same church, the same community, and so on. The parent who can provide continuity may be favored for custody.

 Where the children live matters. In their study of California families, Maccoby and Mnookin found that custody was awarded to the parent with whom the children were living 77% of the time.[1] As they stated in *Dividing the Child,* "In cases where parents had conflicting requests, physical custody was more likely to be awarded to the parent with whom the children were living at the time of initial separation—in other words, 'possession' was 'nine tenths of the law.'"

Logistics

Judges may also consider the *logistics* of parenting. Logistics typically include which parent has more free time or a more suitable work schedule, or which parent lives closer to the child's school or day care facilities, or how much driving each parent has to do. The parent in a more favorable position has an advantage.

Religion

Under normal circumstances, a parent's religion should not influence custody. However, if a child has been raised in a particular religion, that may be a reason to maintain continuity in the child's life. But if a parent subscribes to a nontraditional or unconventional religion, the judge must decide if the religion will threaten the health or well-being of the child. If so, it may be a factor. For example, a judge may decide that a religion that advocates avoiding doctors may put the child's health at risk.

 Custody disputes are as old as time. The story of Solomon: Two women came to King Solomon, each claiming they were the mother of a baby. To settle the dispute, Solomon ordered the baby cut in half and divided between them. One woman screamed, "No, give the child to her!" Solomon knew only the real mother would give away her child rather than let it be harmed. He gave her the baby.

Remarriage

If one of the biological parents has *remarried,* it may influence custody. This is based on the belief that two adults can more easily raise a child than one. The remarriage may also create an issue when the morals or behaviors of the new mate are questioned.

Sex

This factor is vague, but generally, only behavior that affects the child is relevant. This factor can either be positive or negative.

For example, when a parent becomes involved with a new partner, it can demonstrate a positive, healthy relationship. In other cases, the sexual activities of the parent and the new partner may place the child in an embarrassing, stressful situation.

However, if the parent takes a new partner who is of the same sex, that will influence custody. A number of courts will deny custody to a homosexual parent, based upon the reasoning that children of gay parents live in an immoral environment, and that the children will be harmed by the ridicule of other children.

Drinking and Drugs
When a parent abuses alcohol or drugs, this behavior creates a dangerous environment for the child and it will influence custody. Be aware, however, that some judges believe that if one parent uses drugs, the other parent probably does, also.

Four Factors That Do Not Influence Custody

1. *Gender.* There is no legal preference for awarding custody to either parent based on their sex. Mothers and fathers have an equal right to custody of their children.

2. *Race.* Judges may not use race as the sole basis for making a custody decision.

3. *Physical Disability.* A judge cannot base a custody decision solely on a parent's handicap that only affects his or her ability to play with the children in physical activities.

4. *Not Married.* Custody cannot be denied to either parent because they were unmarried when the child was born.

Abuse and Violence
When deciding custody, judges must consider whether either parent has been *violent* or *abusive.*

Violence. While domestic violence usually influences custody, there are some judges who believe that spousal battering is not relevant to the decision. However, if a parent has battered the children, they may lose be denied visitation, or be restricted to supervised visitation.

Child Abuse. Child abuse is any behavior that harms a child. *Physical abuse* is physically hurting the child, and includes punishments that bruise or burn the child. *Emotional abuse* is speech intended to humiliate, or to lower the child's self-esteem. *Sexual abuse* is any behavior by an adult directed toward a child for the adult's sexual gratification. All forms of child abuse will influence custody.

Work and Income

In theory, your *work and income* shouldn't influence custody. In reality, they might. Some judges may feel that the parent with more money can take better care of the children. The reasoning is that this parent can afford a better house in a better school district. This penalizes the lower-income parent, who may have chosen a less demanding—and less rewarding—career in order to devote more time to the children. In either case, children require parents who have time for them, and a parent with an involving, time-consuming job is at a disadvantage.

School

Since children spend most of their awake hours at school, the *educational opportunities* each parent offers may be a factor. School issues can include curriculum differences, such as which school has an enriched or specialized program, or pupil performance, such as which school has a higher-scoring student population. School may also become a factor when the child has perfect attendance while living with one parent, but a record of tardiness and absences when residing with the other.

Children's Wishes

Children's wishes are always a factor. While children don't have the final say on custody, their preferences will be considered.

When a child expresses a preference, the judge must decide if the child is of sufficient *age and capacity to reason* to make a choice. This usually means the child has turned twelve years old, though some judges have listened to children as young as seven.

In addition to hearing the stated preference, the judge must assess the child's maturity, insight, and ability to reason. For example, if a child wants to be with the parent who will let him do "whatever he wants," the judge may not approve. Or, if a child's preference for one parent seems rehearsed and artificial, the judge may decide the child was coached, and discount his or her statements. On the other hand, if a child genuinely feels closer to one parent, this preference may be respected.

Special Interest Support Groups

In the area of child custody, many advocacy groups exist. Some argue for fathers, while others advocate for mothers. And some, such as the *Children's Rights Council* and *Joint Custody Association,* promote shared parenting.

Here are some support groups with a point of view:

National Congress for Men and Children
2020 Pennsylvania Avenue N.W.
Suite 277
Washington, DC 20006
(800) 733-DADS

Men's Defense Association
17854 Lyons St.
Forest Lake, MN 55025-8107
(602) 464-7663

National Organization for Women (NOW)
1000 16th St. NW
Washington, DC 20036
(202) 331-0066

National Organization of Single Mothers
P.O. Box 68
Midland, NC 28107
(704) 888-KIDS

Children's Rights Council
220 Eye St. NE
Washington, DC 20002
 (800) 787-KIDS

Joint Custody Association
10606 Wilkins Avenue
Los Angeles, CA 90024
(310) 475-5352

Interviewing the Children

Asking children what they want poses problems.

The children are harmed because they are being forced to take sides. This makes them feel trapped, or that they are pawns, or that if they tell the truth, they will hurt one of their parents.

The professionals who interview the children also have difficulties, because they know children have a natural instinct for survival, and will say whatever they must to appease their parents.

Nevertheless, children are routinely asked their preference. One way they can be asked—by taking the stand as a witness in open court—is generally avoided. Instead, judges commonly rely on the following methods to learn the child's views on custody:

Judge
Sometimes the judge will talk to the child *in camera*—in the judge's chambers. This is a private meeting between the child and the judge. The lawyers may be allowed to attend, and either parent can request that a court reporter make a record.

In the meeting, the judge may want to hear the child's wishes first-hand, or might want to give the child a chance to express an opinion so that he or she doesn't feel left out. Or, perhaps the judge wants to explain why the child will not be granted his or her already-expressed preference.

 A *guardian ad litem* is someone appointed by the judge to represent the child's best interests. In custody disputes, the guardian ad litem may make a recommendation to the judge.

Mental Health Professional
If the judge has appointed a mental health professional to make a custody evaluation, the report may include the child's custody preference.

Attorney
If the judge has appointed an attorney to represent the child, the attorney may convey the child's wishes.

Judge's Bias

In addition to the factors mentioned above, there are other elements that may play a role in the custody decision. One element is *judicial bias.*

When deciding custody, a judge is supposed to base the decision on the facts. He or she plays the role of an impartial arbiter who listens to each side and then makes a decision.

In reality, deciding custody is difficult. A judge must choose between two imperfect people, and he or she must do so without having much in the way of concrete facts.

The judge will interpret the evidence based on his or her own standards, beliefs, and prejudices.

The legal standard that judges must follow—what is in the best interests of the child—allows plenty of discretion in deciding custody. Some judges will approach the decision already assuming that mothers are better than fathers at raising children. Other judges will assume that fathers are better than mothers when it comes to raising sons.

Whatever the presumption, judicial bias is unavoidable in an area as subjective as family law.

Custody Evaluations

When parents dispute custody, it's quite possible the judge will order a *custody evaluation.* A custody evaluation is a report used by the judge to help with the custody decision.

Judges order custody evaluations in order to relieve some of the court congestion while still keeping control of the final custody decision. They also order evaluations when one parent accuses the other parent of behavior that harms the child.

The Evaluator
The custody evaluation will usually be made by a *mental health professional*—typically a licensed psychiatrist, psychologist, or social worker. These forensic mental health professionals may also specialize in child psychology.

The choice of evaluator is crucial, because there is a wide range of ability levels. Some are extremely competent, and possess an almost uncanny insight into the families they analyze. Others are utterly incompetent, and may make a devastating evaluation that defies all judgment and common sense. Because the quality of the evaluation is so critical, the choice of who will do the evaluation plays a significant role in the final custody decision.

 Here's what one divorce lawyer has to say, "Trial judges, when faced with a hotly contested custody case, solve the vagueness dilemma by overreliance on expert opinions of mental health professionals. The advantage of psychological evaluations for family law judges is that a custodial decision rests in scientific evidence and expertise. In turn, the evaluator rests in the knowledge that the custody decision really lies with the family law judge." Michael Brennan

Gathering the Information
The purpose of the evaluation is to assess each parent's ability to be a parent. To do that, the evaluator has many ways to gather information, including:

Conducting Interviews. The evaluator may interview everyone who is relevant to the custody decision, including:
- Parents.
- Children.
- Grandparents.
- Stepparents.
- Teachers.
- Neighbors.

Reviewing Documents. The evaluator may review all appropriate papers, including documents related to work or financial matters, medical records, and school reports.

Administrating Psychological Tests. The evaluator may administer psychological tests to the parents and interpret the results. Interestingly, these tests do not test parenting skills, but instead, measure personality characteristics associated with parenting.

Writing the Report
Once the evaluator has gathered the information, he or she must write the report. Depending on the purpose of the report, it may be limited it to the child, one parent, or all family members.

The report will be detailed, and may include a recommendation. The recommendation will be based on the evaluator's own opinions—a combination of interpretations from the psychological tests and impressions from first-hand interviews and observations. In the recommendation, the evaluator may suggest which parent should be granted custody, as well as how much time the noncustodial parent should be allowed for visitation. If the report does not contain a custody recommendation, the evaluator has decided to leave that critical decision to the judge.

Using the Report
The custody report will be given to the judge, and copies will be supplied to the attorneys for both parents.

Recommendations from custody evaluations are routinely adopted by the court. This is because the report is considered an unbiased report by an objective, neutral expert. Even if the expert is wrong, their opinions are important. Also the judge appointed the evaluator to help reach the correct decision. It doesn't help to ignore the advice that was sought. And finally, when a judge rejects a recommendation from an evaluator, lawyers take notice. The judge knows that—by rejecting the recommendation—he or she encourages other lawyers to challenge future evaluations.

After submitting the report to the court, the evaluator is considered an *expert witness*—someone with special training—who can be cross-examined under oath by either attorney.

 "The judge follows the recommendation of the custody evaluator at least 86 percent of the time in permanent custody disputes, and 99.9 percent of the time in temporary awards of custody pending settlement or trial of the case." *California Divorce Handbook*

Parenting Books

"Does Wednesday Mean Mom's House or Dad's?", Marc J. Ackerman, John Wiley and Sons, $16.95. Written by a clinical psychologist, this is a good primer for understanding the reality of custody and the legal system.

Families Apart, Melinda Blau, Perigee, $12.00. A very clear and well-written book that explains how to overcome the animosity in divorce and cooperate "for the sake of the kids."

The Good Divorce, Constance Ahrons, Basic Books, $14.00. Written by a social scientist, this book focuses on the relationship between ex-spouses after divorce.

Helping Your Kids Cope With Divorce the Sandcastles Way, M. Gary Neuman, Patricia Romanowski, Times Books, $25.00. An excellent book that describes the Sandcastles program, a national divorce program for children. It includes games and activities parents can do with their children.

Mom's House, Dad's House, Isolina Ricci, $13.00. This book describes the problems of divorce and what to do about them in a way that is clear, so straightforward, and so balanced—it's routinely used in divorce classes and recommended by mediators.

Second Chances, Judith S. Wallerstein, Sandra Blakeslee, Houghton Mifflin, $12.95. A classic, this book is full of emotional insights about the long-term effects of divorce.

Vicki Lansky's Divorce Book for Parents, Vicki Lansky, Book Peddlers, $5.99. A very sensible and well-written book that reminds parents to pay attention to how divorce affects the children. A terrific book to read anytime during or after a divorce.

---

1 *Dividing the Child,* Correspondence of actual residence at time 1 and time 3 with physical custody decrees (table 8.1, page 166).

Chapter 5
Modifying Child Custody

No matter how detailed your custody arrangements are, things are bound to change.

One parent might want to remarry and start a new family, or the other parent might want to move away. Or either parent might start a new job and work different hours.

And even if the parents don't change, the children will change. As they grow older, they will find new hobbies, interests, and activities. School, friends, and sports will all evolve as the children grow. The schedule that worked one year won't work the next.

The only thing certain in child custody is that nothing is certain.

When change occurs gradually—such as the children growing older—simple inertia may prevent you from renegotiating custody. But when a distinct event occurs—such as a residential move or a remarriage—it may be time to update the arrangement.

Because custody modifications disrupt a child's life, many judges are reluctant to change the arrangements. This reluctance is intended to promote stability and discourage the parents from constantly returning to court. To successfully modify custody, the parent seeking the change must show that a *significant change of circumstances* has occurred.

This chapter discusses modifying child custody.

Significant Change of Circumstances

When you are handed your court orders, your lawyer will tell you that child custody is *subject to modification* at any time. That's true, but it's misleading.

While custody orders can be modified at any time, that doesn't mean they will be. When you try to modify custody, you must demonstrate there has been a *significant change of circumstances.*

A significant change of circumstances is some event or change that has such a profound impact on the child that a change of custody is necessary.

It's more difficult to change custody than it is to gain custody in the first place.

That's because, when custody is first decided, the judge assumes both parents are equally fit. But once custody is settled, and one parent is deemed to be more fit, it becomes the responsibility of the other parent to prove that something has occurred that alters the basis for the original decision.

 Occasionally, a custodial parent is temporarily unable to care for a child—such as having to go on a trip or into the hospital. If that happens, the parent may seek a temporary modification giving custody to the other parent. The order can specify the date or event when the modification ends and custody reverts back.

Of course, the parents do not have to return to court if they can agree on how to change custody. If the parents agree and wish to file their decision with the court, they can present the new arrangement—called a *stipulated modification*—to the judge. Unless the arrangement is not in the child's best interests, the judge is likely to approve it.

If the parents do not agree, one parent must file a *motion to modify.* Filing a motion will require that both parents attend a hearing. At the hearing, the parent requesting the change must demonstrate why the change should occur.

Factors That Influence a Modification

When considering a request to change custody, the judge will look to see if there has been a *significant change of circumstances.*

What constitutes a significant change of circumstances is different in each state. Generally, however, the judge follows the same standard in deciding whether to change custody as he did in setting custody the first time—*the best interests of the child.*

The parent seeking the change must usually demonstrate that something has occurred in the custodial parent's life, and that this change has resulted in the child's present environment endangering his or her physical, mental, moral, or emotional health.

Here are some typical factors a judge will consider:

Residential Move

When parents move, they often force a change in the court orders. That's because a residential move may require that a new schedule be created. If the custodial parent wants to move, and their new home is so far away that the noncustodial parent is practically prevented from seeing the children during the school year, the judge will have to decide how to change the custody orders.

Also called a *long-distance move* or *moveaway*, generally the move must force the noncustodial parent to drive at least an hour to see the children.

In resolving a moveaway dispute, a judge has many options. One alternative is to award the noncustodial parent more time with the children over the summer and during the holidays as compensation for the time lost during the school year. If a judge chooses this option, he may also require that the moving parent pay for all additional transportation costs so the children can visit the noncustodial parent. Another option is to switch custody completely from one parent to the other. A third option is to bar the custodial parent from moving away beyond a given distance—say fifteen miles. This restriction maintains the capability of both parents to continue seeing their children.

The flip side to a moveaway is that the same restrictions against moving away placed on the custodial parent are usually not placed on the noncustodial parent. That's because—if the noncustodial parent seeks to move away—they are not interfering with the custodial parent's access to the children.

Destabilized Household

Any significant event that *destabilizes the household* of either parent may affect custody. If the custodial parent's home is destabilized, the noncustodial parent may be awarded custody. If the noncustodial parent's home is destabilized, the custodial parent may seek to have visitation restricted or prevented. Destabilizing events include any devastating event, such as:

- Death of a household member.
- Arrest of the parent for a crime.
- Parental desertion of the children.

Five Bad Reasons to Seek a Modification

1. To raise or lower child support.

2. To maintain contact with the other parent through ongoing litigation.

3. To relieve your loneliness.

4. To prove you're the "better" parent.

5. To punish or get revenge on the other parent.

Custodial Interference

If the custodial parent *interferes* with the noncustodial parent's efforts to visit the children, the judge can respond by awarding custody to the noncustodial parent.

Remarriage

If a parent *remarries,* it may affect custody—but not in a direct way. That is, it's not the marriage that justifies a change in custody, but the changed circumstances in the household that may justify a change.

For example, if the custodial parent remarries, that event may create a healthy environment for the child. But if the new mate endangers the child, or if the custodial parent and their new mate argue in front of the child or begin neglecting the child, there may be a reason to change custody. Conversely, if the noncustodial parent remarries, their household may now represent a more stable home environment for the child—and that may be a reason to change custody. However, the remarriage of the noncustodial parent does not alter the household of the custodial parent, and the custodial parent may well argue that if they were the appropriate caretaker for the child before, they continue to be.

Sex
Only a few states consider cohabitation with a *new mate* reason to modify custody. However, if a parent suddenly reveals a homosexual preference, the judge may decide a change is appropriate. If the custodial parent demonstrates homosexual desires, they may lose custody of the children. If the noncustodial parent announces a same-sex preference, the effect on custody will be less pronounced because this parent presumably has less of an impact on the children's lives.

In *Palmore v. Sidoti,* the U.S. Supreme Court ruled that race could not be the sole basis for a modification of custody. In that case, a white couple had divorced and the mother was awarded custody of the child. She then married a black man. The father sought custody, won at trial, but the Supreme Court reversed the decision.

Drinking and Drugs
If a parent *drinks to excess* or *abuses drugs,* it's likely the judge will change custody. If the custodial parent abuses substances, that parent may lose custody. If the noncustodial parent abuses alcohol or drugs, visitation may be severely restricted or stopped completely, or the visitation may be supervised by a third party.

Abuse and Violence
Whenever a parent endangers the children by being *physically* or *sexually abusive,* a judge will likely change custody. If the custodial parent abuses the children, the judge may remove the children from the home and award custody to the other parent. If the noncustodial parent engages in abusive behavior towards the children, the judge may restrict visitation, order supervised visitation, or stop visitation altogether.

Work and Income
Change in a parent's *income* generally is not a significant change of circumstances. Rising income of the noncustodial parent or falling income of the custodial parent do not usually trigger a change of custody. However, work may be important if it means a change in the household of either parent. For example, if the custodial parent suddenly has to work long hours and leave the children home alone, that may be a reason to change custody. Or, if the noncustodial parent is injured and goes on disability, they may suddenly be unable to provide supervision of the children.

Children's Wishes
Finally, since *children's wishes* almost always play a part in custody decisions, if a child wishes to change custody, that may constitute a change of circumstances. However, a judge still has to evaluate if the child is of sufficient age and capacity to reason to make a choice, and there is no guarantee that it will happen.

 The more things change. In their study of divorcing families, Maccoby and Mnookin found that 28% of the children switched homes within three years after the divorce, and 45% changed the amount of visitation with the noncustodial parent—about two-thirds decreasing the amount of time and the rest increasing it. *Dividing the Child*

Reluctance to Change Custody

When it comes to the children's living arrangements, judges are typically conservative and try to avoid making frequent changes. They do this for the following reasons:

Stability
Judges know that a divorce unsettles the children, and they try to promote stability in the child's life by maintaining the *residential status quo*. By avoiding constant changes in the living arrangements, the judge tries to minimize the harm to the child's emotional development.

Avoiding Litigation
Judges also know that some parents will fight over the children no matter what they put in custody orders. They recognize that custody of the

children is not the real issue, but rather, the parents have an underlying, hidden agenda for the dispute.

For these parents, the judge wants to discourage the endless litigation that simply uses up valuable court time without genuinely resolving the conflict. Thus, the judge avoids changing custody to discourage the parents from initiating endless lawsuits.

 In *Perreault v. Cook,* one judge said he would only change custody when "Circumstances affecting the welfare of the child have been so greatly altered that there is a strong possibility [that] the child will be harmed if he continues to live under the present arrangement."

Modifying Visitation

In addition to changing custody, parents may also need to change visitation.

As with custody, visitation can be modified any time there is a *significant change of circumstances.* When deciding whether to change visitation, a judge will use the same standard to make his decision—what is in the *best interests of the child.*

Here are some common reasons to modify visitation:
- The custodial parent is interfering with the "reasonable" visitation of the noncustodial parent.
- The noncustodial parent is harming or endangering the child during their visitation.
- The children wish to see more—or less—of the other parent.

Custodial Interference
When the custody order calls for the noncustodial parent to have *reasonable visitation,* it may not specify the exact days and times when visitation will occur. While the intent is to let the parents work out the schedule themselves, this may create conflict when they cannot agree on what is reasonable and what is not. Thus, there may be times when the noncustodial parent is frustrated in their attempt to see the children.

Under these circumstances, the noncustodial parent may seek visitation orders that secure more reliable access to the children. This means asking the judge to create a more detailed schedule—one that contains the exact days and times for visitation.

A modification generally becomes effective on the date the judge signs the order. However, the judge can also make the effective date retroactive to when the parent filed the motion. If child support is involved, this might create an immediate arrearage for the paying parent.

Child Endangerment
Another reason for changing visitation is when the noncustodial parent *endangers the child.*

Behavior by the noncustodial parent during visitation that may endanger the child includes neglect or abandonment, drinking, drug use, molestation, or other criminal activities.

A parent not only has the right, but the obligation to protect their child. If the noncustodial parent is endangering the child, the custodial parent must notify the court of the problem.

When a judge is convinced a threat exists, he can take many steps to protect the child. Among other things, he can order the noncustodial parent be allowed only supervised visitation—which means a neutral third-party must be present during the entire visitation period. Or, the judge can terminate companionship, which means the noncustodial parent is barred completely from seeing his or her children.

However, because custody law encourages contact between children and their parents, even in the case of genuine endangerment, it's possible the noncustodial parent will be allowed to seek counseling or take other steps before a judge permanently bars them from seeing their children.

Child's Wishes
A final reason to change visitation is when the children want to. When a child expresses a preference, the judge must evaluate the child's ability to understand the choice and consider whether the child is making the

choice of his or her own free will or is being coerced by a determined parent. Also, the judge is more likely to grant the preferences of an older child over a younger one.

Gender Wars

Books for Women

Cutting Loose, Ashton Applewhite, HarperCollins, $13.00. An upbeat and inspiring book that debunks the myth that divorce causes emotional and economic ruin.

Suddenly Single, Kerry Hannon, John Wiley and Sons, $14.95. A financial writer tells women how to handle their money for the first time.

What Every Woman Should Know About Divorce and Custody, Gayle Rosenwald Smith, Berkley Publishing Group, $14.00. Crucial advice from judges, lawyers, and therapists on how women can protect themselves in prolonged divorce or custody proceedings.

Books for Men

Divorced Dads, Sanford L. Braver, Diane O'Connell, Putnam, $24.95. A psychology professor dispels the popular myths about divorce, including that men abandon their children.

Fatherless America, David Blankenhorn, HarperPerennial, $14.00. A thoroughly researched book that argues that many problems in families are caused by the lack of active, involved fathers.

Fathers' Rights, Jeffery Leving, Kenneth A. Dachman, Basic Books, $12.50. *Fathers' Rights* accurately describes the legal system from a man's point-of-view. A must-read for men who go to court for custody of their children.

Screw the Bitch, Dick Hart, Victor Santoro, Loompanics Unlimited, $17.95. Despite an awful cover, this book contains solid advice for men who want to "get lost" and not be found.

Single Parenting Web Sites

Alliance for Non-Custodial Parents Rights
www.ancpr.com
Dedicated to preserving and promoting the inalienable human rights
of noncustodial parents.

Single Dad's Index
www.vix.com/pub/men/single-dad.html
Part of the World Wide Web Virtual Library, this site opens the door
to plenty of interesting and factual articles on custody, support,
visitation, and more.

Single Fathers
www.single-fathers.org
A site designed "to support those fathers who have accepted the
responsibility of raising their children alone."

Single Mothers by Choice
www.parentsplace.com/readroom/smc/index.html
Also a part of *ParentsPlace.com,* this site is home to this woman's
support group.

Single Parent Resource Center
www.singleparentresources.com
Providing links and information to provide support to single parents
on topics such as divorce, parenting, single dads and moms,
counseling, organizations, publications, spirituality.

Single Parents Association
www.singleparents.org
International nonprofit organization devoted to providing educational
opportunities and fun activities for single parent families.

Solo Parenting Alliance
www.solo.org
Grassroots organization run by and for single parents.

The Story of Jessica and James

Break Up

When Jessica Rorhman first saw Jim Miller's paintings hanging on the walls of the Madison University student union, she fell in love with him.

One afternoon, Jessica dropped by the union to check out the work of the other students in the fine arts program, and when she saw Jim's watercolors, she simply stopped. Jim had painted bare trees standing starkly in the snow. Jessica stared at the paintings. The trees were so dark—*so brave,* she thought—unmoving in the broad expanse of delicate, unbroken snow. Jessica was touched, and she knew she had to meet the artist.

A few months later, she finally did meet him. There was a party one night in a dorm, and when a girlfriend pointed him out, she went right up to him to talk to him. She felt very brave doing that, but because it was really about art, she decided it was okay.

Jim didn't enjoy parties much, preferring instead to hang out with his roommate or spend time in the studio, but when this attractive girl came right up to him and began talking to him, he couldn't help but be interested. She really liked his paintings, and Jim felt for the first time that someone understood what he was trying to do. Jessica liked the calm look in his eyes, and—as she would laugh about later—found his hands unbelievably sexy.

Fourteen years later, Jim sat in his favorite chair and looked at the watercolors Jessica had admired so much when they first met. Their house was quiet, empty, save for him. A car drove down the street and was gone. Somewhere in the distance, a bird sang out.

As Jim looked at the paintings, he felt numb, cold, empty. Jessica had just moved out. And she had taken their only child.

*   *   *

For the next few days, Jim walked around the house aimless, disconsolate, purposeless. One moment he felt depressed and miserable, and the next he was outraged that she could walk out so easily. Jim desperately missed his son, Julian, and more than anything else, wanted to talk to him.

At first, Jim tried calling Jessica, but the answering machine was always turned on, so all he could do was leave long, rambling messages. Jessica never called back.

Several times during the week, Jim went by the doctor's office where Jessica worked as a records technician, but Monica, the receptionist, always said she was too busy to see him.

Finally, on Friday, Jessica called. Jim was in his studio—which was nothing more than a spare bedroom with some glazed windows and a rickety, broken-down easel—when the phone rang. He rushed into the bedroom and sat on the edge of the bed.

"Hello?"

"Hi."

"Where are you?" Jim asked.

"Home," said Jessica.

"I called," said Jim accusingly. "You never called back."

"I know," Jessica responded simply. She didn't elaborate, and that made Jim more nervous.

"Where's Julian?"

"With me."

"Can I talk to him?" Jim asked.

"Not right now."

Jim struggled to stay calm. "I want to see that he's all right."

"He's fine," Jessica said defensively. "You don't have to worry about him."

"I'm not. When am I going to see him?"

"I thought that you could have him for the weekend. I'll drop him off tomorrow morning, and then pick him up Sunday night."

Jim fell silent. As he sat on the bed, he stared at the pictures of Jessica and Julian on top of the dresser. Julian was smiling, his eyes bright and shining. Jessica had a more serious expression, with her lips pressed tightly together, but the corners of her mouth wrinkled up in an involuntary grin.

"Well?" she asked. "Is that okay?"

"Do I have a choice?" said Jim, his eyes pulling away from the picture.

"Don't make this harder than it already is." The tension in Jessica's voice was palpable. Jim realized how difficult it was for her.

"All right," he finally said.

"Good," said Jessica. "See you tomorrow." She hung up.

"Bye," said Jim. He hung up the phone and fell back on the bed.

Then he began to cry.

*   *   *

Creating a Parenting Plan

Chapter 6
Negotiating Your Parenting Plan

When you separate or divorce, you are handed a custody order that spells out the rights and responsibilities you have for your children.

That's fine as far as it goes, but no court order can account for the complexity of raising children in two homes. Inevitably, many issues will not be covered, and if you litigate every disagreement, you will be in court for the rest of your natural life.

That's where a parenting plan comes in.

A parenting plan is an optionally negotiated agreement that describes how to handle specific issues. It can be as simple as a few sentences, or as formal as a notarized contract. It can be as short as a quick note, or as long as an unedited novel. In short, the plan can be whatever you want it to be.

More than anything else, a parenting plan allows you to continue to do business with the other parent.

This chapter discusses the benefits of a parenting plan.

Parenting Apart

When parents live together, they raise their children together. When one parent is working or sick, the other can care for the children. When one parent is angry or depressed, the other can intercede to protect the children. This *parental alliance* allows the parents to complement each other's strengths and insulate each other's weaknesses.

But when you separate or divorce, this alliance is broken. The arrangement that allowed you to work together has changed. The old system is gone.

Now, you must create a new structure to raise the children. This rearrangement of responsibilities goes by many names, including *co-parenting, parenting apart, parenting agreement,* or—more simply—*parenting plan.*

Whatever it's called, it simply means that you have to identify the discrete parenting issues and decide how to handle them.

The issues generally fall into two categories:
• Decision-making issues.
• Living arrangements.

Shadow of the Law

Believe it or not, the laws and courts actually encourage you to create your own parenting plan. Judges know that if they impose a custody decision, it's much less likely to be obeyed, but if you create your own agreement, it's much more likely to be obeyed.

That's why custody laws permit parents to create an agreement on how to raise their children. However, while you can create your own agreement, you can't make it legally binding. Only the court has the final say on what will happen to the children.

To make a parenting plan legally binding, it must be submitted to the judge, who will accept or reject it. This supervision by the judge means that—when creating a plan—you must create an agreement that is acceptable to the judge. When you negotiate with one eye on the law, you are said to be bargaining in the *shadow of the law.*

What a Parenting Plan Will Do

There are a number of advantages to making a parenting plan. By creating one, you can:

Reduce Conflict
Negotiating a parenting plan requires each parent to think through the issues that are important. This activity directs you away from *blaming behavior* and towards a constructive goal. By listing your priorities, you may discover you have some misconceptions about the other parent—and you may be surprised when you unexpectedly agree on some issue.

Increase Fairness
Everyone knows what's most important to them, and when you compare priorities, you may realize you don't have mutually exclusive goals. In negotiating a parenting plan, you may be able to achieve those items you regard as most important, while agreeing to the items most important to the other parent. This *win-win* result lets each of you achieve an agreement you feel is fair.

Account for the Uniqueness of Your Situation
No two children are the same, and no two family situations are the same. When third parties—such as judges or mediators—make custody decisions, they necessarily revert to model agreements and schedules. This *one-size-fits-all* approach happens because others don't have the time to learn about your unique family.

Since no one knows your children better than you, a parenting plan can deal with any special circumstances you choose. Parents can accommodate the psychological makeup of their children, or allow for a child's particular hobbies or interests, or even account for unpredictable work demands.

Avoid Court
A final reason to create your own parenting plan is that—by making the decisions yourself—you avoid having the judge do it. As skilled as some judges are, they make mistakes, too.

Also, when you go to court, you spend more time and money to arrive at a decision. Custody law is complex, family courts are crowded, and you will expend a lot of money to have the legal system run your life.

What a Parenting Plan Will Not Do

Of course, while a parenting plan can make your life easier, it won't do everything. Among the things a plan won't do are:

Resolve Incompatible Values or Parenting Styles

No parenting plan—no matter how detailed or inclusive—can resolve the dilemma of incompatible values and beliefs. While one parent may prefer that the children have plenty of freedom and few restrictions, the other parent may want the children to lead highly structured, organized lives.

If you were incompatible before the divorce, it's a safe bet you will be afterwards. It's unrealistic to imagine that a piece of paper will change the core values of an adult. A parenting plan can influence the *behaviors* of the other person, but it will not change their *beliefs*.

Shield the Children from the Other Parent

Practically speaking, there's not much you can do when the children are with the other parent. If that individual is unstable or dysfunctional, a parenting plan will not buffer the children from the harmful effects. A parenting plan does not give you control over them, and it won't provide a way to shield the children from a parent who is depressed, abusive, or neglectful.

© 1993,1994 AL ROSS

***"I'm also available as an expert witness
In custody battles."***

Making Changes to Your Parenting Plan

As the needs and interests of your children change over the years, you'll need to update your parenting plan.

Here are some examples of the nearly limitless reasons why you might need to change your parenting plan:

- One parent moves away.
- One parent starts a new job with different work hours.
- One parent remarries.
- The child joins a team or other organized activity.
- The child gets a part-time job or begins dating.
- New, unexpected issues suddenly become important.

Five Big No-No's With Your Children

1. Don't give them messages to give to the other parent.

2. Don't recruit them to be your confidant.

3. Don't tell them what you really think of the other parent.

4. Don't assume they'll stay the same. The arrangement that worked fine when they were in preschool won't cut it when they're teenagers.

5. Don't compete for them with the other parent. Each parent is naturally better at certain things.

Because it's impossible to anticipate everything involved in raising children, you can establish a *periodic review* of the plan. The review can be scheduled for regular times, and/or triggered by certain events.

For example, because your life will be uncertain immediately following a separation or divorce, you can review the plan every few months. Then, once a new equilibrium is established, the review can occur less frequently—say once a year. Also, you can automatically review the plan when a specific event occur, such as when the children begin school, or when they become old enough to drive.

A parenting plan is a work-in-progress, and the benefit of making the plan is that it gives you a place to start.

Children's Developmental Stages

Another reason why you might want to change your parenting plan is that *children grow older each year.* The plan that worked fine when they were in preschool won't work at all when they're teenagers. When making your plan, consider the needs and interests of the children at their various ages and stages of development.

Here's a brief summary of expert opinion on the developmental stages of children and how it affects custody arrangements:

Birth to 3 Years Old
Infants and very young children are completely helpless, and must rely on their parents for everything. A parent who cares for a small child must provide food, clothing, a safe physical environment, constant attention, love, and nurturing—as well as handle the more mundane tasks such as changing diapers and toilet training.

Quality of care and *consistency of care* are the two most important factors when designing a parenting plan for very young children. If the parents are highly flexible and cooperative, a bird's nesting arrangement—where the children stay in one home and the parents move in and out from a separate apartment or home—is ideal. If the parents live nearby, joint physical custody may work, but the parents should buy the same crib, blanket, highchair, and so on. If the parents are not equally interested in caring for the child, one parent should be the primary caretaker, and the other parent should visit frequently—one to two hours three days a week.

3 to 5 Years Old
Preschool-aged children can accomplish some tasks on their own, but still need their parents to provide a safe and supportive environment. Parents must provide the child's meals, clothes, books, and toys—as well as an unending supply of love and nurturing. Because preschoolers are very physically active, parents will need to keep up with them.

Consistency of care is the most important need for preschoolers, and parents should consider the same arrangements recommended for younger children, for the same reasons. Because preschoolers have a limited grasp of time, parents with joint custody may want to use visual aids—such as large wall calendars and color-coded lunch boxes—to remind the child when it's time to go with the other parent. If one parent becomes the primary caretaker, the other should consider taking the child for a minimum of two full weekends a month. Parents should try to maintain similar routines for bedtimes, TV-watching, meals, and so on.

5 to 12 Years Old
Grade-schoolers and preteens still require their parents to meet their physical needs, but now they have more complex emotional needs. On the one hand, parents must be ready to give both unstinting reassurance and guidance, while on the other, they must allow the children to start to pull away, beginning to lead lives independent of parental control. Parents must be ready to actively participate in their children's school and extracurricular activities during these years.

 When designing your plan, consider how resilient the children are. In *Second Chances,* Judith Wallerstein reports that flexible children are much more likely to succeed with a schedule that requires a lot of exchanges. "Not all children have the flexibility to go back and forth between homes and to adjust to two different environments. Indeed, a child's basic temperament is a major contributing factor to his or her adjustment. Children who succeed... have an elusive characteristic that we are not used to considering in psychological assessments—flexibility."

Consistent contact with both parents is the most important consideration for children of this age. Because children can readily understand and follow schedules, joint custody is ideal. If the parents do not want joint custody, they should each plan to spend a significant amount of time with the children.

12 to 18 Years Old
Teenagers require much less active care from their parents—but much more patience. Parents of teenage children must learn to gradually relinquish control over their children's lives, yet still provide supervision. Parents can expect that teenage children will challenge their authority in surprising and exasperating ways. At this age, children are struggling with

both hormonal changes and feelings of wanting to be accepted by their peer group, so parents must allow them the limited freedom to arrange their own social lives.

Allowing teenagers to *make their own decisions* is the most important factor when creating a parenting plan for them. They will want to choose where they live. Because teenagers are very independent, joint custody tends to create logistical problems for them—such as having to carry clothes and schoolbooks back and forth between the two homes—so they often choose sole custody for purely practical reasons. Also, because the teenager is spending less time with both parents, the noncustodial parent can expect to see less of their child during this time.

Children's Books

At Daddy's on Saturdays, Linda Walvoord Girard, Judith Friedman (Illustrator), Albert Whitman and Co., $5.95. This gentle tale is filled with appealing watercolors that will help children cope with divorce.

The Boys and Girls Book About Divorce, Richard A. Gardner, Bantam, $5.99. At 150+ pages, this clearly-written divorce book is more suited for children who read at the "young adult" level.

Dear Mr. Henshaw, Beverly Cleary, Demco Media, $9.60. The famed children's book author has written an excellent book that describes the daily problems of a ten-year-old boy as he copes with his parents' divorce. A *Newberry Medal* winner.

Dinosaurs Divorce, Marc Tolon Brown, Laurence Krasny Brown, Little Brown and Co., $6.95. This classic book addresses divorce issues through the drawings of very humorous dinosaurs.

Divorce, Fred Rogers, Jim Judkis (Illustrator), Putnam, $5.99. Mr. Rogers (yes, *the* Mr. Rogers), gives out much-needed information for children about how divorce affects them. Recommended by *American Bookseller* and *School Library Journal.*

Mom and Dad Don't Live Together Anymore, Kathy Stinson and Nancy Lou Reynolds (Illustrator), Firefly Books, $5.95. A short picture book that helps young children cope with divorce.

Chapter 7
Making Decisions

While it may not always seem so, most decisions involving the children are pretty minor.

What to wear to school, when it's time for dinner, how much TV to watch... in the bigger scheme of things, these are not exactly life-changing. On the other hand, there are decisions that many parents believe are vital to the raising of their children.

When parents create their parenting plan, they are free to include as many—or as few—issues as they want.

The advantage to including a large number of highly specific, detailed issues is that it lets everyone know what should be done in any given situation. In that sense, it takes some of the uncertainty out of the co-parenting relationship.

The disadvantage with a highly detailed plan is that it can become overwhelming and burdensome, restricting the parents with too many rules and regulations.

The ideal parenting plan achieves a balance between too much and too little detail.

For separated or divorced parents, the importance of a good parenting plan cannot be underestimated, because you may have to live longer with the divorce than with the marriage.

This chapter discusses issues to include in a parenting plan.

Issues to Consider

When constructing a parenting plan, it's useful to consider the following items, even if you eventually decide not to include them:

Education
School may be the single most important issue simply because it accounts for most of the child's awake time. There are many topics in this category, and you may include any or all of them.

Choice of School. The child has to go to some school, but which school is a decision that must be made. Not all private schools are better than all public schools, and many large school districts have specialized—or magnet—schools with enriched programs. With so many tradeoffs, you should consult as early as possible.

School Records. Normally, the school will send home tons of paperwork, including report cards, papers, notices, and so on. Someone has to read and respond to it all, and you must decide who that someone will be.

School Conferences. Whether they call you in to tell you what a well-behaved genius your child is, or something worse, someone has to show up for the face-to-face meetings with the teachers. Meetings usually require appointments, and whichever parent has the less-demanding work day may find it easier to attend.

School Activities. School is more than academics, and you will inevitably have to attend ball games, concerts, plays, and much, much more. Also, in the early grades, some schools encourage the parents to volunteer as classroom aides.

School Emergencies. By definition, emergencies require fast action, so you should determine your respective authority ahead of time, and then notify the school. If you have joint legal custody, both of you should be contacted in an emergency. Otherwise, the school needs to be told exactly what the arrangement is.

Special Needs. If your child has some special educational needs, the parenting plan is an ideal place to address them. Whether it's advanced coursework or remedial assistance, it can often be accounted for in an agreement.

Paying for College. If you only have young children, this may not seem like something worth discussing for a while. However, if you take a look at tuition costs, you'll realize that someone has to start saving when *the children are born.*

 In many states, a divorced parent may be ordered to financially support their child beyond high school. In those states, as long as the child remains in college, the parent must pay support until the child turns at least 21.

Religion
If you both feel strongly about your faith, and you have *different faiths,* this is a great issue for a parenting plan. Religious training usually boils down to one of three choices:
* Teach one religion.
* Teach both religions.
* Don't teach any religion, and let the child choose when they're older.

In addition, if one parent wants the children to attend a parochial school, or if the other parent celebrates religious holidays that don't fall on weekends, these issues can be addressed.

Medical Care
Medical topics go beyond who takes the children in for checkups. You may also wish to consider the following issues:

Medical Providers. Choosing the child's doctor, dentist, and optometrist, is critically important, and this issue must be decided before it comes up. If you use different doctors, the doctors must be told so they can exchange medical information.

Medical Decisions. If you have joint custody, this may not be an issue, because generally both parents must be consulted on medical treatments. Otherwise, you must decide who calls the shots on shots, physicals, etc.

Medical Emergencies. When a child is hurt, someone has to be in charge. If there is a reason why one parent shouldn't make emergency medical decisions, then the other parent must always be available. Alternatively, the decision-making parent can sign a medical release.

Medical Records. It's hard to imagine why, but one parent may have a reason to prevent the other from getting copies of the children's medical records. Otherwise, this issue requires coordination, since some doctors won't willingly supply duplicate records.

Insurance
With medical costs come insurance costs, and you should assume you will have to share the burden of the premium payments. Typically, the parent with the better medical plan will carry the children, and other payments between the parents will be adjusted accordingly. Insurance can include all of the following:
- Life (for the parents).
- Major medical.
- Dental.
- Vision.
- Prescription drugs.

 When establishing child support, many judges will order one of the parents to pay for the children's health insurance. Also, the noncustodial parent may be ordered to carry life insurance naming the children as irrevocable beneficiaries until child support is terminated.

Child Care
With the exception of some teenage children, most children cannot be left home alone. That means that parents who work—or who have some other reason why they cannot care for their children—must find appropriate child care. Child care decisions bring up many items, including:

Child Care by a Professional. In choosing a care provider, you must decide on the minimum qualifications they require. For example, one parent may feel that paying a teenager $5 per hour to watch the children is fine. But the other parent may not agree to anything less than a state-licensed and bonded, full-time care provider. If you live close by, using the same care provider can provide extra stability for the child.

Child Care by the Other Parent. If you are on good terms and live nearby, you may decide to use each other for child care. This arrangement has many advantages, including *continuity* and *consistency,* and a lowering of child care expenses. The disadvantage is that it requires you to cooperate fairly well. If you don't get along, the children are exposed to the very conflict the divorce was supposed to prevent.

Child Care by a New Mate. When parents remarry, the new mate may be willing to care for the children. While this sounds like an advantage, frequently the "other parent" will not want the new mate to meddle with the children.

Exchanges
When parents live in separate homes, the children almost always have to go back and forth between them. This means the children have to be *exchanged.*

Exchanging the children requires you to coordinate many items, such as where to exchange, when to exchange, who drops off, who picks up, and so on. Here are some problem areas:

Number of Exchanges. The number of exchanges clearly involves tradeoffs for everyone. The greater the number of exchanges, the less time the children wait before seeing the other parent, but the more time someone has to spend moving them back and forth. And, the fewer the exchanges, the longer the children have to wait, but the less time the parents spend moving them.

For example, if you live near each other, and share the children each week, they may be exchanged two times per week. But if you live far apart, they may be exchanged a few times per year.

 Exchanges can add up. Imagine that you divorce when your child is exactly two years old. If you begin twice-monthly visitation, and maintain it every month thereafter, by the time your child turns 18, he or she will have been exchanged 768 times.

Exchange Point. When deciding the exchange point, you can account for everything from the location of your homes to your respective work schedules. A very important item is whether you can cooperate enough to exchange the child at the front door of each home.

If you cannot cooperate, then the exchange point can be a neutral
location, such as a:

* School.
* Day care setting.
* Relative, friend, or neighbor's house.
* Curbside (rather than the front door).
* Mall.
* Library.
* Police station lobby.

If you choose a neutral location, then you both must drive there to meet
and swap the children.

 In their study of divorced California families reported
in *Dividing the Child,* Maccoby and Mnookin found
that the vast majority of parents lived close enough to
exchange the children by car. Initially after the
divorce, the average drive time from one household to the other was
18 to 20 minutes. After three years, the parents moved slightly
farther apart, and the average drive time increased to 25 to 29
minutes. Maccoby and Mnookin also found that—for the majority of
families where the children lived primarily with one parent—the
noncustodial parent did most of the driving.

Transportation. How the children get to the other parent's house is
important because it must be safe, secure, reliable, and it will happen
many, many times. When the two homes are close, older children can
travel back and forth by bicycle, city bus, and so on. Otherwise, someone
has to move the children, and that means deciding who does it. Though
one parent can assume the sole responsibility, it will clearly become a
burden over time, and that parent may eventually wish to share the
responsibility. Also, if one parent is responsible for transportation, and the
other parent moves away, the transporting parent is forced to seek a
modification of the agreement.

An alternative to the parents do all the driving is to have a third party
transfer the children. The advantage of using someone else is that you
can avoid face-to-face exchanges, but then you will have to rely on yet
one more person—further complicating the logistics of exchanges.

For those who don't want to exchange the children at all, the children can remain with the custodial parent, and the noncustodial parent may visit. In those cases, the visiting parent can rent a room in a nearby hotel or stay with a friend.

Transportation Costs. You will also have to decide who pays for the transportation of the children. As a general guideline, transportation costs are often apportioned by the relative income and ability to pay of each person.

Five Tips for Easier Exchanges of the Children

1. *Make it natural.* Time the exchanges to coincide with a drop-off or pick-up from some other activity.

2. *Make it quick.* The best exchanges are the simple ones—short and pleasant.

3. *Don't talk.* Don't use exchanges to discuss issues with the other parent.

4. *Don't worry about it.* If the child leaves an item at the other parent's house, the child is responsible for retrieving it—not you.

5. *Time to get ready.* Remind the children fifteen minutes before they will be picked up.

Schedule Changes

Ironically, two people who could not get along well enough to stay married or live together must now somehow cooperate when exchanging the children. This may be too much to ask, and for some people, last-minute *schedule changes* will occur frequently.

When parents are picking up the children, they may find the children are not ready on time—or not home at all. When they are waiting for the children to be picked up, they may find the other parent arrives late—or not at all. And, of course, when parents wait for a child to be returned, the other parent may show up late.

Because last-minute changes are inevitable, you must decide how the other parent will be notified, and who will pay any extra costs associated with the change.

Travel
While travel shouldn't normally be a problem, it's possible that one parent may be planning to travel abroad with the children and then abduct them to another country. If that's a possibility, the parents can agree to restrict access to the children's passports.

Moving
Nobody stays put forever, and sooner or later someone may want to move. Moving is complicated, and involves many issues. For example:
- If the move will take the children away from where the other parent lives, then the visitation schedule may need adjusting.
- If the move will increase the transportation costs for visitation, then someone has to cover those extra costs. Often, the moving parent is required to pay the increased costs.
- If the parent wants to move, but the children don't, then the move may trigger a change of custody.

 When exchanging the children, realize that toys, clothes, books, and blankets will go back and forth. Clothes that you dressed them in may not return. Toys that you bought for them will be left "over there." After a while, you may not even know who bought what. It's normal that items bought for the child will end up at the other parent's house.

Sharing Information
Children's lives are very active, and when parents share children, they have to *share information*. The information to be shared includes school progress, school activities, illnesses, sports, friends, and so on.

The simplest way to communicate is directly with each other. A brief phone call, a short chat, a quick note—all can pass along vital information. If these approaches fail, other methods include:
- Writing a formal letter.
- Meeting with a counselor or mediator.
- Communicating through attorneys.

Because older children can talk for themselves, some parents may use them to convey information. But relying on children to carry messages poses problems, not the least of which is that the message may be distorted or incomplete. In addition, older children use leverage to get what they want, and using them may create more problems than it solves.

Making Decisions
Because you can't anticipate every possible issue that will come up, you will need to *decide how to decide* future issues.

For the sake of simplicity, the elements of a decision and the types of issues involved can be charted. For example:

Decision-Making Checklist

	Either Parent Decides	Parents Must Agree
Day-to-Day		
Meals	X	
Clothes	X	
Etc.	X	
Major Decisions		
School		X
Religion		X
Etc.		X

Generally, day-to-day issues correspond to *physical custody*, and include what the children eat, what they will wear, what time they go to bed, etc. Major issues generally correspond to *legal custody*, and include the choice of schools, elective medical attention, when to allow the child to get a driver's license, and so forth.

"Good decisions take your values and needs, and your children's values and needs, into consideration. Good decisions also stand the test of time because everyone involved gains something important. Whenever possible, the advantages of a decision should outweigh the disadvantages for everyone concerned." Mimi Lyster, *Child Custody*

If you can agree on most major items, a useful division is to allow whichever parent is caring for the children to have day-to-day authority, and for both parents to jointly decide the important issues. However, if you cannot agree, the dispute will have to be resolved with the help of a third party. If one parent is not interested in making decisions about the children, the other parent may make all the decisions.

Resolving Disputes
And finally, when you cannot agree on an issue, you may be able to agree on how to resolve the disagreement. Some options include:

Custodial Parent Decides. Allowing the custodial parent to make the decisions may be best when the children live primarily with that parent, and only occasionally visit the other parent.

Decide With a Third Party. Many different professions help parents resolve their disagreements. For example, the parents may turn to a:
- Mediator.
- Counselor.
- Lawyer.
- Member of the clergy.
- Respected friend.

When parents turn to a third party for help, they can retain the ultimate control over the decision. After that, if they still cannot agree and must turn to litigation, the final decision-making authority is taken away from them.

When You Want a Detailed Parenting Plan

Child Custody: Building Agreements That Work, Mimi Lyster, Nolo Press, $24.95. An enormously useful book for creating a highly detailed parenting plan.

Chapter 8
Creating a Schedule

After resolving the decision-making issues, you must also decide the living arrangements of the children. This usually means *creating a schedule.*

A schedule tells you how much time you have with your children, and the children how much time they have with you. A schedule answers the question: where will the children live?

The schedule can be as rigid and specific—or as loose and vague—as you want. There is no correct or incorrect schedule, and different families will create different schedules.

Because school accounts for most of the year, many different arrangements have been created. An alternate weekend schedule allows the children to live primarily with one parent, and to visit the other parent every other weekend. But this is not the only possibility, and the children can be shared in many other ways.

When school is out, such as during holidays and vacation, you can create more imaginative schedules. Vacation time allows you to "balance the books" by allowing the noncustodial parent to have more time with the children.

This chapter discusses what to consider when creating a schedule.

Dividing the Child

There are only so many hours in a child's life.

When you share children, you must decide where the children will be each part of the day. Practically speaking, if the children are with one parent, they are not with the other. And, of course, when they are in school, that time is not being spent with either parent.

Creating a schedule means dividing a child's life.

Think of the child's life as a pie from which you and the other parent are each taking a slice:

Dividing the Child

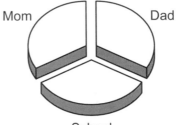

Mom   Dad

School

Because there is only so much time to divide, you will have to share. That's why some parents look at custody as a *zero-sum game*—a competition to acquire as much of the children's time as possible at the expense of the other parent.

Unfortunately, there is no magical solution to this dilemma. More time cannot be invented, nor can the child be cloned. The only thing you can do is create the best schedule possible.

 Children need time alone with you. If you have two or more children, your schedule may not allow them to have private time with you. One solution is to plan a separate visit with each child. Another is to stagger the pick-up times so that each child has a little time alone with each parent.

Creating a Schedule

When deciding how the children's hours will be divided, you will each have needs and agendas.

One parent may want a highly detailed and specific schedule, describing exactly where the children will be every moment of the day. The other parent may want a loose, unstructured schedule that lets him or her adapt to the children's needs moment-by-moment. Or both parents may want the children during a majority of the children's awake hours—something that cannot happen.

There is no one correct schedule. If a lawyer or mediator hands you *a model agreement,* you do not have to accept it.

Every family is unique, and the schedule that works best for you may not work for someone else. At best, your schedule is a compromise. It is a resolution of your different—and at times incompatible—desires.

 "There is no substitute for fixed schedules. Everyone, particularly the children, needs to know what is going to happen and when. The parent who demands unlimited access is either unrealistic or has a hidden agenda. Young children need to know when they are going to see you because they have a poor sense of time. Older children also need to know so they can make their own plans." Sam Margulies, *Getting Divorced Without Ruining Your Life*

Counting the Hours

When making a schedule, you must add up all of the hours each parent spends with the children. You must do that because all of the time in the children's life has to be accounted for, and the only way you create a useful schedule is to actually add it all up and divide it.

Here are some handy amounts to remember when counting the hours and days.

Time

First of all, there are 24 hours in a day and 365 days in a year, or 8,760 hours in a year. Also, there are 168 hours in a week, and approximately 730 hours in an average month.

Time Chart

	Day	Week	Month	Year
Hours	24	168	730	8,760
Days		7	30.4	365
Weeks			4.3	52
Months				12

To use the chart, look down the left-hand column for *units,* then across the top row for the *period.* For example, there are 168 hours in one week.

The amounts in a month are an *average.* If you need to add up the months exactly, use the following:

Days	Month
28	February (leap year has 29 days)
30	April, June, September, November
31	January, March, May, July, August, October, December

If you want to use months as a basis for creating a schedule, remember that there are more 31-day months than 30-day months.

Two-Week Periods

Most schedules are based on a *two-week period.*

Basing the schedule on a two-week period allows the children to see both parents within a fairly short period of time, and allows the year to be divided up evenly. If the time periods are something else—say months—the mathematical divisions might produce a remainder—that is, part of a day.

For purposes of counting the hours, a two-week period has 336 hours. But since children obviously aren't awake that long, you can divide the time based on just the awake hours or on the total number of hours.

Counting the hours may influence child support. In some states, the percentage of time spent with the child is a factor in the child support guidelines.

School Year

Typically, the *school year* is divided up into two-week periods.

Since a schedule covering the school year accounts for more than half the year, there are many different arrangements for the time, including:

Single Primary Home
Also called *home base,* a single primary home means the children live with one parent most of the time, and visit the other parent for specific periods.

Single primary home arrangements have several advantages. They are often best when one parent is not interested in raising the children, or when one parent has an erratic work schedule, or when the parents live too far apart to make more frequent exchanges practical. Also, if the parents simply cannot cooperate on even a basic level, a single primary home may be best because it removes the children from the middle of the conflict.

The disadvantage of a single primary home is it eliminates one parent from the child's day-to-day life. This parent loses the opportunity to stay connected to his or her child, and the child loses the benefit of consistent contact with their parent. In single primary home arrangements, it's common for the visiting parent to feel tremendous loss and to drop out of the child's life after a while.

Transitions are difficult on everyone—especially the children. To make it easier, try not jumping into an activity right away, but instead, allow them some quiet time, such as reading, taking a walk, or watching TV. They need time to adjust to being with you, too.

Some variations on a single primary home include:

Alternate Weekends. The children live with one parent most of the time, and visit the other parent every other weekend. Here's how it looks:

Alternate Weekends

		Mon	Tue	Wed	Thu	Fri	Sat	Sun
Week 1	Parent A	X	X	X	X	X	X	X
	Parent B							
Week 2	Parent A	X	X	X	X	X		
	Parent B						X	X

Typically, the alternate weekends begin on either Friday night at 6 p.m. or on Saturday morning at 8 a.m. And they often end either on Sunday night at 6 p.m., or—if the visiting parent can bring the children to school— Monday morning.

Alternate Weekends and Weeknight. When parents live near each other, the visiting parent may see the children one weeknight, as well.

Day Visits. One parent may be prevented from bringing the children to their home. This may happen when parents have supervised visitation, or when one parent lives very far away. With day visits, the visiting parent travels to see the children rather than have the children travel to him or her.

School Year/Summer. When parents live very far apart, sharing the children during the school year may be impractical. One solution is to allow the children to remain with one parent during the school year, and then live with the other parent during the summer.

Dual-Homes
When children spend a more equal amount of time in each parent's home, the arrangement is called *dual-household.*

Dual-household arrangements may be any division of the child's time, up to and including an exact fifty-fifty split. The difference between dual-home and primary home arrangements is that the children generally spend a minimum of four overnights with each parent in a two-week period—but usually more. Dual-household indicates the parents are participating more equally in the raising of the children.

Dual-home arrangements allow the children to have a meaningful relationship with both parents, but for a dual-home schedule to work, the parents must live near each other, and they must usually cooperate on the frequent exchanges.

Some typical variations of two-home arrangements include:

Split Weeks. This can be a weekly schedule of 3 1/2 days with each parent, or 4 days with one parent and 3 days with the other, or anything similar. Often, these schedules alternate or divide the weekend days so that both parents get weekend time with the children. With this schedule, the parents must live very close, and both must be able to drop off and pick up the children from school.

Here's an example of a split-week schedule where the children live with one parent from Tuesday afternoon through Saturday afternoon—4 days— and with the other from Saturday afternoon through Tuesday afternoon—3 days:

Split Week: 4/3

		Mon	Tue	Wed	Thu	Fri	Sat	Sun
Week 1	Parent A	X	1/2				1/2	X
	Parent B		1/2	X	X	X	1/2	
Week 2	Parent A	X	1/2				1/2	
	Parent B		1/2	X	X	X	1/2	X

Weekdays/Weekends. Parents can also share the children on a weekday/ weekend schedule. In this schedule, the children stay with one parent during the school week, and go to the other parent's home every weekend.

Alternating Periods. Children can move back and forth between their parents' homes every week, every two weeks, every month, every two months, every six months, every year, and so on. If the children switch often, the parents have to live in the same school district.

Bird Nesting
This is where the children remain in one home and the parents alternate moving in-and-out. The period of time each parent stays in the home can vary. When parents choose this arrangement, each needs a separate home or apartment to stay in, or a friend or relative to live with.

Free Time
Some parents toss off the structure of a fixed-schedule and let the children stay wherever they want. This arrangement requires that both parents be extremely cooperative and involved with their children. While it gives the children the best chance of having a relationship with both parents, it also forces the parents to remain connected to each other's lives.

 Who watches the children? School is in session about 180 weekdays a year, but a year has 260 weekdays. That means your children don't have school about 80 weekdays a year. If you get two weeks' vacation plus the standard 12 holidays, you only have 22 weekdays a year off from work. That leaves 58 weekdays a year when your children are off from school, and you can't be home to supervise them.

Holidays and Special Occasions

After deciding how to divide the school year, you also need to share the children during holidays and special occasions.

Traditional holidays and school holidays might include:
- Thanksgiving Holiday.
- Hanukkah Holiday.
- Christmas Holiday.
- New Year's Day.
- Martin Luther King Day.
- Presidents' Day.
- Memorial Day.
- Independence Day.
- Labor Day.
- Winter Vacation.
- Spring/Easter Vacation.

Special occasions include days important to the family, such as:
- Child's birthday.
- Parent's and sibling's birthday.
- Mother's Day and Father's Day.
- Other religious, cultural, or heritage-related days .
- Family celebrations.
- School activities.

Here are some common ways to share the holidays:

Alternate Years. Many holidays are shared by alternating the year. For example, during even-numbered years the children stay with one parent during a given holiday, and in odd-numbered years, the children stay with the other parent. Holidays and special occasions shared this way usually include Thanksgiving and the child's birthday.

Five Ways to Keep in Touch with Your Children

1. Schedule a time when you can call them.

2. Let the children call you.

3. Plan a mid-week dinner with them.

4. Send post cards, letters, or even taped greetings.

5. Go to school events, church gatherings, and team games.

Divide in Half. Some holidays, such as Christmas and Spring Vacation, are long enough for the parents to divide in half. Specifically, Christmas is often divided by giving the child to one parent from the close of school until noon on Christmas day, and then to the other parent for the rest of vacation until school starts in January. The arrangement is then reversed the following year.

Celebrate Twice. Another way to share the holidays is simply to allow each parent to schedule nonconflicting time with the children. During the time, each celebrates the holiday. For example, one parent can celebrate

Christmas with the children a few days early, and the other parent can celebrate on Christmas Day.

Repeat Every Year. Finally, some days are often scheduled with the same parent every year. Examples include each parent's birthday, Mother's Day, and Father's Day.

Also, when a holiday falls on Monday or Friday, it's customary that the children remain with the parent scheduled for the weekend. For example, if a parent has the children on a weekend and the following Monday is a holiday, that parent will keep the children that extra day. Conversely, if a parent has the children on a weekend and the prior Friday is a holiday, they start the weekend a day early.

Summer Vacation

After scheduling the child's time during the rest of the year, you also need to account for summer vacations.

With the wide-open days of summer, you can let children see more of the parent they have not seen during the school year. Here are some typical ways of scheduling the summer vacation:

Block of Time. If parents share the children during the school year, then a standard summer schedule allows each parent to have the children for an uninterrupted period of time. The block of time can be any length, but thirty-day or six-week blocks are common. If the block is six weeks long, often the other parent is granted visitation on alternate weekends. The dates during the summer when the parents take their children can be fixed or discretionary, and if they are discretionary, each parent usually must notify the other from one to two months in advance. When parents disagree on when to take the children, one parent's wishes may have priority in even-numbered years, and the other parent's wishes may have priority in odd-numbered years.

Compensating Time. If parents do not share the children during the school year, then the summer can be used to give the noncustodial parent extra time with the children. For example, if the children see only one parent during the school year, then they may spend the entire summer with the other parent.

The Story of Jessica and James

Separation

The first few months of their separation went calmly—almost eerily so. Whenever Jessica and James talked on the phone, they remained muted and restrained. As if by some unspoken agreement, they decided to try and remain friends, and went about the business of exchanging Julian without any arguments.

For his part, Julian—who was four—was very curious about why he was suddenly living with his mother in a small apartment, instead of with his mother and father in his own home. But whenever he asked, Jessica quickly assured him that it was only temporary, and that it was being worked out. It didn't take Julian long to conclude that it was better not to ask his Mom too many questions.

As a thirty-one-year-old woman, Jessica was relieved to be away from Jim and the constant tension she had felt in the marriage. As the marriage had developed, she had felt increasingly suffocated by Jim, a man whom she began to believe was more interested in his work than in his family. The chance to move out on her own and start her life over again was exhilarating, and Jessica was determined to avoid repeating her mistakes. With an energy level that often surprised her, Jessica happily rose each morning to the challenge of being a single mother out on her own.

Jim, on the other hand, was not so happy. As the days stretched into weeks, and the weeks into months, he wasn't sure what to do. While Jessica hadn't filed for divorce, she hadn't given him any signs that she wanted to get back together, either. As Jim saw it, Jessica was being maddeningly indecisive, and it was making him more frustrated with each passing day. Finally—angry at the lack of resolution—he called Jessica and demanded that they meet. To his surprise, she agreed.

*　　*　　*

Jessica wasn't sure what she would say when she met with Jim. When he had called and insisted on talking, she had agreed, but now she had second thoughts. What if he gets angry? Or what if he tries to take Julian? Throughout the week she constantly considered calling it off, but at the last minute, decided to go through with it.

The doorbell rang. Jessica took a deep breath, then opened the door.

"Hi," she said.

"Hi," said Jim. "Where's Julian?"

"Sleeping. Don't wake him up."

Jim stepped inside. "I won't."

He walked over to Julian's room and peeked in. Jessica followed, watching as he stood over the sleeping boy's bed. He gently touched the child's hair, then stepped back and closed the door.

"You want a soda?" Jessica asked.

"No, thanks."

"How about a beer?"

Jim was surprised. "You know I don't drink. When did you start?"

"I don't. It's for friends."

"Oh." Jim glanced at her suspiciously. "Friends."

He walked around the tiny living room, looking at the paintings hanging on the walls. They were his. He smiled, and sat down on the sofa. Jessica perched on a high-back chair. They remained motionless for a few moments.

"You're the one who called," she finally said.

"I know," said Jim. "Look, Jessy. This is crazy. You're not happy. I know that. But this is no good."

"It's fine with me."

"What about Julian?"

"What about him?"

"What do you want?" said Jim. "Do you want a divorce? Do you want to get back together? What?"

"I don't know. I just don't want to argue anymore," she said firmly.

"Neither do I."

They stared at each other for a few moments. Jessica thought he looked sad. His clothes were wrinkled and he needed a haircut. Jim started tugging at an imaginary piece of string on his pants leg. Jessica knew he did that when he was nervous.

"I want to see Julian."

"When?"

"Every day."

Jessica stiffened. "That's not a good idea."

Jim's fingers twirled faster around the imaginary string. "Why not?"

Jessica remembered the speech she had practiced. "It's not a good idea for Julian to see us fighting."

"I'm not going to fight."

"Neither am I."

They lapsed into quiet again. Jim finally broke the silence. "So, why can't I see him?"

"I think it's best for Julian if he lives with me." She walked over to the counter, picked up a carefully drawn calendar, and gave a copy to Jim.

"Here. I've made a schedule. You can have him every other weekend. I'll take him during the week. If anything comes up and I can't take him, you can baby-sit. Also, if he has to go to the doctor, I'll take him, but I'll tell you about it so you can be there."

Jim stared at the paper. "I see Julian on weekends?"

Jessica corrected him. "Every *other* weekend. I need my time with him, too."

"But you have him all week long."

Jessica said nothing. She waited for Jim's reaction. Jim's fingers were in constant motion around the thread. Jessica's stomach tightened.

"And I want custody."

Jim stopped playing with the thread. He stared at the paper, frozen.

"He lives with you? That's it?"

"Unless you have a better idea."

Jim exploded. "Yes, I have a better idea! He can come home. To his home. Where he lives. And you can too, Jessy. We have a home. It's not a great home, but it's our home!"

Jessica grew angry. "No, it's not. This is my home now."

"But that's my son!"

"He's my son, too."

"But you can't just take him!"

"I don't want to be married to you, Jimmy. I'm tired of waiting for you to get it together. Julian needs a stable home environment. I can give him that."

Jim tried to answer back, but his response was meek. "I can take care of—"

"How long have you been out of a job? One year? Two years?"

"There's been a recession—"

"Don't give me that!" Jessica was fired up. "How much did you earn last year? Nothing! What are we supposed to live on, food stamps? The house is broken. There's no money in the bank. If I didn't have a job we would have starved!"

"I have a job interview next—"

"Knock it off! You don't want to work. You don't want to get a job. My mother was right about you. You're lazy!"

Jim's voice grew louder. "You knew I was a painter when you married me! What do you want from me?"

"Get a job!"

From inside the bedroom door they heard Julian. "Mommy?"

Jessica hissed at Jim. "See? You woke him up!"

"I want to see him."

"No! Go!" She turned and went into Julian's bedroom. "I'm coming, sweetheart."

"Is that Daddy?"

"It's nobody." Said Jessica. "Go back to sleep." Then she closed the door to the bedroom.

Jim stood for a moment, then he turned, shook his head, and left.

✳   ✳   ✳

Hiring a Lawyer

Chapter 9
Finding a Lawyer

Because child custody is so inextricably bound up in the laws, it's likely that at some point you will want to talk to a lawyer.

A lawyer is someone who represents you in legal matters. Lawyers—or attorneys—are people who have usually completed four years of college, three years of law school, and passed a special test called a bar exam.

In a few states—notably California—people can pass the bar and practice law without having completed law school. In other states, graduates of certain law schools are automatically admitted to practice without having taken the bar. But most lawyers have completed three years of law school and passed the bar.

When you go out to find a lawyer, you'll have many choices. Some lawyers have a general practice, while others specialize. Some work by themselves, while others work in a partnership of lawyers, called a law firm.

You'll have to choose your lawyer, and that will not necessarily be an easy decision to make.

Deciding which lawyer to hire will be the single most important decision you make.

This chapter discusses how to find a lawyer.

What Your Lawyer Will Do

Generally, a lawyer has two main jobs: to uphold the law and to protect a client's rights. More specifically, your lawyer should do the following:

Give Legal Advice
One of the main reasons why you hire a lawyer is to tell you what the laws are. Family law is a quagmire of exceptions, and a knowledgeable lawyer will *advise you* on what you can and cannot do. You can ask questions in advance, or simply review decisions you've already made. And because the lawyer is objective—and you're not—he or she can help by telling you precisely what you don't want to hear. A lawyer's job is to help clients adjust their expectations to the legal realities.

Lawyers know the laws and you don't.

Do the Legal Work
A second reason to hire a lawyer is to handle the legal work. Legal work that lawyers do typically includes:
- Investigating the facts in the case.
- Researching prior judicial decisions.
- Reviewing new laws that may apply to the case.
- Writing and preparing legal documents.
- Delivering documents to the court and to the other party.
- Arguing to the judge in favor of your side.
- Questioning witnesses.
- Objecting to improper testimony, exhibits, or arguments made by the opposing attorney.

Not only do these tasks require unique knowledge, but the lawyer must adhere to precise standards mandated by the court. While you could theoretically do all of these things yourself, it may be easier to hire someone who already knows how to do them.

 Nothing in life is free. If you are accused of committing a crime, you have the right to be represented by a lawyer. Unfortunately, the right to a public defender applies only to criminal law, and family law is civil law. That means if you need a lawyer—you have write that check.

Negotiate for You

Since most family law cases never make it to trial, a critical job of your lawyer is to *negotiate* for you. Deciding child custody is a contentious subject—to say the least—and long after the lawyers go home, the parents must still deal with each other. By helping you avoid dealing with the other parent, lawyers can deflect some of the blame that you and the other parent might direct toward each other. Also, if one parent is in a weak bargaining position—either because of income, knowledge, personality, or guilt feelings—hiring a lawyer can help equalize the negotiations.

Work the "System" for You

And finally, a lawyer can *maneuver you* through the legal system. Local family court is a small community, with the same judges and lawyers working together for many years. A good lawyer will know both the local court procedures and the personal preferences of the local judges. This knowledge may allow him or her to maneuver the case in front of the judge most likely to issue a favorable ruling. Also, by knowing the inclinations of the judge, the lawyer can give the client the most realistic advice possible about the outcome of intended litigation.

This knowledge—by the way—works both ways. While the lawyers are getting to know the judges, the judges are getting to know the lawyers. A lawyer with a good reputation imparts both credibility and believability to his or her clients.

"The problem was that damn level playing field."

What Your Lawyer Will Not Do

"Win" Your Case

As odd as this sounds, your lawyer doesn't win your case. *You win your case.* That is, your lawyer can only give you a tactical advantage for a short period time. Over the long run, you will probably get the result you are genuinely entitled to. Your lawyer does not create the facts—he or she only presents those facts in the best possible light.

Reduce the Cost

Lawyers are *trained adversaries,* and it's their job to aggressively pursue your interests. Frequently, that means making unreasonable demands, filing excessive motions, and choosing litigation over settlement—all of which raises the financial and emotional cost to you. Also, because lawyers must guard against future malpractice claims, they will protect themselves by doing everything they possibly can.

Solve Your Emotional Problems

Simply put, your lawyer is not your therapist. If your problems cannot be solved by an application of the law, then your lawyer cannot solve them. Because family law has a superheated emotional component, this is one of the most common misunderstandings about lawyers.

 "Your lawyer is your lawyer. She is not your therapist, your plumber, your best friend, your lover, your doctor, your car mechanic, your social escort. She is a professional as a lawyer and an amateur at all those other things." Patricia Phillips and George Mair, *Divorce: A Woman's Guide to Getting a Fair Share*

Do Your Work for You

While lawyers can handle many tasks, it's your job to meet with the attorney, find and prepare documents and other evidence, give depositions, attend other hearings where your presence is required, and so on. Hiring a lawyer means that you must supervise her—managing how she spends her time and your money, and deciding what needs to be decided.

Types of Lawyers

There are many different types of lawyers, and some are more suited for your needs than others. Here's a general guide:

Size of Practice
Of all the lawyers you can hire, about half work in a solo practice, and the rest work in firms or partnerships of different sizes.

Practice	Number	%
Solo	269,280	46%
2-10 attorneys	147,360	25%
11-99 attorneys	114,240	19%
100 or more attorneys	57,120	10%
Total	588,000	100%

Sole Practitioner. A sole practitioner is a lawyer who works for himself. Because he must do everything himself, a sole practitioner can get stretched pretty thin, but he can extend his capabilities by hiring other lawyers and paralegal assistants. Many excellent family lawyers are sole practitioners.

Small Firms. Two-to-ten lawyers constitutes a small law firm. Small firms—or boutiques—are where you'll find many top family lawyers. Small firms let the lawyer get involved in the entire case, but still use other lawyers as needed.

Medium-Sized Firms. Twenty-to-fifty lawyers constitutes a medium-sized firm. In these firms, only about a third of the lawyers are partners—the rest are associates. Associates are younger, less experienced, and may do most of the work on your case.

Large Firms. Over fifty lawyers is a large firm, and over one hundred lawyers is a megafirm. Firms of this size have many highly specialized lawyers working in multiple departments. The advantage of such firms is that they are full-service—offering you legal expertise in many different areas.

Law Clinics. Law clinics handle simple, uncomplicated legal matters. They keep costs down by using standard forms and using plenty of paralegal assistants. The advantage of law clinics is that their work will often cost less overall than the alternatives. The disadvantage is that clinic lawyers are usually not exceptional family lawyers, and are often overworked.

Specialization
The law is so broad and so deep that no lawyer could possibly know it all. While a general practitioner will usually handle any type of case, practically speaking, every lawyer concentrates on some area of the law.

Some areas of *lawyer specialization* include:
- Domestic relations: divorce, child custody, child support.
- Estate planning: wills, probate.
- Real estate: developing, buying, and selling property.
- Criminal law: crimes.
- Personal injury: injuries, workers' compensation.
- Business law: corporations, mergers and acquisitions, taxes.
- Intellectual property law: patent, trademark, copyright.

Certified Specialist
In some states, when lawyers have pursued extra training and passed extra exams, they can call themselves certified specialists. Certified specialists in family law have not only passed a comprehensive examination, but must continue to study each year to stay current on changes in the law. They must know about child custody, child support, property division, alimony, and more. The standards for certification are set by the state bar.

The American Bar Association reports that "Seventeen states have specialization programs that certify lawyers as specialists in certain stated types of law. These states are: Alabama, Arizona, California, Connecticut, Florida, Georgia, Idaho, Louisiana, Minnesota, New Jersey, New Mexico, North Carolina, Ohio, Pennsylvania, South Carolina, Tennessee, and Texas."

How to Find a Lawyer

Finding a lawyer is easy. Finding a *good* lawyer isn't.

To find a good lawyer, you'll have to spend considerable time and effort following up on many leads. That's the bad news. The good news is that lawyers need you as much as you need them, so they'll make it easy for you to find them.

Here are some traditional ways to find a lawyer:

Personal Referrals
The best approach is to ask someone. "How did you like your lawyer? Did she do a good job?" There's nothing quite like the personal touch, and if you know someone who was satisfied with their lawyer, you may be, too. If their lawyer doesn't handle family law, or can't take your case, they may refer you to another lawyer who can.

You can ask family, friends, counselors, or even ministers for the name of a good lawyer. Here's a tip: call a local paralegal or legal typing service. They work with local lawyers every day, and may know who will be right for you. When pursuing a recommendation, remember that your case may not turn out the same. Also, because personal chemistry is so important, you may not be as comfortable with the same lawyer someone else was.

 Loose lips sink ships. When asking others for a personal referral, be careful what you say. If you let slip something that could hurt you, they can be ordered to appear and testify in court. Only conversations with your lawyer are protected by attorney-client privilege.

Yellow Pages
Lawyers are almost always listed in the *yellow pages.* The yellow pages are a great place to find family lawyers because they usually advertise, and they train their receptionists to handle callers who saw their ad. The advantage of using ads is that they may contain useful information—such as initial consultation rates. The disadvantage is that they don't tell you how competent the lawyer is.

If you look under the heading "Attorneys" in the yellow pages, you may find that family law lawyers are listed under a subheading such as:
- Divorce.
- Family Law.
- Family Law—Board Certified.
- Marital and Family Law.

Advertising
In addition to using the yellow pages, you can also find a lawyer through *advertising.* To get your attention, lawyers can advertise in newspapers and magazines, or on billboards, radio, or TV. While an ad will tell you the lawyer's area of practice, it probably won't tell you much about the lawyer's competence.

Publicity
Another way to find a lawyer is by reading and watching the *news.* News stories often contain the names of the lawyers involved in a local case, or some other useful quote by a lawyer. If the legal matter is similar to yours, you can contact the lawyer. Unfortunately, many news stories about lawyers are not really news, but are reprints of press releases put out by a public relations firm paid by the lawyer to get his or her name in the paper. This means that some of these lawyers want only high-profile cases, and if yours is not high-profile, they may pass your work on to an assistant.

 Think the world is full of lawyers? In fact, the labor force numbers 119 million, but only 777,000 are lawyers.[2] That's only .65% (a little over one half of 1 percent). *The other 99.35% are probably being sued.*

Legal Plans
Sometimes you can find a lawyer by signing up for *legal insurance* or a *legal plan.* These are programs offered by employers, labor unions, credit unions, credit card companies, and so on, that allow you to pay a small membership fee in exchange for a basic amount of legal service. If you need additional legal work, you'll have to pay more. A legal plan may be a bargain if it offers the services you need. Otherwise, you must use the plan lawyers, and they may not always be as good as you want.

What Others Think of Your Lawyer

Martindale-Hubbell Law Directory
If you want to find an attorney, try the Martindale-Hubbell Law Directory. This set lists almost 800,000 lawyers.

From Martindale-Hubbell you can get:
- Date of birth.
- Undergraduate and law school degree.
- Year of admission to practice.
- Bar association membership.
- Certification.
- Peer rating.

Two pieces of information are especially valuable. The *year of admission to the bar* says how long the lawyer has been practicing. The *peer rating* will tell you what other lawyers think of their colleague. These are confidential ratings, and they can be useful.

Peer rating is divided into legal ability and general recommendation. Legal ability "takes into consideration experience, nature of practice, and qualifications relevant to the profession." Legal ability ranges from "A" to "C." General recommendation evaluates, "faithful adherence to professional standards of conduct and ethics of the legal profession, professional reliability and diligence, and standards relevant to the attorney's discharge of his or her professional responsibilities." The only general recommendation rating is "V." About 30% of the lawyers score at the top: A-V.

The directory is organized by city and state, so you'll need to know the city the attorney practices in.

To view Martindale-Hubbell online, go to:
www.martindale.com

To read a large bound copy, try:
- Public library.
- Courthouse law library.
- Law department in a large corporation.

Support Groups
You can also find a lawyer by contacting a *support group.* A support group is an organization that helps people with a specific problem. Some support groups help victims of domestic violence, while other groups help people deal with drug or alcohol abuse.

Examples of support groups include:
• Parents Anonymous
• Batterers Anonymous
• Parents Without Partners

To find a support group, look in the phone book under community groups, crisis intervention services, or family services.

Online
If you have access to a computer, you can also find a lawyer *online.* The *American Bar Association* has a database that contains the name and vital information for every licensed lawyer. You can search for a lawyer based on location, expertise, and more, and then send e-mail to the lawyer at an Internet address. Also, the major online services, such as *America Online* and *Prodigy,* provide access to legal directories. And finally, lawyers may be listed on private computer bulletin boards run by special interest groups.

Lawyer Referrals
You can also find a lawyer through a *lawyer referral service.* A lawyer referral service will help you find a lawyer in your area. The person who answers the phone is not a lawyer, but is a counselor trained to help determine if you need a lawyer, and if so, what kind. They'll give you the names, addresses, and phone numbers of several lawyers near you. If you go to see one, you'll usually have to pay a small fee to the referral service—say $25—that entitles you to a thirty-minute consultation.

Calling a referral service is best when you're not sure if you need a lawyer, or if you can't get a recommendation from anyone you know, or when you're new to the area. The problem with lawyer referral services is that the lawyers they refer you to are not always the most experienced or most competent. It all depends on the lawyers who participate.

Usually, state bar associations have referral services, as do many local bar associations. In addition, there are some private referral services.

You can find a referral service by looking in the yellow pages under:

- Lawyer Referral Service.
- Lawyers.
- Legal Assistance.
- Any city, county, or state bar association listing.

Two Places for Lawyer Referrals

American Academy of Matrimonial Lawyers
20 North Michigan Avenue
Chicago, IL 60602
(312) 263-6477
If you want an exceptional attorney, choose from among the members of the American Academy of Matrimonial Lawyers. A fellow of the Academy can only be invited to join after showing outstanding ability in family law. All the members are board-certified specialists.

American Bar Association
750 N. Lake Shore Dr.
Chicago, IL 60611
(312) 988-5000
(800) 621-6159
www.abanet.org
The national organization for lawyers. Lists attorneys licensed to practice. If you are looking for a recommendation, state and local bar associations will refer you to attorneys in your area. They can also tell you about alternative dispute resolution, lawyer discipline, and more.

---

1 *American Bar Association Membership and Marketing Research Department,* Chicago, 1993.
2 *Newsweek,* July 31, 1995

Chapter 10
Hiring a Lawyer

Once you get the names of several lawyers, you'll have to decide which one to hire. Because each lawyer is different, the only way you'll know if you've found the right lawyer is to interview him or her.

During the interview, be sure to ask questions about your case, and about fees. Take good notes when they explain how they will charge you and what they will do for the money.

When interviewing a lawyer, the important thing to remember is that you are the one doing the hiring, and the lawyer is the one being hired.

It's your money—spend it wisely.

This chapter discusses how to hire a lawyer and how lawyers charge clients for their work.

The Interview

Once you have the names of several lawyers, you'll have to decide which one to hire. You make this decision after the *interview.*

Generally, lawyers will agree to meet with you for an initial interview, or *consultation,* so you can evaluate them—and they can evaluate you.

Some lawyers charge you a small amount—$25 to $50—to have this meeting, while other lawyers don't charge anything. It all depends on the common practice of lawyers in your area.

Because hiring a lawyer is so important, and each lawyer is different from the next, it's desirable to interview at least three lawyers before making a hiring decision.

Interviewing three lawyers is time consuming and expensive, and may not seem worth doing. On the other hand, if you fail to perform *due diligence,* you can wind up with the wrong lawyer, and that may ultimately affect your life and the lives of your children.

Choose your lawyer carefully.

The interview will give you the opportunity to talk to the lawyer. You can tell him or her about your case, ask questions, and observe how well you and the lawyer communicate.

Because much happens during the interview, and hiring interviews are generally brief, it's vital that you prepare for the meeting ahead of time.

 Whatever you say to a lawyer during an interview cannot be repeated. This protection—known as attorney-client privilege—extends to conversations you have even if you don't hire them. Interestingly enough, this also means that lawyers you interview are sometimes prevented from being hired by the other parent. As a general rule, for a lawyer to become off-limits, you must have revealed very damaging or confidential information during the interview.

Preparing for the Interview

If you walk into a lawyer's office unprepared, you will use the meeting time badly—possibly not even finding out what you need to know. That's why you must *prepare for the interview.*

Here are some ways to prepare:

Why You Want a Lawyer
The first thing to do is to identify your reasons for hiring a lawyer, and what outcome you hope to achieve. You might realize that you don't even need a lawyer, but another professional—such as a financial advisor or therapist.

If you're sure about needing a lawyer, you then must decide the *level of service.* Believe it or not, you don't have to dump your whole life on a lawyer and let them sort it out. You can hire a lawyer for more limited service, such as consultation, where you seek information or advice only, or negotiation, where you want the lawyer to negotiate for you.

Information for the Lawyer
The lawyer can't give you useful answers without knowing something about you. That means you must tell them about yourself. But unless you're a lawyer, you don't know what legal issues affect you, so you'll spend valuable time conveying legally irrelevant information.

The solution is to assemble the important information ahead of time. Look around and dig up valuable documents, write down vital information, and so on.

Here is a list of the information and documents you may need to provide:
- Personal: names, addresses, phone numbers, ages.
- Marriage: date, place, length, date of separation or divorce.
- Children: birthdates, ages, schools.
- Work: employers, addresses, wage statements.
- Financial: tax returns, checking and savings accounts.
- Legal: prior court orders, papers you've been served with.
- Medical: insurance, illnesses, disabilities.

You won't need all of this for the initial interview, but if you're involved in a legal action, you'll eventually need to provide it.

If some information reflects badly on you, be especially sure to tell the lawyer. It's a given that the other parent will mention it, and you want your lawyer to be prepared with a response.

In addition, if you expect to dispute child custody, you'll need to tell the lawyer the reasons why the other parent may not be fit for custody. This is the stuff of tabloid newspapers, and it's not hard to imagine what it might include. For example:

- Does the other parent abuse drugs or alcohol?
- Do they have a mental illness?
- Have they attempted suicide?
- Are they a spouse or child batterer?
- Are they a sexual abuser?
- Do they have a criminal record?

While this information is useful to the lawyer, if you cannot substantiate the allegations with objective confirmation, then they remain just that—*unsubstantiated allegations.* However, keep in mind that while a great deal of testimony under oath is unsubstantiated, it is assumed to be "true" if it is not refuted.

 Inadmissible evidence. In many states, it is illegal to record a telephone conversation without the other party being informed. If you make a recording without their approval, it may not be allowed as evidence in court.

Questions to Ask the Lawyer

Besides answering questions from the lawyer, you get to ask your own questions. If you have prepared the questions ahead of time, you'll be better able to assess the lawyer's expertise.

Consider the following subjects when creating your questions:

Lawyer's Knowledge and Experience. You want to know all about the lawyer's background and expertise. Ask how long he or she has been practicing, length of time with the firm, what percentage of the practice is in family law, and what bar and professional associations they belong to. If you expect to dispute custody, ask how much experience the lawyer has had with contested cases.

Lawyer's Style. In addition to finding out about knowledge and experience, you also want to know how the lawyer works. Find out if he or she will be handling your case alone, or if it will be given to someone else—say a junior associate. Ask if paralegals and law clerks will be involved, and what they will do. Ask how the lawyer feels about settling, and if your case will go to trial if it isn't settled. And finally, find out how return phone calls are handled, and whether the lawyer will automatically send you duplicates of all correspondence.

Case Questions. You'll want to know about your case, so ask plenty of legal questions. Ask the lawyer what his or her opinion of the case is, and what the likely outcome will be. Also ask how long it will take to complete. In addition, find out how the local judges have decided recent cases similar to yours. Also—if mediation is ordered—ask if the recommendations will be confidential, or if the judge will be given a report. Finally, if custody is in dispute, ask how evaluations are handled.

Client Participation and Problems. Be sure to find out what you are expected to do, and what decisions you will need to make. Also, if it turns out that you have a problem with how your case is handled, you'll need to know if the lawyer will submit to binding arbitration over the fees.

Fees. No interview is complete until you've settled fees. Most family lawyers charge by the hour, so be sure to find out the rate. Also, ask about other expenses, such as paralegal work, filing fees, and phone calls. Be sure to get the lawyer to give you a total estimate, even if it's only a ballpark figure. Ask about a retainer, and how—or if—it will be refunded if it's not used up. Finally, check on billing practices, and if you can pay in installments.

There are way too many questions to ask during a brief meeting, so you'll need to prioritize your questions. If you run out of time, consider making a second appointment—at the lawyer's full rates.

 Friend or foe? Family lawyers practice against each other every day, and you should ask if your attorney has a significant relationship with the other attorney. For example, if the two attorneys are bitter enemies, that does not bode well for a peaceful settlement.

What the Lawyer Is Looking for During the Interview

During the interview, while you're evaluating the lawyer, he or she is evaluating you. Lawyers can—and do—turn down cases, and the lawyer will be deciding if he or she wants you as a client.

Generally, lawyers want calm, businesslike clients who are organized and rational. What lawyers don't want are clients who:
- Have a case without merit.
- Are motivated by revenge.
- Complain about the legal system.
- Have fired previous lawyers.
- Won't pay for what they need.

If you fit the above—you may have trouble hiring a good lawyer.

If you are turned down, just keep going. There is a lawyer for every case.

After the Interview

After you finish the interview, you'll have to *evaluate the answers*.

If you have interviewed several lawyers, you need to compare their responses and decide whom to hire. Here are some criteria to consider when evaluating the answers:

Competence. If you're not a lawyer yourself, you can't really judge competence. However, because the basis of law is what a reasonable person would do, almost every answer should make sense. If the lawyer is a specialist, you can assume he or she is current on child custody, otherwise, compare how different lawyers answered the same question. Also, make sure the lawyer can practice in the court where your case is.

Communication. Did the lawyer answer your questions—and did you understand the answers? If communication wasn't good during the interview, it may not get any better.

Availability. Decide if the lawyer is too overloaded to handle your case, or may shunt you off to a junior associate. Keep in mind that good lawyers are busy, and lack of availability may be the price you pay for hiring a top lawyer.

Style. If you want to settle, make sure the attorney prefers negotiation. If you want to fight, make sure the lawyer is a litigator.

Honesty. You need a lawyer who is honest, even if you don't like what you hear. Try to distinguish between lawyers who agree with you, and lawyers who remain objective. If the lawyer "guaranteed" you would win, be cautious. The judge decides the case—not the lawyer.

Objectivity. If the lawyer has a gender bias, make sure that it doesn't clash with your gender bias. Hiring a lawyer of the same sex does not automatically improve your chances of winning.

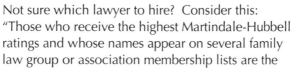 Not sure which lawyer to hire? Consider this: "Those who receive the highest Martindale-Hubbell ratings and whose names appear on several family law group or association membership lists are the ones most likely to meet your expectations..." Leonard L. Loeb, President, American Academy of Matrimonial Lawyers, 1988-89, Chairman, American Bar Association, Family Law Section, 1978-79

Why Parents Should Not Use the Same Lawyer

If you have little disagreement over custody, it's sometimes appealing— even enticing—to save money by sharing a lawyer.

Unfortunately, now that you and the other parent are apart, you have *competing interests.*

If a lawyer actually agreed to represent both parents simultaneously— which they normally won't do—it represents a *conflict of interest.* Lawyers are bound by their ethical code to not represent both sides of a dispute or negotiation at the same time.

Of course, you can work around this restriction by *waiving* the conflict, but doing so may create even more problems. Often, parents without their own competent lawyer—or any lawyer—either agree to an unreasonable settlement, or demand an unrealistic settlement. One of the advantages of involving lawyers is that they bring a businesslike demeanor to the negotiations.

Also—and for the same reasons—don't hire a lawyer recommended by the other parent. Your attorney is your attorney, and you need to hire this person on your own.

What Lawyers Cost

No doubt about it—lawyer's fees are a touchy subject. Lawyers don't work for free, and unless you earn very little or the judge awards you attorney's fees—you'll have to pay.

Hiring a lawyer really means making a *cost vs. benefit* decision. On the one hand, you don't want to pay more than you have to, but on the other, you want to get the best lawyer possible.

Also, since lawyers are not a standardized product—like, say a McDonald's hamburger—you can't get their prices off a big shiny board. Each lawyer is unique, and can charge whatever he or she wants. All you can do is ask the price, and then see how it compares with those of other lawyers nearby.

When you hire a lawyer, you'll have to pay *fees* and *expenses.*

Types of Legal Fees

There are some fairly standard ways lawyers charge their clients. While there are major differences between the following arrangements, the goal remains the same.

Lawyers are selling their time. The more people who want that time, the more the lawyer can charge.

Here are some common fee arrangements:

Hourly
The most common arrangement for family lawyers is to charge an *hourly fee.* Under this agreement, the lawyer charges you for each hour they work on your case. Rates vary depending on many factors, including how experienced the lawyer is, and whether the lawyer works in a large city— where everything seems to cost more—or a small town. Also, some lawyers charge more for time in court, and less when meeting a client in their office.

Hourly fees are typical in family law cases because so many unpredictable things happen. Custody battles, parental kidnappings, moveaways—all require a sudden and unplanned legal response. For their efforts, lawyers typically charge from a low of $75 per hour, to a high of $350 per hour. Top family lawyers in a large city can even command as much as $500 per hour.

Hourly rates are often divided into time units of 10 or 15 minutes. Thus, if your lawyer charges you $200 per hour in 15-minute intervals, and you talk to her on the phone for 6 minutes, your next bill will show a charge for $50.

 Career day. Here's what your high school guidance counselor never told you. As reported in the *Los Angeles Times,* in one year California lawyers made $16.3 billion dollars in legal fees. That's more than the Gross Domestic Product of any three Third World nations. With 134,983 lawyers, it works out to approximately $120,000 annually per lawyer. New York lawyers lagged behind at $14.3 billion.[1]

Contingency
Contingency fees are paid to the lawyer only if the client "wins" in court or is given money in a settlement. The lawyer takes a percentage of the amount awarded. Since many states forbid contingency fees in most family law cases, it's unlikely you'll find a lawyer to work for one. One exception is when a parent pursues a support delinquency. In those cases, the lawyer may take 20% to 50% of the final collected amount. More typical contingency fee cases include personal injury or medical malpractice, and workers' compensation.

Fixed
If a lawyer is willing to charge you a set amount for the legal work, that is a *fixed fee.* Fixed fees are common when the legal matter is routine, and the lawyer can use standardized forms. Because any legal matter can escalate unexpectedly, fixed-fee agreements often have loopholes that allow the lawyer to charge extra if it becomes necessary. Examples of fixed-fee arrangements include uncontested divorces, simple wills, and some personal bankruptcies.

Referral
If you are referred to another lawyer, there may be a *referral fee.* Generally, you don't pay this, but rather, one lawyer pays the other. A referral may happen when another lawyer has the special skills or experience you need. Many states have specific rules governing how lawyers split fees, and it's prohibited when it does little more than increase your overall costs.

Statutory
If the fee for a particular type of work is set by statute, it is known as a *statutory fee.* These fees are approved by the court.

Types of Legal Expenses

In addition to paying your lawyer's professional fee, you'll also have to pay your *legal expenses.*

Expenses are direct costs paid by the lawyer. Sometimes you'll have to pay the expenses up front, and sometimes you'll have to reimburse the attorney. Some expenses are fees paid to third parties, while other expenses are internal to the law firm. Because these expenses are in addition to the lawyer's professional fee, you are usually billed separately.

Examples of legal expenses include:
- Checks written to the court clerk's office for filing fees.
- Expenses incurred for the service of subpoenas.
- Wage assignments or writs of execution.
- Expenses for court reporters for depositions.
- Fees and expenses for expert witnesses.
- Copying.
- Phone calls.

 If you have little money, you may qualify for a *pro bono* or *legal aid* lawyer. Pro bono lawyers volunteer their time to help low-income litigants. Law firms use this charitable donation to train their junior lawyers. Legal aid is a social program that offers legal services to the poor. To get a pro bono lawyer, call a large law firm and ask to be included in their pro bono program. To find legal aid, look in the phone book under *Legal Aid.*

Legal expenses can add up pretty quickly in family law cases. Because lawyers are always mindful that they can be sued for malpractice, they don't mind relying on many types of experts, including accountants, appraisers, actuaries, and psychiatrists. When you use experts, you'll have to pay for the time to prepare them, the time they testify, and their travel time.

Five Mistakes Made When Hiring a Lawyer

1. Hiring the first lawyer you meet.

2. Hiring a lawyer based on price.

3. Hiring a lawyer who only practices family law part-time.

4. Hiring a litigator when you want to settle, or the other way around.

5. Hiring the same lawyer as your ex.

Fee Agreements and Retainers

When you hire a lawyer, you sign a contract, or *fee agreement*. The fee agreement describes exactly how much you will be charged and for what.

The fee agreement will typically include the lawyer's hourly rate—if you are being charged that way—as well as any additional legal expenses you must pay. The fee agreement is very important, and if you do not read it carefully, there may be some unpleasant surprises awaiting you.

At the time you sign the contract, you will often have to pay a retainer fee. A *retainer fee* is the money you pay the lawyer so they will take your case. It's usually a lump-sum amount—typically between $1,000 and $15,000.

Retainer fees are generally credited against future work. That is, when the lawyer begins work, he or she first spends the money you paid them in retainer. When that money is used up, the lawyer starts billing you.

Many lawyers insist the retainer fee is *nonrefundable,* and that they can keep any amount you don't use. Others insist that only a portion—such as 80%—is nonrefundable. Whatever the amount, you can always negotiate this point.

Billing

Once you know what you'll pay, you have to determine how you'll pay.

While a law firm can establish any billing method they choose, most lawyers allow clients to pay in *monthly installments.*

For the client, monthly billing allows payments to be spread out more evenly over time. You can also can keep better track of expenses by requesting an *itemized bill.*

For the lawyers, monthly billing poses problems. They realize that the legal work doesn't always keep pace with the payments, and they may have to do most of the work at the beginning of the case, only to wait a long time to be paid. This may encourage some clients to not pay at all.

Unfortunately, lawyers have little choice about monthly payments. Few clients have large sums of excess cash lying around just waiting to be spent on a lawyer.

 The bottom line. Here's what one attorney had to say (in a journal for attorneys) about retainers: "The fee, which often is substantial, should neither be payable in installments nor refundable. If the client cannot afford the retainer, he or she can borrow from parents or relatives, sell a piece of jewelry or securities, refinance a car, or obtain a personal bank loan." Willard H. Da Silva, *Family Advocate*

If You Don't Pay

There's a certain irony in your relationship with your lawyer. Generally, this person will be your best friend until you have spent all your money, and then they will drop you... *just like that.*

If you do not pay your lawyer, he or she can stop working for you.

There are a few exceptions that require lawyers to continue working without pay, but they only apply if your case would be prejudiced by the lawyer's discharging you. In family law, a lawyer must usually remain on your case only if a trial is imminent. Otherwise, they can drop you at any time.

Read Before Hiring a Lawyer

Finding the Right Lawyer, Jay G. Foonberg, American Bar Association, $19.95. Written by a lawyer who teaches at a law school, this book not only gives advice on hiring a lawyer, it reveals how lawyers look at clients. *Can you spell money?* Order directly from the ABA.

Divorce Lawyers, Emily Couric, St. Martin's Press, $14.95. This book describes 10 couples going through a divorce. Some are fighting for custody, others are battling over property distribution, one is a parental kidnapping. In all the examples, you not only meet the couples and follow their problems, but you learn a lot about divorce laws and how they influence the outcome.

---

1 *Los Angeles Times,* January 15, 1995

Chapter 11
Working With Your Lawyer

Hiring a lawyer doesn't end your troubles, any more than getting married and having a child begins a lifetime of happiness.

It's going to take a great deal of work to achieve your desired outcome. You can't do it alone, and your lawyer can't do it alone. You have to work together.

Working with a lawyer is different from anything you've ever done before. As you'll quickly discover, you have certain obligations to them, and they have certain obligations to you.

Besides the obvious obligation of paying the bills, you'll have to furnish the lawyer with information, and you'll have to tell the truth—even if it embarrasses you. You'll also have to be flexible and accept what is realistically obtainable.

Your lawyer, on the other hand, must give you useful guidance on your situation, follow your directions, keep your intimate secrets truly secret, and keep you up to date on all developments in your case.

This chapter offers a guide to working with your lawyer, as well as some tips on how to save money on your legal fees.

What You Must Do for Your Lawyer

It's not what your lawyer must do for you, it's what you must do for your lawyer.

You hired your lawyer to help you achieve a goal, and now you must do what it takes to make that happen. Here are some responsibilities you have to your lawyer:

Tell the Truth
You should tell your lawyer the truth for a number of reasons. First, if the other parent knows you're hiding something, they'll almost certainly mention it to their lawyer. And when it comes out—and it will come out—your lawyer won't have a good response. Second, because very few cases go to trial, your lawyer will be negotiating for you. If you tell him what your real objectives are—in your order of priority—he can fight for what you care about and give in on what you don't. And finally, because the court maintains jurisdiction over the children, if your deception is discovered later on, you can lose what you have gained.

Adjust Your Expectations
Your lawyer can only do what the law allows. If you cling to an unrealistic goal, you will probably fail, and you will make things harder for your lawyer. Child custody laws do not seek to exact revenge, but to assure the children are adequately supported and have regular contact with both parents. It's your job to listen to your lawyer when he or she explains that to you.

Provide Information
Your lawyer only knows what you tell him, so it's your job to walk around the house, go through your files, and look in your closets. You must pull together the pertinent papers, organize them, and hand them over.

Hidden costs. Legal actions cost more than the lawyer's hourly rate. If you work a regular weekday job, you'll probably have to miss work to talk to the lawyer, be deposed, and go to court. It's not unusual to take a day off work, wait all morning in court, and then watch as your case is continued to another day.

Listen to Advice
When you hire a lawyer, you're in charge. You're paying the bills, so the lawyer is working for you. But it's more complicated than that because you're buying professional expertise. You want guidance. So, if your lawyer tells you to do something, you might want to do it.

Give Support
Let your lawyer do what you hired him to do. If you feel absolutely compelled to negotiate a side deal with the other parent, be cautious and check it out with your lawyer first. It couldn't hurt.

Ask Questions
Giving your lawyer authority doesn't mean giving him carte blanche. If you don't understand something—ask. The lawyer doesn't know what you don't know, so you must ask.

Pay Your Bill
And finally, you must pay your lawyer. This is his day job, and he has financial responsibilities just like you.

 There's no place like home. Avoid securing payment of legal fees with a lien on your home. While many lawyers will accept a lien, if you decide to change lawyers, it will create added complications.

What Your Lawyer Must Do for You

Of course, your lawyer has responsibilities, too. Here are some of those obligations:

Give You Guidance
When you hire a lawyer, you're hiring a specialist to help you reach your goals. The lawyer has a responsibility to do competent work. The lawyer must analyze the legal issues, research and study the laws, and explain your rights and obligations.

Follow Your Directions
You—not your lawyer—have to live with the final court orders, so the final decisions must be yours. It's your lawyer's job to explain the options and then pursue your wishes.

Keep Your Secrets
You cannot be honest with your lawyer if he or she can reveal what you say. That's why *attorney-client privilege* prohibits lawyers from sharing your intimate secrets with the world. However, if you mention something over the phone, that privilege is lost.

Keep You Up to Date
Your lawyer must eventually return your phone calls, inform you about any settlement offers, and give you copies of everything that relates to your case.

Be Your Advocate
Your lawyer's job is to represent your best interests. He or she must handle your case quickly and carefully, and must not accept your case if there is a *conflict of interest.*

Charge You Fairly
Finally, your lawyer must clearly explain how you will be charged, and the amount he or she charges must be *reasonable.*

School daze. Impressed with your lawyer's law school? Don't be, says attorney Jay G. Foonberg in *Finding the Right Lawyer,* "Very few law schools flunk out students, so no matter how stupid the student is, or how little the student learns in law school, chances are the student will graduate with a law degree." On the other hand, class standing is important. "I have found a very high correlation between academic achievement in law school and being a good lawyer. Good class standing is, in my opinion, indicative of excellence."

When You're Unhappy with Your Lawyer

Probably more than in any other area of law, attorney-client relations in family law are influenced by *personal chemistry.* While you can act as badly as you want, your lawyer is held to a *code of professional conduct.*

If the lawyer is the problem—and not you—you can usually attribute it to one of two areas: he or she is *incompetent* or *unethical.*

Incompetent Lawyer

If you're not happy with how your case is being handled, it may be because you hired an *incompetent lawyer.* A lawyer may be incompetent through lack of skill at being a lawyer, or through lack of knowledge about the area of law. Family law is a quickly changing field, and a lawyer who only practices part-time may not be current.

There are good lawyers and there are bad lawyers.

Examples of incompetence include missing filing deadlines, missing settlement meetings or court appearances, failing to keep you informed, and consistently forgetting the facts of your case.

If you're not happy with the outcome of your case, don't automatically assume your lawyer is incompetent. There are two sides to every case. If you lose, it may not be because you had a bad lawyer. *You may have had a bad case.*

Unethical Lawyer

Lawyers can be more than just incompetent—they can be *unethical.* Most lawyers are human, and humans are often weak.

Examples of unethical behavior include:
- Lying to you.
- Misusing or stealing your money.
- Abandoning you.
- Having sex with you.

Having sex with your lawyer is a particularly incendiary topic, and in some states, it is expressly forbidden by statute.

Your lawyer can also act unethically by refusing to hand over your case file after you have fired him, making a settlement offer without your permission, or colluding with the other party.

 Sex trap. "Perhaps the single most frequent ethical abuse by attorneys in the context of emotionally troubled clients involves sexual overtures toward the client. The emotional difficulties of divorcing clients render them particularly vulnerable." Lynn Feiger, *Family Advocate*

How to Solve Problems with Your Lawyer

If you feel that the problems with your lawyer are severe enough, you need to take some action. Here are some options:

Talk with Your Lawyer
If the problem is caused by a lack of communication or a misunderstanding, *talking* to your lawyer may solve it. If she doesn't call you back promptly, send her a letter.

Mediate or Arbitrate
If you genuinely disagree on some issue—probably fees—and you feel it's possible to reach an agreement, try *mediation* or *arbitration.* Most state bar associations have programs. Fee arbitration hearings are less formal than court hearings, you don't need to hire a lawyer to present your side, and—in some states—the lawyer must agree to participate.

Fire Your Lawyer
You have the right to *fire your lawyer* for any reason. When you fire your lawyer, you must pay for the work already done, and you must notify the court of the change. In many states, your lawyer must give you your case file—even if you still owe some money. Aside from that, firing your lawyer may affect your case. The first time you fire your lawyer, the new lawyer will need time to get up to speed on your case. After that, if you continue to fire lawyers, you will alert the judge to the fact that you are an *unstable litigant.* And finally, after you go through a few lawyers, new lawyers won't want you as a client.

"Most judges believe persons who go through several attorneys during one dissolution often are neurotic or unreasonable. They are considered problem clients by the bar as well as by the judges. You will understand how badly a second or third change of attorney has prejudiced your case when you hear your spouse's attorney emphasizing in all pleadings and at oral arguments before the judge that your current lawyer is your 'fourth.' Such a statement carries with it the inference that you lack stability, or your demands are unreasonable, or both." Judge Stewart, *California Divorce Handbook*

File a Complaint

Because lawyers are licensed to practice, you can also *file a complaint* with the state bar. Lawyers are *officers of the court,* and must adhere to a *code of professional conduct.* When you file a complaint of lawyer misconduct, the lawyer is investigated—usually by the disciplinary board of the state bar or the state supreme court. If the investigator finds evidence of unethical behavior, the lawyer can be disciplined. Typical discipline includes private warnings, probation, suspension, and—for the most egregious cases—disbarment. Lawyers take complaints very seriously, and you will undoubtedly get their attention if you file one.

To file a complaint against a lawyer, contact the state bar association.

 As reported in the *Los Angeles Times,* in one year the California state bar received 75,000 complaints against California lawyers. [1]

Seek Available Funds

If your lawyer has stolen your money or your property, you can contact your state's *client security fund* or *client assistance fund.* Practicing lawyers pay fees to fund those funds, and you may be reimbursed for some—or all—of your loss. For example, in California, clients are eligible for a maximum payout of $50,000. To contact the fund, call the state bar association.

Sue for Malpractice

If your lawyer has made an honest mistake that has hurt you or cost you money, you can *sue for malpractice.* Many lawyers carry malpractice insurance specifically for this purpose. To sue a lawyer, you'll probably need another lawyer—one who specializes in suing lawyers. Ironically, you may be able to get a referral from your state bar's lawyer referral service.

Contact the Police

If your lawyer has committed a crime, you can report it to the *police.* If you are not sure it's a crime, you can always talk to another lawyer.

Unhappy Lawyers. A poll in *California Lawyer* magazine reported that "Seven out of 10 lawyers would change careers if the opportunity arose." A RAND Corp. study found that only half of the lawyers surveyed "would choose again to be a lawyer." [2]

How to Save Money on Legal Fees

Finally, your problem with your lawyer might not be her performance, but that she *costs too much.* Here are some way to keep your costs down:

Communicate with Your Lawyer Efficiently

The first way to save money is to *communicate* with your lawyer efficiently. Whoever said time is money must have been looking at a lawyer's bill. Your lawyer is your lawyer—not your therapist—so if you restrict your conversation to legal matters, you can save money.

Ways to communicate efficiently include:
- Write a letter instead of calling.
- If you must talk, make it brief.
- If you must meet, prepare an agenda beforehand.
- Mail the lawyer a list of important names, dates, telephone numbers, and facts.
- Deal with the secretary as much as possible.

Minimize the Role of Your Lawyer

Another way to save money is to minimize the role of the lawyer. This is simple economics. The more the lawyer does, the more she charges you. The less she does, the less you pay.

You can hire a lawyer to provide information only, to review an agreement you've already drafted, to negotiate for you, or to act as your *legal coach* while you represent yourself.

Watch Your Bill

A simple way to save money on legal fees is to *watch your bill.* Insist on regular billings that itemize your charges. If you see something unreasonable, immediately question it. Details that should appear on your bill include phone calls, messenger charges, and dates and lengths of meetings. You should also watch your bill because—once you see the costs—you can make some changes. You can decide to drop the case, do more yourself, or even hire a less expensive lawyer.

Hire a Specialist
Another way to save money is to hire a *specialist*. Hiring a certified specialist may cost you more per hour—but save you money overall. A specialist is more familiar with the law, and may be able to conclude your case more quickly.

 When *Consumer Reports* polled their readers about their experiences with lawyers in adversarial cases, many were unhappy. Among the reasons: 30% thought the lawyer didn't expedite the matter, 27% thought the lawyer failed to keep them informed, and 25% thought the lawyer charged them unreasonable fees. [3]

Negotiate Your Fee
When a lawyer quotes you a fee, it's just that—a quote. There's nothing stopping you from *bargaining*.

Fee Awards and Sanctions
In some cases, one parent must pay the other parent's attorney's fees. This often happens when one parent earns a little, and the other parent earns much more. By ordering an award of attorney's fees, the judge seeks to remove the advantage of the higher-earning parent. It also happens when one parent is a litigious ex-spouse. A litigious ex-spouse is someone who files frivolous motions intended to harass the other parent. To discourage the litigious ex-spouse from litigating, the judge may order that person to pay attorney's fees. State laws usually authorize awarding attorney's fees, but the decision is at the discretion of the judge.

Besides awarding attorney's fees, the judge can also *sanction* either party. A sanction is a financial penalty for misconduct—either yours or your attorney's. Sanctions are commonly ordered when someone has been frustrating the orders of the court—either by disobeying a court order, or by intentionally delaying a court proceeding. To punish the offending party for their behavior, the judge can order the party to pay, or reduce the amount the party was supposed to receive.

138

Child Custody Made Simple

Five Mistakes Made Working With Lawyers

1. Not telling your lawyer the truth—or not wanting your lawyer to tell you the truth.

2. Having sex with your lawyer.

3. Using your lawyer as your doctor, therapist, friend—anything but your lawyer.

4. Turning your life over to your lawyer.

5. Not paying your lawyer.

---

1 *Los Angeles Times,* October 6, 1995
2 *Los Angeles Times,* June 27, 1995
3 *Consumer Reports,* February, 1996

The Story of Jessica and James

Lawyers

Jessica was mad. And she felt powerless. The one thing she knew was she was not going to let Jim push her around.

Jim was a selfish, pushy man who didn't care about Julian, she told her friend, Monica. Monica nodded her head in agreement. Monica even encouraged her to stand up for herself and not give in. Jessica felt good when Monica said that, because she wasn't planning to. She knew what she needed to do.

The door to Brenner & Marsh was heavy oak, stained dark brown. Jessica liked it the minute she touched it. As she sat on the deep leather couches in the waiting room, she imagined all sorts of powerful, important lawyers working in the offices. But when she saw her lawyer, Ms. Michelle Marsh, she was surprised. She didn't look at all like the lawyers on T V. Ms. Marsh was a middle-aged woman with thick, plastic-frame glasses and coifed hair. When Jessica saw her, the first word that came to mind was frumpy.

"Have a seat," said Ms. Marsh, as she looked over the questionnaire Jessica had filled out. "You were married ten years... you are presently separated from your husband... and you have one minor child?"

"Yes," said Jessica.

Ms. Marsh fixed her gaze on Jessica. "What can I do for you?"

"It's about my son, Julian," Jessica began. "I think he would be better off living with me."

"You would like custody?"

"Yes."

"And what does your husband want?"

"Jim says he wants joint custody. But Julian is too young. He needs his mother."

Ms. Marsh carefully placed her pencil down on her desk.

"Would you like the court to award you sole custody of Julian?"

"Yes. I just want Julian. I don't care about money. I just want my baby."

Ms. Marsh paused. She knew that clients who professed not to be interested in money usually were. "We can certainly ask the court to grant you sole custody, which would entitle you to receive child support, and with a marriage this long, we might be able to get you spousal support. Would that be all right with you?"

Jessica was surprised. "Sure."

Ms. Marsh smiled at Jessica and picked up her pencil. "Tell me what has been going on."

✳   ✳   ✳

When Jim received the divorce papers from Jessica, he knew he had to get a lawyer.

The first lawyer he talked to told him it would cost $3,500 to open the case. It might as well be a million, thought Jim, as he thanked the lawyer and left. After two more lawyers quoted him the same price, Jim knew he had to find a cheaper lawyer.

The next lawyer Jim tried worked in a small office above a little restaurant. The office was dimly lit with thin, ripped carpeting, and the vinyl chairs in the waiting room were cracked, with yellow stuffing poking out. After twenty minutes, Mr. Shepard came out to greet him. He was smoking.

Jim spoke up right away. "I have to tell you, I don't have a lot of money."

Mr. Shepard shrugged. "No one does."

Jim followed Mr. Shepard into a cramped office, and Jim handed him the divorce papers. "Here. She wants to—"

"I can read."

Jim sat quietly as Mr. Shepard flipped through the legal forms. He silently noted the cigarette holes in the carpet and the "tracks" from cigarette ashes burned into the edge of the desk.

Mr. Shepard took a long drag on his cigarette. "Okay. So, what's the problem?"

Jim struggled for the right words. "I never know what's going on in his life. I hardly ever see him. She never tells me anything. He needs his Dad."

Mr. Shepard took a long drag on his cigarette, letting the smoke curl lazily towards the ceiling. "She wants custody and she's offering you visitation every other weekend. That's 20%. I'll be honest with you. That's what most Dads get."

Jim shook his head. "Look, I'm not good at this. I just want to see my son."

"We could try for more visitation. But that'll cost you a thousand, maybe two." He peered at Jim. "You have that?"

"No," muttered Jim.

Mr. Shepard flipped through the papers again. "You're in Department 12. Harold Kaplan." He shook his head. "Tough luck. 'Killer' Kaplan is a 'Mom' judge. He'll never give you more time with the kid."

"So, what do I do?" asked Jim.

Mr. Shepard shrugged. "The legal deck is stacked against you. You want my advice? Give her what she wants. Wait till the kid gets older. Maybe you can get him when he's a teenager."

Mr. Shepard crushed out his cigarette into the overflowing ashtray. The ashes and butts spilled onto his pants.

"Oh, shit."

Yeah, Jim thought. Oh, shit.

*   *   *

Going to Court

Chapter 12
Courts and Jurisdiction

If you've never been to court before, you're in for a strange, confusing—
and possibly frightening—experience.

Courts are a world unto themselves, where people follow highly
specialized customs and speak in highly specialized words. In fact, many
legal words are derived from Latin—a dead language.

*And "dead" is exactly how you may feel after spending a few hours sitting
on a court bench.*

However, if you fight over custody of your children, you have no choice
but to learn about the world of courts.

This chapter introduces the courts, judges, and jurisdiction.

The Adversarial System

To understand what courts do, you first have to understand what our system of justice is based on. To settle disputes, we use the *adversarial system.*

The adversarial system assumes that when two people fight, the truth will emerge. Each side rigorously advances its version of the facts to a third party who listens to the evidence and then decides.

The adversarial system developed many hundreds of years ago when people engaged in *trial by combat* to settle their disputes. Whoever survived the battle was deemed right.

Today, people hire lawyers to fight for them. Each person is an adversary, and the lawyers are their combatants. And when they fight—or *litigate*—they follow certain rules to ensure the fight proceeds in a fair and orderly manner.

The adversarial system resolves many kinds of disputes, but critics say it works poorly when it comes to family law. They point out that parents become enemies, fighting to win their case and beat their opponent. This is the opposite of what is needed, because after divorce parents must cooperate to raise the children.

Regardless of the merits of the adversarial system, it is the basis of our system of justice.

"Counsel may object, but he may not whine."

What Courts Do

If you fight over custody of your children, you must go to *court*. A court is where disputes are resolved.

The *courthouse* is the building where you go to resolve a dispute, and the *courtrooms* are where the court conducts its business.

Courts do many things. For example, they:
- Provide a forum for people to air their disputes.
- Punish criminals by separating them from society.
- Protect individuals from abuse of government power.
- Make a formal record of legal status.

When you go to court to decide custody, the court will decide who has legal custody and who has physical custody, who has visitation, and who pays child support and how much they pay.

By the way, notice that the words *court* and *judge* are interchangeable. This is common parlance. A lawyer may say, "the court ordered something" when she really means the judge ordered it.

Court System

Because there are many different kinds of cases, there are many different kinds of courts.

The largest division of courts is *federal* and *state*. Federal courts hear cases involving federal law, and state courts try issues involving state law.

Federal Courts
Since family law is state law, you probably won't find yourself in a *federal court*. A case can only be filed in federal court if it involves federal laws or the U. S. Constitution.

If you do somehow land in a federal trial court, you will first be heard in one of the 94 U.S. District Courts around the country. If you appeal, you will go to one of the 13 Courts of Appeals. Then, if you decide to appeal again and your case is chosen to be heard, you go to the highest court in the land—the *United States Supreme Court*.

State Courts

More likely, however, when you dispute child custody, you will do so in a *state court.*

Each state has created a state court system to resolve legal disputes not covered by the federal courts. Because federal courts only address a narrow range of legal issues, state courts handle the vast majority of legal problems.

The 50 state court systems handle almost every kind of case imaginable, including cases involving criminal behavior, personal injuries, real estate transactions—and specifically—child custody.

State courts are where the action is. As reported by the *American Bar Association,* of about 20 million civil cases a year, 19,700,000 were filed in state courts, and only 227,000 were filed in federal courts.[1]

Court Structure

Within each state, the courts are further subdivided. Dividing their courts allows states to solve many different types of legal problems more efficiently. Unfortunately, it also makes the court system more difficult to understand.

Since each state is free to create its own court structure—within the limits of the state constitution and the U.S. Constitution—no two states have ended up with exactly the same system.

There are as many different state court systems as there are states.

When you go to court for child custody, the court you go to is determined by how your state has organized its courts. While there is no single model of state court systems, there are many similarities.

Generally, states organize their courts into layers, with the lowest layer being trial courts that hear small problems—such as traffic offenses and small claims—and the highest being the supreme courts that only listen to cases on appeal. This hierarchical organization allows the judges in the upper courts to review the decisions made by the judges in the lower courts.

Here's an example of a typical state court system:

Court System

Supreme Court
The highest court is usually called the *Supreme Court*. These courts do not conduct trials, but rather, review the decisions made by the appellate courts below them. They are often called the *court of last resort* because—if you appeal your case—this is as far as you can go.

Court of Appeals
Below supreme courts are intermediate appellate courts, usually called the *Court of Appeals.* These courts review the decisions of the trial courts below them. Appeals courts do not retry cases, but rather, review the case to see if the law was correctly applied.

Trial Courts
The first two levels of courts are *trial courts.* Trial courts are where you actually file a lawsuit. It is in the trial court that you present your evidence, give testimony on the witness stand, and listen to the judge's decision.

States divide up their trial courts in many different ways. Here are the two most common groupings:

Courts of General Jurisdiction
Courts of general jurisdiction typically hear cases involving serious criminal and civil offenses. These courts go by many names, including *Circuit Court, District Court,* and *Superior Court.* They can usually hear all types of cases, without limits on the type of criminal behavior or the amount of money involved.

Courts of Limited Jurisdiction
The lowest courts are also trial courts, but they are limited to hearing specific types of cases. They are usually called *County Court, Municipal Court,* or *Magistrate Court.* They typically hear civil cases involving small dollar amounts, and also involving minor criminal offenses. Traffic offenses and small claims are examples of cases heard in courts of limited jurisdiction.

Family Court
If you dispute child custody, you may well end up in a *family court.* Depending upon your state, these trial courts can have either limited or general jurisdiction. The proceedings in each family court are different, but generally mediation is encouraged over litigation.

 What's in a name? States can name their courts as they choose. For example, in New York the highest court is called the Court of Appeals, and the Supreme Court is a trial court.

Courthouse

Once you find the right court, you'll have to go inside. While each courthouse is different, they almost all have the same rooms—or departments—that are necessary for the court to function.

When you walk through the courthouse, be sure to look for the *clerk's office.* This is where you go to file your lawsuit, retrieve copies of your *case record,* and pick up a copy of the court rules. The office is only open during posted hours, and there may be long lines.

Most courthouses also have *law libraries* open to the public. Here you can do research or browse through the legal newspapers.

And finally, you'll need to find the *courtroom* where your case will be heard. A courtroom is where the judge works. Judges typically have their own courtrooms, and the judge's name may be posted outside the door. In some places, the courtroom may be called a *department,* but it is still a courtroom.

 You're being watched. Family disputes are so confrontational that some parents smuggle in concealed weapons in order to hurt someone—the other parent, the judge, or maybe even the opposing lawyer. Courts have responded by installing pervasive video surveillance and metal detectors at the door. Some judges even wear a bulletproof vest. You should assume that when you enter a courthouse, your behavior is being monitored.

Courtroom

Like courthouses, *courtrooms* are also laid out in different ways, but they usually have the same elements.

When you first walk in, you enter the *spectator* area—the place in the back of the courtroom where you wait your turn. This part of the court is usually separated by a bar or partition.

While you're waiting, the judge works at the *bench*—a desk or raised platform in front of the courtroom. No one can walk in the area near the bench—called the *well*—without her permission.

When it's your turn, you sit at the *counsel table,* the table where you and your lawyer face the judge. There are usually two tables—one for you and one for the opposing party.

When you testify, you sit in the *witness stand,* a boxed-in area usually next to the judge.

And finally, when it's appropriate to have a conversation "off the record," the judge may have a whispered conversation at the bench, or may adjourn to her *chambers*—a private office near the courtroom.

Court People

Everyone in court has a special name, including you. Here are some:

Parties
You and the other parent are known as parties or litigants. The person who started the lawsuit is the moving party, plaintiff, or petitioner. The other person is the responding party, defendant, or respondent. If you are representing yourself, you are a pro per or pro se. If you are appealing, you are an appellant and the other person is an appellee.

Judge
The judge is the man or woman who supervises the courtroom. Other words for judge include court or bench. If the judge is temporary—such as a lawyer filling in—he or she is a judge pro tem. A commissioner, magistrate, master, or referee is a court-appointed official who handles routine matters.

Lawyer
A lawyer, attorney, or counsel is someone who represents you.

Clerk
A person who keeps track of court documents and physical evidence is called a court clerk, county clerk, civil clerk, or judge's clerk.

Bailiff
A bailiff is a peace officer who keeps order in the courtroom. Bailiffs are usually armed and in uniform.

Court Reporter
A court reporter records every word said during the official court proceedings.

Witnesses
Witnesses are people who testify under oath about information they possess. Ordinary witnesses testify to what they have seen or heard, and expert witnesses testify to their opinions.

Court Rules

When you enter a court, you'll have to obey the *rules of the court.* Some rules are issued by the state, and are called *state rules of court.* Other rules are issued by the court, and are called *local rules of court.*

Court rules can be quite specific, and may include how much time you have to respond to a motion, the size and type of paper you must use, etc. Copies of the court rules are usually available in the *clerk's office* or the courthouse *law library.*

A knowledgeable local attorney is supposed to know the court rules, and if you have hired such an attorney, you may not have to learn the rules yourself. However, if you choose to represent yourself, you will have to learn the rules.

 Justice delayed is justice denied. Don't be surprised if you wait all morning in court, only to have your case continued to another day. In some cities, cases are routinely delayed three or four years before finally coming to trial.

Calendar

When someone files a lawsuit, the court must schedule a time when that suit will be heard. The schedule of cases with their dates and times for hearing or trial is called the *calendar.*

The calendar is prepared each day by the court clerk, who usually posts it near the front door of every courtroom. When you arrive at the courthouse, you must check the court calendar to make sure your case is indeed scheduled for that day.

There are several different ways to schedule—or calendar—cases, but typically courts apportion caseloads in one of two ways:

Master Calendar
When courts follow the *master calendar format,* they divide up the cases among the available judges. Generally, the *master calendar judge* calls

out each case and asks for a time estimate from the attorneys, then assigns the case to an available judge. This method almost guarantees that different phases of your case will be heard by different judges. For example, pretrial motions may be heard by one judge, but if you go to trial, they may be heard by a different judge.

Direct Calendar

The opposite approach is the *direct calendar* system, where the case is assigned to one judge who hears it from start to finish. Usually the judge is assigned by the court clerk in an automatic rotation. Under this format, the same judge will:

- Hear all motions.
- Preside at the settlement conference.
- Conduct the trial.
- Render a decision.

The court calendar determines not just the day you have to go to court, but *which judge will hear your case.*

Judges

Judges are people who have been given the authority to resolve disputes. They are the public officials who remain neutral while the two opposing parties advance their version of the facts.

Because custody cases are decided by a judge, his or her most important role may appear to be that of an *umpire* or a *referee*. But trial judges have many roles, including:

- Presiding over pretrial and settlement conferences.
- Ruling on pretrial motions and discovery disputes.
- Presiding over trials.
- Ruling on trial procedure, such as allowing or excluding evidence.
- In bench trials, deciding who wins, who loses, and how much someone pays.
- Managing the caseflow.

In particular, judges are acutely aware they must manage the flow of cases through their courtroom. This is a response to the belief that most lawsuits drag on and cost too much. Judges can move cases through the system by setting time limits for parts of the case, and then monitoring the progress to ensure compliance.

Because judges do so much, it's impossible to underestimate their importance. When you present your dispute to a judge, he or she will be the sole *fact finder.* The judge will listen to the evidence, decide what that evidence establishes, draw inferences from those facts, and then apply the law to reach a decision.

This makes the individual preferences—or bias—of the judge very, very important in determining the outcome of your case.

Selecting Judges
Since judges play such an important role, it stands to reason they don't become judges by simply walking in and applying for the job. In fact, judges become judges by *appointment* or *election.*

Appointment. In the federal court system, all of the judges are appointed for life by the President. This includes the 649 district court judgeships, the 179 appeals court seats, and the nine seats on the Supreme Court. But in the state court system, only about two-thirds of the states appoint their judges, with the rest requiring the judges to run for election.

When states appoint a judge, typically a panel of lawyers and nonlawyers recruits and evaluates applicants. The panel then recommends the names of the most qualified to the governor, who makes the final selection, subject to the approval of the legislature.

Election. When judges are required to run for election, a judge must win a seat by a majority of the popular vote in a general election. In these states, judges must regularly run for retention, and if they do not get enough votes, the seat may be vacated.

Finally, a few states follow a mixed system, where judges are appointed initially but must run for election thereafter.

I'll take my case to the Supreme Court! If you get an unfavorable judgment in a lower trial court, you can always appeal the decision. But there are limits to how far you can go. Certain high courts—including the U.S. Supreme Court—turn down the vast majority of cases that are submitted to them. This means the decision of the last appellate court stands.

Evaluating Judges
Once a judge becomes a judge, all states monitor and evaluate his or her performance. This not only ensures that people get a fair trial, but that the judge improves over time. Typically, the evaluation program is run either by the highest court or some state association. Judges evaluations are usually composed of anonymous feedback by the same people who appear before them—lawyers, jurors, litigants, and so on.

 Real judges don't do family law. Don't be surprised if your judge doesn't want to be there. Some family court judges don't have the personality to handle social problems, while other judges want to do more prestigious assignments—such as death penalty cases. Still other judges may feel overwhelmed by the workload. That's why, "If you find that your judge appears tired, a bit testy, and willing to approve any settlement terms so long as you settle, keep in mind you are seeing the results of a society that talks a lot about the importance of family and children but has seldom put its money behind either." Judge Stewart, *California Divorce Handbook*

Disciplining Judges
And finally, all states have procedures for *disciplining* judges. Discipline procedures vary from state to state, but every state has a commission that investigates complaints about a judge and recommends possible sanctions—including removal from office.

Sanctioning. If a judge's behavior or performance is problematical, the disciplining body can apply various sanctions, including reprimands, censure, or suspension.

Firing. A judge whose problematical behavior or performance is more serious can be involuntarily retired or fired. In addition, judges who are elected may be subject to recall, where the voters vote in a special election to decide if the judge should be removed from office. Because federal judges are appointed for life, they can only be removed by impeachment, but they are subject to lesser sanctions, including removal of their work.

Because they work in a public setting, judges are constantly being watched and evaluated.

Non-Judges

Faced with an overwhelming number of cases and a limited supply of full-time judges, many courts solve the problem by assigning cases to other court officials, such as a:

Judge Pro Tem
A judge pro tempore is a temporary judge. He or she is often a practicing attorney, and may know the law as well as a regular judge. A judge pro tem has all the powers of a regular judge, but typically serves only with the consent of the parties—which means you can insist on having a permanent judge.

Master or Referee
A master or referee is generally a court-appointed official who handles routine, uncontested matters. In some courts, masters hear pretrial motions, rule on discovery issues, and more.

Commissioner or Magistrate
A commissioner or magistrate is often someone who helps the judge determine the facts in a case. Depending on the court system, this individual may also conduct trials.

Jurisdiction

When you file a lawsuit, you must also decide which court to file it in. Not every court can hear every case. Generally, you must file your case in the court that has *jurisdiction*. Jurisdiction is the authority of the court to decide a particular case.

Deciding where to file your case is one of most important decisions you will make.

Jurisdiction can be very simple or very complex—it all depends on your circumstances. For example, if both you and the other parent have never been involved in custody proceedings before, there is no custody proceeding going on somewhere else, and you have both lived in the same state for the last six months, then jurisdiction may be straightforward. But if someone has moved, or if there are prior orders from a different court, or if custody is currently in dispute in a different court, then determining which court has jurisdiction can get complicated.

For the court to have jurisdiction over your case, it must have authority over both the legal issues raised and the people involved. This is called *subject-matter jurisdiction* and *personal jurisdiction.*

Subject-Matter Jurisdiction
Subject-matter jurisdiction simply means the court can hear that type of case. For example, family courts can hear child custody and child support cases, but not bankruptcy cases. Subject-matter jurisdiction is usually determined by state statutes. For a court to have subject-matter jurisdiction, a party to the suit must generally have lived in the state six months, though some states allow as little as 90 days, while other states require a full year.

Personal Jurisdiction
The court must also have the authority to make orders involving the people named in the lawsuit. This *personal jurisdiction* is usually established when the respondent is either personally served with an order from the court within the state, or it is demonstrated that they have had minimum contacts in the state. If the court does not have personal jurisdiction over someone, it cannot make enforceable orders against that person.

Because we live in a highly mobile society, jurisdiction can easily become a problem. For example, when some parents disagree with a custody decision, they simply move to a new state and file for a modification there. Other parents take the law into their own hands and kidnap the children to a different state, where they seek a change in orders.

Jurisdiction can become a nightmare if two states each enter separate—and different—custody orders. Because federal courts do not have the authority to decide custody or settle a custody dispute caught between different states, the case could conceivably bounce back and forth indefinitely.

Because state borders have become such huge obstacles to deciding and enforcing child custody, uniform laws have been adopted to resolve the problem.

Uniform Child Custody Jurisdiction Act (UCCJA)

The *Uniform Child Custody Jurisdiction Act (UCCJA)* is a uniform law that has been adopted by every state . This law provides a set of guidelines for deciding initial child custody. It lists four factors that determine when a court has jurisdiction, or when it must defer to another court.

Under the UCCJA, a court can decide custody only if it meets one of the following tests:

- *Home State.* The court is in the child's home state. "Home state" means the child has lived there for the past six months. If the child has been removed from the home state by the other parent, it still qualifies as the home state if six months have not yet passed since the child was removed.

- *Best Interest.* The court can decide custody if it is in the best interest of the child to do so. This usually means the child has *significant connections* to other people in the state, or that it will harm the child's "future care, protection, training, and personal relationships" if the case is tried elsewhere.

- *Abandonment.* The court can also assume jurisdiction if the child has been abandoned, or if there is reason to believe that the child will be abused or neglected if returned home.

- *No Other State.* Finally, if no other state meets the above tests—or if another state meets the tests but chooses not to decide custody—the court has jurisdiction.

The act discourages one parent from moving to another state to gain a favorable custody decision. If the other parent files within the six-month period, jurisdiction remains with the first state.

 To quote from the UCCJA, home state is "the state in which the child immediately preceding the time involved lived with his parents, a parent, or a person acting as parent, for at least six consecutive months, and in the case of a child less than six months old the state in which the child lived from birth with any of the persons mentioned."

Parental Kidnapping Prevention Act (PKPA)

The *Parental Kidnapping Prevention Act (PKPA)* concerns cases where a custody order has been made—or is pending—in one state, and a subsequent suit is filed in a different state. The PKPA doesn't just cover kidnappings, but all cases where one court is asked to modify or enforce an order from a court in a different state.

Generally, the PKPA assigns *continuing jurisdiction* to the court that issued the original order. However, to decide this subsequent jurisdiction, the court must ask three questions:
- Did the first state have jurisdiction?
- Is the custody case in the first state finished?
- Does the second state now have jurisdiction?

For example, if the first state had jurisdiction, and the case is still pending, then the second state must defer to the first state. However, if the case is over, the second state must determine if it has jurisdiction by the tests in the UCCJA. If it does, it can hear the case. Otherwise, it can't.

On the other hand, if the first state didn't have jurisdiction, and the second state does, then the second state has jurisdiction. But if the first state didn't have jurisdiction, and the second state doesn't either, then the second state still can't hear the case.

When circumstances cause the UCCJA and the PKPA to overlap, the PKPA takes priority.

"Full faith and credit law requires that a judgment from one state have the same effect in a second forum as it has in the forum that rendered the judgment. Title 28 U.S.C. section 1738 (general full faith and credit statute) provides that a judgment shall have the same full faith and credit in every court as they have "by law or usage in the courts of such State ... which they are taken." This has always been interpreted to mean that forum two must give forum one's judgment the same degree of finality as it would receive in forum one." *National Conference of Commissioners on Uniform State Laws*

Venue

Aside from jurisdiction, you may also have to decide *venue.* Venue is the city, county, or district where you file your lawsuit.

Venue is established by state law, and—unlike jurisdiction—can easily be changed. Parents can file a motion for a *change of venue* simply for the convenience of going to a more accessible courthouse, or even for the convenience of their witnesses.

Venue is typically changed in high-profile criminal trials so that the defendant can find a less biased jury.

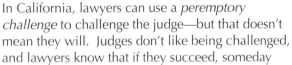 In California, lawyers can use a *peremptory challenge* to challenge the judge—but that doesn't mean they will. Judges don't like being challenged, and lawyers know that if they succeed, someday they'll appear before that judge again... and he'll remember. That's why "there is a saying among lawyers that once you challenge a judge, you must do so whenever assigned to that judge for the rest of your career." Judge Stewart, *California Divorce Handbook*

Forum Shopping

When judges make custody decisions each day, they acquire a reputation among the lawyers who appear before them. This preference—or judicial bias—of the judge will influence the outcome just as assuredly as any statute or precedent. That's why some lawyers try to maneuver the case so that it will be heard by a judge who is more likely to decide in their favor. This is called *forum shopping.*

A *forum* is the court where the hearing or trial takes place. Forum shopping is the effort to move the case to another courtroom, and hence, another judge.

Many lawyers consider forum shopping a legitimate tool to aggressively represent their client. Most judges, however, object to forum shopping because it implies they won't make an impartial decision.

How the court assigns cases dramatically influences your chances to
forum shop:

Master Calendar

When cases are assigned under the *master calendar* system, attorneys
have many ways to forum shop. For example, when the master calendar
judge calls out for a time estimate, the lawyer can estimate less time to get
assigned to the judge who is hearing short motions, and more time to get
assigned to the judge who is hearing long motions. Also, since the judges
under this system routinely rotate assignments, the lawyer can delay filing
a motion, or get "sick" for a short time, thus waiting for a new judge to be
assigned. Or, the lawyer can wait for the judge to go on vacation,
knowing another judge will be assigned.

Direct Calendar

When courts assign cases under the *direct calendar* format, there is much
less opportunity to forum shop. Under this format, judges are usually
assigned in automatic rotation, and then remain with the case until it
completes. To choose a particular judge, an attorney would have to stand
in the clerk's office watching the order of judges being assigned, and then
suddenly leap into line at the appropriate point. This may happen, but it's
probably unusual.

View from the Bench

*California Divorce Handbook: How to Dissolve Your Marriage
Without Financial Disaster,* James W. Stewart, Prima Publishing,
$18.95. Judge Stewart offers fascinating glimpses into the daily life of
a family court judge.

---

1 *Law and the Courts: A Handbook of Courtroom Procedures,* American Bar
Association, 1995. If you're wondering where the other 73,000 cases were filed—
the ABA didn't say.

Chapter 13
Pretrial

When you go to court to decide custody of your children, you will have to follow many court rules and regulations. These rules are designed to move people through the legal system as smoothly as possible.

The rules of *civil procedure* determine how you begin a case and what you do each step along the way. Depending on your case, you may have to file *pleadings, conduct discovery,* make *motions,* and attend various *hearings.*

And if the dispute is not resolved during pretrial, you will have to prepare for *trial.*

This chapter discusses the pretrial phase of a civil case.

Civil Procedure

When you take a dispute to court, you must follow a specific set of rules that govern how the dispute is handled. These are the rules of *civil procedure.*

To some people, procedure can seem like red tape or technicalities. Certainly, procedure can be complex, and at times may appear to fly in the face of common sense.

However, procedure is critical in helping the judge reach a fair decision. With a few exceptions, following procedure means the judge must wait until both sides have had a chance to tell their story before making a decision. This protects your rights as well the rights of the other parent, and it is the essence of our system of justice.

Because custody and support disagreements are private disputes between two individuals, they are governed by civil law, and are controlled by the *rules of civil procedure.*

These rules come from laws passed by the state legislature or from rules issued by the State Supreme Court. They include:
- Who can sue whom, and for what.
- What documents you need to file, and when.
- How much time you have to bring a lawsuit.
- What kind of trial you can have.
- What kind of remedy you can ask for.
- What you can do if you lose.
- How you can enforce a judgment.

No matter how good a case you have, you must follow the rules.

Generally, the rules of civil procedure for state courts are modeled after the *Federal Rules of Civil Procedure,* but each state can have its own version. To find out the rules for your state, look in the state statutes for a section called civil procedure or court rules.

How a Civil Case Proceeds to Trial

Unless you're in court regularly, you may not know how a civil case proceeds to trial. Here's a diagram:

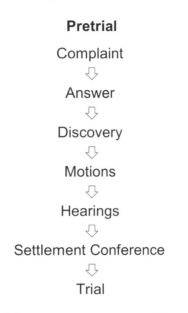

Pretrial

Complaint
⇩
Answer
⇩
Discovery
⇩
Motions
⇩
Hearings
⇩
Settlement Conference
⇩
Trial

Generally, the *pretrial* phase encompasses everything that happens before the trial, and the *posttrial* phase encompasses everything that happens after the trial.

This chapter discusses the pretrial phase.

Pleadings

You begin a lawsuit by filing a legal document with the court. Each side submits one or more documents that state a version of the facts and what needs to be done. These initial documents are called *pleadings*.

Complaint

The first paper filed in a lawsuit is a *complaint* or *petition*. You do this by completing a form and giving it to the clerk of the court, along with a filing fee. The person who makes the complaint is the *petitioner* or *plaintiff*, and the other side is the *respondent* or *defendant*.

The complaint contains several important pieces of information. First, it has the plaintiff's version of the facts. The plaintiff describes what happened and what wrongs were committed. The specific offenses are listed in a series of *counts*. Second, the complaint states the legal basis for the lawsuit, including the laws that apply, and shows that the court has jurisdiction to hear the case. And finally, the complaint ends with the *prayer for relief*. This is what the plaintiff wants the court to do—either make a monetary award or a court order. In a custody suit, the *remedy* sought might be for sole custody or increased visitation.

Summons and Service

After the complaint is filed, the other person must be told about the lawsuit. In federal and state courts, the clerk of the court issues a *summons,* which contains the name of the plaintiff, the name and address of the plaintiff's lawyer (if there is one), the case number, and how much time the defendant has to respond.

Because our system of justice is based on a struggle between two combatants, it's only fair that the person being sued knows about it. That's why there are very strict rules about how the summons and complaint are given to the defendant. The lawsuit will not proceed unless the court is convinced the other party has been given *notice.*

The summons and complaint can be *served* on the defendant by:
- A sheriff, marshal, or constable.
- A process server.
- Certified or registered mail.
- A private person, over 18 years old, who is not a party to the action.

 A plaintiff or defendant in a lawsuit generally can't serve his or her own pleadings or motions on the other party. At the very least, another adult must do it. Some states allow any adult not connected to the suit to serve legal papers.

Answer

If you receive a complaint, you have an opportunity to file your response—called an *answer.* While the amount of time varies, you'll typically have between two and four weeks.

In your answer you respond to the allegations made against you. You can admit some charges, deny others, and say you can't respond to the rest because you don't have enough information. If you do not respond to something, that can be interpreted as an admission that it's true. Also, you can add facts which may prove that you're not at fault, or offer a reason which may justify your actions.

If you don't respond to a complaint, and you don't show up for the hearing, the plaintiff can get a *default judgment*. This means the plaintiff wins the suit without having to prove anything. If that happens, you can try to get the judgment *set aside* by offering valid excuses for your oversight, such as being in the hospital or that your attorney failed to act in a timely manner.

 Instead of filing an answer, you can challenge the complaint with various kinds of motions, such as a motion to dismiss, a motion to strike, or a motion for a summary judgment. You argue that the court does not have jurisdiction, or that the complaint does not state a legally valid claim. You can also file a motion to quash service by insisting that you were not served notice properly.

Counterclaim and Reply

If the defendant answers the complaint by making his or her own claims against the plaintiff, those complaints are contained in the *counterclaim*. Sometimes the counterclaim is part of the answer, sometimes it is filed separately.

When one side raises new allegations, the other side can file a reply to the new allegations raised, which means the plaintiff can reply to the counterclaim.

Discovery

After the pleadings have been filed, each side tries to learn more about the facts in the case. You do this through *discovery*.

Discovery is a set of legal procedures that each side uses to force their opponent to reveal information. Through discovery, you can learn what the other person is claiming, what potential witnesses have to say, and whether any physical evidence exists. Discovery lets you find out what evidence the other side will present, thus ensuring you won't face any surprises at trial.

Because you don't know what the other side knows, the rules limiting discovery are quite broad and generally allow one side to seek any information that is "reasonably calculated to lead to the discovery of admissible evidence." Thus, you can ask for information that is not admissible itself, but may lead to something that is.

Discovery is a necessary part of trial preparation because most people are reluctant to reveal information. By letting each side force the other to answer questions, the judge can see everything important and— hopefully—reach the correct decision.

Unfortunately, discovery can also be used as a weapon to harass the other side. Aggressive attorneys wage discovery wars where they seek reams of information about everything possibly related to the case. This inundates the other side and creates huge legal fees.

To combat such abuses, many courts require discovery to be completed within a short period of time. Each side must quickly disclose everything relevant to the case. If the lawyers disagree over what needs to be revealed, those disputes can be brought to the judge's attention in a short discovery motion hearing, or can even be discussed over the telephone. If the judge finds that one side has failed to cooperate (for example, by giving evasive or argumentative answers), that side can be fined.

Here are the most common forms of discovery:
- Depositions.
- Interrogatories.
- Request for admission of facts.
- Request for production of documents.
- Subpoenas.

 Discovery can easily cost more than $10,000 in lawyer's fees, and you'll pay extra for the expert witnesses and the court reporter. Also, don't forget to include the time you lose from work while you are being deposed.

Depositions

A widely used form of discovery is a *deposition*. A deposition is when someone is asked questions by an attorney. That person is placed *under oath* by swearing to tell the truth. A court reporter records all answers.

The main difference between a deposition and live testimony is that the deposition occurs outside court—usually in a lawyer's office. However, the person answering the questions is still under oath, so the answers must be as truthful as if that person was actually testifying in court.

Who Can Be Deposed

Both the plaintiff and the defendant can be *deposed*. In addition, anyone else not named in the lawsuit—but who might be a potential witness or who might possess useful information—can be ordered to answer questions. If an important witness cannot testify at trial, a deposition can be taken and read in court.

 *Paper trail.* If you are representing yourself, be sure to keep good records of all requests and agreements. When the other side promises to do something, send them a letter confirming what they said.

The Purpose of a Deposition

The main reason for "taking a deposition" is to prepare for trial. Depositions allow each side to know what a witness will say in court, thus helping to prepare the case.

But depositions are also used to undermine the opposing party. The questions asked are designed not only to elicit helpful information, but to find information damaging to the other side.

Lawyers try to get the person being deposed to make an inconsistent statement or an admission against interest.

Because every answer in a deposition is being recorded, one of the goals of the opposing lawyer is to trap the person into making an inconsistent statement. Anything said in a deposition can be read back at trial, so if the person changes an answer, the opposing lawyer can argue that—at the very least—everything this person says is unreliable, and at worst—this individual is a bald-faced liar. Lawyers actually practice how to successfully impeach a witness during trial.

How a Deposition Is Taken

Typically, a deposition is taken at one of the lawyer's offices, but it can also be done in a hotel room or even your home. A court reporter is present to record the questioning, and whoever is being deposed can have a lawyer there. In addition, the other party has the right to attend.

Most depositions only last a few hours, but conceivably they could stretch to a few days, or even a few weeks. After the questioning is finished, the court reporter types up the transcript, and the witness signs a copy in front of a notary. This makes the answers as important as if they were said in a courtroom.

If you are being deposed, you will first receive a *subpoena* and a *notice,* and you will generally have at least ten days' warning.

What Can Be Asked at a Deposition

When you are questioned during a deposition, you can be asked about any aspect of the case. The scope of questions allowed is quite broad, even if the questions themselves would not be allowed at trial. You may also be required to bring copies of any documents relevant to the case. These can include financial records or other documents in your possession. If you must bring something, it will be specified in the subpoena or notice.

While you generally must answer what you are asked, your attorney can object to improper questions. For example, if you are asked to reveal privileged information—such as conversations protected by attorney-client privilege—you don't have to answer. Or if a question is totally irrelevant, you can refuse to answer. Also, your attorney can object to questions that are confusing, vague, or ambiguous.

If the attorneys disagree over whether a question can be asked, they may have to resolve the dispute in front of a judge.

In addition to questions about your home, work, and income, you may be asked about raising the children.

For example, you could be asked:

- Who takes the children to and from school?
- Who is the primary contact with the teachers?
- Who makes the children their meals, washes their clothes, and helps them with their homework?
- Who takes the children to their after-school activities?
- Have you ever hit, confined, or physically disciplined your children?
- Have you ever kissed, caressed, or fondled your children in a sexual manner?
- Have you ever been arrested, convicted of a felony, or served time in prison?
- Have you ever used alcohol, drugs, or illegal substances?

How to Answer Questions at a Deposition
There are some specific strategies that you can pursue when you are deposed. As a general rule, the more information you give the opposing lawyer, the more it can hurt you—so you want to answer honestly but briefly.

First, plan on *practicing ahead* of time with your lawyer. If he or she grills you like crazy in private, you'll be better equipped for the opposing attorney.

Second, when asked a question, *listen carefully.* Many questions are trick questions designed to trap you. The classic trick question is, "Do you still beat your wife?" By answering with a simple "No," you've agreed with the questioner's implied assumption that you beat your wife at one time.

Third, before answering, *pause a moment.* This gives your lawyer time to object to an improper question, and keeps you from tossing out an off-the-cuff response.

Fourth, when answering a question, *stay calm.* The other lawyer will be watching you for signs of stress. Don't give any clues as to what's important. Try to answer with the same inflection and timing in your voice, and try to keep your body language consistent.

Fifth, when you answer a question, *don't volunteer* anything. Answer what is asked, and nothing more. Try to answer "Yes," "No," or "That's not correct" as much as possible. If you decide to explain something, you will give the other side more material, and they will also know this is an area that concerns you. That can only lead to more questions you may not want to answer.

And finally, *avoid admissions against interest.* In a deposition, frankness is deadly. You have to tell the truth, but don't bring up anything that can hurt you. And when you do reveal something negative, try to make it sound as positive as possible.

Three Steps to Formulating an Answer

Step 1. Do you understand the question?

"I don't understand the question. Please explain."

Step 2. Do you understand the question but don't know the answer?

"I don't know."

Step 3. Do you understand the question and know the answer?

Answer it.

Interrogatories

Another way to pry information loose from the opposing party is through *interrogatories.* Interrogatories are written questions that you send to the other side. The other party must answer all of your questions in writing, and—as with depositions—the person is under oath to answer truthfully when answering.

The rules governing interrogatories vary from state to state, and include how many questions you can ask and how much time the party has to answer. You can use this discovery method along with a deposition, or instead of one. Generally, however, you can only direct interrogatories to the other party named in the lawsuit, and not at third parties.

Interrogatories are a much less expensive way to gather information than depositions, but they have their drawbacks. Because you're not present when the other side responds, you may get vague or incomplete answers. The solution is to phrase very specific questions asking for factual information.

What You Can Ask in an Interrogatory

Generally, you can ask the same questions as in a deposition, but you may not want to. Interrogatories are best suited for nailing down factual information or establishing the validity of documents for trial.

The type of subjects you might want to cover in an interrogatory include the person's vital statistics, employment history and income, financial information, and any arrests or convictions.

If you receive an interrogatory, it's a good idea to review it with your lawyer before answering. You may be able to save a lot of time by answering many questions "N/A" for *not applicable.* For example, if a series of questions ask about a criminal past, and you have no criminal past, you can mark the answers "N/A."

 Fast track. Many courts have rules designed to move a case through the court system as quickly as possible. These include: deadlines on when each phase of the case must be completed, limits on how much information can be requested from the opposing party, and mini-trials or neutral evaluations that encourage the parties to settle.

Request for Admission of Facts

You can also get information by asking the other side to agree to certain facts. When one party to a lawsuit asks the other side if some statements are true, it's called a *request for admission of facts.*

Typically, the other side either admits or denies the statements you make. You can use whatever facts they admit to as evidence in the trial without having to prove it. This discovery tool has limited usefulness, but it can save some time and money.

Request for Production of Documents

When you need copies of certain documents, you can make a request to *produce documents*. This is a written request you make for the other party to hand over copies of relevant papers.

When child support is an issue—which it almost always is—the income of the other parent is extremely relevant, and you can request copies of bank statements, pay stubs, and so on.

What You Can't Do with Discovery

1. *Ask for privileged information.* You can't ask the other side to reveal confidential conversations, such as between lawyers and clients.

2. *Overwhelm the other side.* You can't inundate the other party with discovery requests beyond their resources to comply.

3. *Be abusive.* You can't seek information solely designed to embarrass or harass the other party.

4. *Request irrelevant information.* You can't ask for facts unrelated to the case.

Subpoenas

A final way you can secure information is with a *subpoena.* A subpoena is a court order that requires someone to do something. You issue a subpoena when you want a witness to give testimony—either at a deposition or in court.

You can also issue a special type of subpoena called a *subpoena duces tecum.* This subpoena allows you to secure copies of documents that are in the exclusive control of someone else. That might include school records, business records, police records, bank records, and so on. If you use these records at trial, you may also have to subpoena the *keeper of the records*—the official who maintains the files—to vouch for their authenticity.

To subpoena someone, have your lawyer prepare the subpoena, then arrange for it to be served on the witness. Generally, you don't need the court's permission to issue a subpoena unless you're trying to get copies of government documents. If the other party ignores the subpoena, they can be held in contempt, and a sheriff can be ordered to bring them to court.

 You must serve a witness subpoena or a subpoena duces tecum far enough in advance for the other person to have time to respond. Court rules often specify the number of days ahead of time you must serve the subpoena for it to be considered good service.

Motions

Once the pleadings have been filed, you can ask the court to do certain things. These include stopping the other parent from doing something—such as moving away with the children—or forcing the other parent to do something—such as answering discovery questions. You file a *motion* to ask the court to issue orders.

Typically, you make pretrial motions when you want to:
- Ask that the lawsuit be dismissed.
- Enforce discovery by requiring the other side to answer certain questions or to produce certain documents.
- Limit discovery by protecting yourself from having to answer certain questions or having to produce certain documents.
- Maintain the status quo by ordering the other side to refrain from doing something.

How to File a Motion
Either party can file a motion before, during, or after the trial. Depending on what you want, you usually submit your motion to the court in writing, and the other side files a response. If the other side objects to what you're asking for, the judge holds a brief hearing where each side makes a short oral argument. Finally, the judge either grants or denies the motion.

If you have an urgent need, you can make an emergency motion, such as a request for a *temporary restraining order (TRO)* or a *preliminary injunction.* If the court approves these motions, they stop the other party from taking certain actions prior to the trial.

You don't always have to file a motion to get what you want. If you can reach an informal agreement with the other party, you may be able to notify the court by filing a *stipulation.* A stipulation is an agreement between the parties that certain facts are true or that a certain procedure will be followed. Typically, both parties sign the stipulation and file it with the clerk.

Here are some common pretrial motions:

Motion for a Summary Judgment
If there is no disagreement over the facts in the case, either party can file a *motion for a summary judgment.* This tells the judge that everyone agrees on the facts, and the only thing left to do is to decide how the law should be applied. If the motion is granted, the judge reads all of the written arguments and evidence, and then makes a ruling—without having a trial. If the motion is denied, the parties proceed to trial.

The advantage of a summary judgment is that it saves everyone a tremendous amount of money. Also, because most of the legal activities are skipped, the litigants get a much quicker court decision. On the other hand, because summary judgments are just as final as if you had actually gone to trial, if you get a decision you don't like, you can't change your mind and opt for a trial.

If you file a summary judgment motion, you attach supporting documents, such as *affidavits* or *declarations*—sworn statements under oath—and other written evidence. If the other party has filed a summary judgment motion, and you want a trial instead, you respond by arguing that some facts in the case are in dispute.

Motion to Quash Service
If you want to dismiss the lawsuit without having to answer, you can file a *motion to quash service.* This motion argues that the defendant was not served properly, or that the case is outside the jurisdiction of the court. If this motion is granted, the lawsuit may be thrown out, and the moving party has to start all over again. If the motion is denied, the lawsuit continues.

Motion to Dismiss

Another motion filed before the answer is a *motion to dismiss for failure to state a claim.* This is where the defendant asks the judge to dismiss the lawsuit because the complaint states a legally meaningless claim. In other words, the motion argues that even if the allegations were true, it doesn't matter—the plaintiff isn't entitled to anything.

If a motion to dismiss, or *demurrer,* is granted, the lawsuit may be thrown out, or the plaintiff may be given the chance to amend the complaint and file it again. If the motion is denied, the defendant will usually get some time—such as 30 days—to answer.

Motion to Strike

You file this motion when some parts of the complaint are flawed, such as when the allegations have already been decided by another lawsuit. If the motion is granted, the deficient parts of the complaint are removed.

Motion for Preliminary Orders

When parents first separate and can't agree on custody of their children, either one can file a *motion for preliminary orders* that asks the court to create temporary orders. These orders can include child custody, child support, or any other issue that needs a temporary resolution until trial.

Motion for a Protective Order

A parent who is feeling threatened or harassed by the other parent can file a *motion for a protective order.* This motion asks the court to protect the victimized parent. If the parent is alleging domestic violence or other physical harm, the court can issue a temporary restraining order. If the parent seeks protection from unreasonable discovery requests, the court can limit the scope of discovery.

Motion to Compel Discovery

When there is a dispute about discovery, the opposite of a protective order is a *motion to compel discovery.* This motion asks the court to force the other side to answer certain questions or to produce certain documents. For example, if you send an interrogatory, and the other side refuses to complete it, you can file a motion to compel. If the judge grants the motion, the party will be ordered to answer the questions. A person who refuses can be fined or held in contempt of court, which can mean a jail sentence.

If you file a motion to compel, be sure to include a request for sanctions. This request asks the court to punish the other side by giving you something—such as attorney's fees.

Motion for Examination by a Mental Health Expert
In custody disputes, it's normal for one side to file a motion requiring all parties to submit to a psychological examination. These examinations are usually performed by a mental health expert, who may rely on interviews and psychological tests to reach a conclusion. The recommendations made by the custody evaluator are evidence, and may be adopted or rejected by the judge.

Motion for a Paternity Test
When paternity of the child is in doubt, either party to the suit can make a *motion for a paternity test.* This motion asks the court to order the man— ostensibly the father—to undergo a paternity test. Paternity tests have an extraordinary degree of accuracy, and for legal purposes, are usually the only evidence relied on to prove or disprove paternity. Mothers may file this motion to establish a father's responsibility, while fathers may file to either disprove their responsibility, or to secure rights to a child when the mother denies his fatherhood.

Motion for a Continuance
This motion asks the court to delay the impending hearing, conference, deposition, and so on, because the party needs additional time. Either side can file for a *continuance,* and if it is granted, the case will be delayed a certain length of time.

Motion for Sanctions
A final motion is a *motion for sanctions.* This asks the court to punish the other side because they have misused the legal process. Typical examples include if one side files frivolous motions—that is, motions without a valid legal basis—or if one side files for repeated continuances seemingly to delay the proceedings. If the motion is granted, the penalized party may have to pay a fine, may be limited in their discovery, or may be found in contempt.

Court Papers

Everything in court has a name. Here are some terms:

Affidavit
An affidavit is a written statement wherein the author swears under penalty of perjury that the facts stated are the truth. The affidavit must be notarized.

Brief
A brief is a written legal argument submitted to the court.

Case
A case is a dispute taken to court.

Case File
A case file is the folder that contains all the legal documents relating to a case.

Case Number
A case number is the unique number assigned by the court clerk when the case is filed.

Case Record
The case record includes all papers filed with the court. This includes transcripts of all hearings and trials.

Declaration
A declaration is the same as an affidavit, except that it does not have to be notarized. Affidavits and declarations are often used in place of live testimony.

Docket Sheet
A docket sheet is the court paper that lists everything that happens in a case. Case files and docket sheets are usually public records.

Petition
A petition, or complaint, is a legal document filed with the court that requests some action.

Hearings

Both before and after the trial, you may have to attend one or more *hearings.* A hearing is any appearance you make before a judge or other court official where you present your case.

Pretrial hearings are usually limited to deciding specific issues prior to the trial, while posttrial hearings often involve enforcing or modifying the court judgment. An example of a pretrial hearing might be to establish child support, while a posttrial hearing might be to adjust the support amount.

Court hearings are serious, and you must appear when scheduled. If you don't go, the judge can issue a *bench warrant* authorizing the police to arrest you and bring you to court. If you don't have a good reason for missing the hearing, the judge can declare you in contempt.

In addition to attending hearings to decide various motions, you may also have to attend several other kinds of hearings:

Pendente Lite Hearing

A *pendente lite hearing,* or temporary hearing, is when the judge first makes temporary custody and support decisions. At this pretrial hearing, the judge seeks to create orders that maintain the status quo in the children's lives.

Judges know that when parents first separate, everyone's life is blown apart. The parents have to set up two households where there formerly was one, and the children have to go back and forth between them. It's hard on everyone, and it takes time to adjust. The last thing the judge wants to do is change the home of the children—or their school. Thus, in a pendente lite hearing, the judge seeks to stabilize the children's lives. If the children were living primarily with one parent before the hearing, the judge may want that to continue.

Temporary orders have a lasting impact on future decisions.

Because most custody decisions seek to avoid disrupting the children's lives, the temporary hearing may be the *single most important* hearing you have. All future custody decisions will take into account the existing arrangements of the children.

Order to Show Cause Hearing

Another type of hearing is called an *order to show cause hearing,* which occurs when someone files an order to show cause.

In family law, an order to show cause hearing usually involves enforcement of the current orders, or it occurs when someone wants to change the current orders. The responding party must show cause why the motion should not be granted.

 Don't rush back to court. As one lawyer says, "Judges do not want the court system overburdened by litigants who request multiple pre-trial hearings. Judges are happy to help in fine-tuning previous orders, but are loathe to revisit problems that have been adequately assessed at previous court hearings." *Custody for Fathers*

Ex Parte Hearing

The essence of our judicial system is fairness, which means both sides get a chance to talk to the judge. However, there are times when one side alone can talk to the judge. A hearing where only one side may be present is called an *ex parte hearing.*

Ex parte hearings occur under very specific circumstances. Generally, they are used to resolve crisis situations where someone may be harmed—such as when there is a threat of domestic violence. An ex parte hearing is considered an emergency proceeding, and can happen with little or no notice to the other side.

If an order is issued at an ex parte hearing, it will generally last only until both sides attend a full hearing. This may be a few weeks or even longer, depending on how busy the court is.

By the way, if one side doesn't show up, and the other side wins by default, that's also considered an ex parte hearing.

In Camera Hearing

A final type of hearing is an *in camera hearing.* This is when the judge meets privately with someone in his office. Often, lawyers meet with the judge to resolve issues, or the judge may speak with the children. This hearing is not open to the public, giving the parties involved privacy.

"Judges in family law deal with large volumes of
cases and only remember the difficult ones that
appear repeatedly in court. A judge hearing a case
from beginning to end will make a determination
early on as to which parent is being difficult. So, do not lose your
temper and act irrational in court with a judge who you will be
seeing again and again." *Custody for Fathers*

Conferences

In addition to hearings, you may also have to attend *conferences*. A
conference is less formal than a hearing, and may occur without the
judge. Conferences are a useful part of the litigation process because they
create opportunities for the parties to settle, or—at the very least—simplify
the issues involved.

Pretrial Conference
Depending on the local court terminology, a *pretrial conference, status
conference,* or *issue conference* is when the parties meet to decide the
issues that remain to be resolved. The goal of the conference is simply to
narrow down the dispute to the core issues. The more that can be agreed
on ahead of time, the less that needs to be decided at trial.

If this conference occurs just before the trial, you may have to prepare a
pretrial memorandum that lists the issues still in dispute and the evidence
you plan to introduce.

Settlement Conference
A *settlement conference* is a final chance to settle the dispute and avoid
trial altogether. The goal of the conference is to bring the parties together
to see if there isn't some way to resolve the lawsuit. Depending on the
court, the settlement conference can be voluntary or mandatory.

Settlement conferences are a very useful way to resolve disputes, and—in
some courts—the judge can exert considerable pressure on the parties to
settle. While the judge has no official power to force an agreement, he or
she may be able to comment on the reasonableness of each parent's
position. This sobering view of how the judge might rule can dislodge an

intransigent parent from a hardened position and cause the parties to move towards an agreeable middle ground.

In some courts, the settlement conference has evolved into a mini-trial, where each side actually presents their evidence and the judge makes an intended ruling. While this is not a complete trial, when the likely ruling is indicated by the judge, the parents are further encouraged to settle.

 Race to the courthouse steps. The moving party has a distinct advantage in the legal process. By striking first, the moving party puts the responding party on the defensive, and makes that party answer the allegations within 30 days. This can lead to an early, favorable ruling. Then, the moving party delays trial as long as possible, and when it finally does come, argues that there is no change of circumstances.

Orders

The purpose of all this activity is to create *orders*. A court order is an instruction from a judge. The judge can tell you to do something or order you not to do something, and if you ignore what the judge says, you can be held in contempt of court.

Depending on when they're made, orders may be called something else. Orders made before a trial can be called *temporary orders,* while orders made at the end of a trial are called *judgments,* and orders made thereafter are called *post-judgment orders.*

Here are some typical orders:

Pendente Lite Orders
Pendente lite means *pending the litigation,* which is another way of saying these are temporary orders. Temporary orders are only intended to stabilize the situation, and will generally last until you reach an agreement or complete a more extended hearing or trial. Pendente lite orders may include custody arrangements, support amounts, legal fees, expert witness fees, and more.

Show Cause Orders
An *order to show cause* is an order that requires you to appear before the judge and explain why the judge should not do something. Show cause orders may be issued either when someone violates a court order, or when someone wants to change the existing order. For example, a show cause order might be issued when one parent is ordered to pay child support but doesn't do it. The other parent may insist that the non-paying parent violated the order, and the judge has to resolve the dispute.

Ex Parte Orders
Ex parte orders often arise from emergency situations. Generally, they occur when someone is in danger or something is at risk. The emergency may involve violence, such as one parent hitting the other, or other danger, such as a parent threatening to kidnap the children.

Ex parte means "by one side," and ex parte orders arise when only one side has had a chance to tell their story. That's designed to prevent the other side from doing something by not giving them advance warning. Because ex parte orders are based on the story told by one side, they usually last only until a hearing when both sides can be present. At the hearing, the judge can drop the orders or keep them.

Like all court orders, ex parte orders are not enforceable until they have been properly served. If the other parent cannot be served, you may have difficulty enforcing the orders. However, once the orders have been served, and the other parent violates them, the judge can hold that parent in contempt of court.

 A protection order doesn't guarantee your protection. If the other parent decides to ignore the order, you are still at risk until the police arrive. In addition to obtaining the order, use common sense to safeguard yourself and your children.

Restraining Orders
Restraining orders are orders that stop someone from doing something. If the orders are temporary, they are called *temporary restraining orders,* or TROs. Restraining orders can apply to both parents equally, or to either parent individually.

In some states, certain types of mutual restraining orders automatically take effect when the parents file for divorce or a paternity action. These stop the parents from:

- Removing the children from the state without prior written permission from the court or the other parent.
- Disposing of any marital property.
- Altering insurance policies held for the parent or the children.

Other restraining orders occur after a hearing—ex parte or not. And still other restraining orders originate when the court is not in session, and the judge verbally issues the orders over the phone to a law enforcement officer. These truly emergency orders may not last long, but they give the parent time to get into court to file for more permanent orders.

Restraining orders can cover a variety of situations, but they are commonly used to protect one parent from the other. Typically, the allegations include that one parent has beaten the other parent, beaten the children, threatens to kidnap the children, or harasses the parent at work or on the phone. To prevent further assaults, the judge issues an order restraining the conduct of the dangerous parent. The order may even require this parent to leave the family home and not return—it's otherwise known as a *kick-out order.*

If you have been issued a restraining order, be sure to give a copy to the police department. If there is a disturbance and you call them, they will need to see a certified copy of the order before they can act on it.

 Resist mutual restraining orders. "Some judges prefer to issue temporary restraining orders against both parties when one party files papers with the court requesting protection against domestic violence. You should protest this practice (which equates your conduct with the abuser's) and remind the judge that the law allows mutual restraining orders only if both parties appear and show evidence justifying the mutual orders." Patricia Phillips and George Mair, *Divorce: A Woman's Guide to Getting a Fair Share*

Contempt Orders

A judge who feels that someone is challenging the court's authority can declare that party to be in *contempt of court*. Contempt of court is serious, and the person charged with contempt must convince the judge to withdraw the order or be punished. Possible punishments range from a stern lecture by the judge, to a substantial fine, to several months—or longer—in jail. The punishment is intended to pressure the defiant parent into obeying the judge's orders.

Depending on the nature of the misbehavior, contempt can be criminal or civil. *Criminal contempt* typically occurs right in front of the judge—such as when someone "loses it" and starts yelling at the judge. *Civil contempt* often occurs away from court—such as when a parent fails to pay child support. With this indirect contempt, the judge must see sufficient evidence before finding the person in contempt. Also, while there is some latitude in punishments, someone who is found guilty of criminal contempt may be jailed on the spot. Someone who is found guilty of civil contempt may get a limited amount of time to comply.

In family law, contempt actions typically occur when a judge needs to enforce a child custody or child support order. Typically, if one parent fails to pay support, or the other parent fails to comply with visitation orders, a contempt action is brought by the other side.

How to Save Money During Pretrial

The simplest way to save money during pretrial is to settle. As a general rule, the longer the dispute drags on, the more it will cost you, but the quicker you reach an agreement, the more you'll have left in your pocket.

Of course, for you and the other parent to reach an agreement, the other person must be reasonable, and that may not always happen. In the real world, people engage in litigation for all sorts of reasons. Maybe someone has an ax to grind or is out for revenge.

So, if you can't settle, here are some other ways to save money.

Mediate First

Even before you hire a lawyer, you may be able to work out a solution with a *mediator*. In some courts, you'll be ordered to see the court-appointed mediator anyway, and the mediator may be empowered to make a recommendation to the judge that will likely be adopted. For this approach to work, both parents must take it seriously. A parent who has already decided to litigate "no matter what" will see this as just a momentary diversion.

Make a Cost vs. Benefit Decision

If mediation fails and litigation is in your future, you need to make a *cost vs. benefit decision.* Admittedly, this is immensely difficult when caught up in the heat of the moment. Child custody being what it is, money may seem to be of secondary importance at the time. *It's not.*

You don't help yourself or your children if you wipe out just to gain an advantage. Custody orders can be reversed on appeal, or they may be modified a few years down the road. That satisfying victory you gain today may be very fleeting indeed.

To make a good decision, you first need to decide on your goals. Do you want sole custody, or can you live with joint? Is the other parent truly unfit, or are they just different from you? Do you need to control the children all the time, or can you let them go with the other parent and not worry?

Once you have decided—or at least thought through—your goals, you need to test those goals against reality. For example, you may want sole custody— but is it likely to be granted? Or you may want to cut off the other parent from having access to the children—but is it possible? The answers to these questions will probably come from an experienced family attorney, and you may have to interview several.

When you test your goals, keep in mind that courts only deal in financial and practical solutions. The judge decides a schedule for the children, orders

someone to pay support, and that's about it. If you want something more, you may want the court to do something it can't do.

Also, when you talk to a lawyer, ask about costs. The real costs. For example, it's not uncommon for certain kinds of motions to run as much as twelve hours of attorney time. At $250 per hour, that's $3,000. Depositions, expert witnesses, attorney preparation—all are costs someone will have to pay.

Once you have set your goals and tested those goals, you have to make a decision. *Is what you hope to gain worth what you will have to spend?*

Only you can answer that question. If you decide that it makes sense— that is, it's *cost-effective*—to engage in full-scale litigation, then do it. However, if you can achieve most of what you want at lesser cost, consider that. You can save money during pretrial by simply being rational and not engaging in needless legal battles.

 Litigation blues. "Part of the problem is the American legal system. Majestic in many respects, it provides lawyers with procedural options that can make the client's pretrial experience far more time-consuming, expensive, and vexing than the trial itself. Everything from a motion to dismiss to a five-day deposition can put every other aspect of your life on hold: forget about getting any work done, forget about spending time with your family, forget about your vacation plans." *You Don't Always Need A Lawyer*

Limit Discovery

If you still must continue with a lawsuit, there are other ways to save money. One way is to *limit discovery.*

You can limit discovery by agreeing to exchange information quickly and inexpensively. This may not work if you have substantial disagreements with the other party, or if the other party is not being forthcoming. But you can save on your attorney's fees if you provide your attorney with all the information he or she needs, and the other side with all the information to which they're entitled.

You can also limit discovery by using a single expert. It's amazingly expensive to use three different experts—yours, the other parent's, and the judge's. By using one impartial expert to resolve issues, you eliminate duplication of effort and cut costs by two-thirds. For this to work, the other parent has to agree, and you both have to be prepared to live with an opinion you may not like.

Make Regular, Reasonable Settlement Offers

Throughout pretrial, you can continue to make regular settlement offers to the other side. If you make offers by mail, the opposing lawyer cannot ignore the letters, even if the other parent wants to. Also, if you try to schedule a private conference and the other side refuses to attend, you can document that effort.

Key moments when conferences are useful:
- When you first hire your lawyer—to settle as many issues as possible.
- When a minimum amount of discovery is finished—to stop the litigation before the bills really go through the roof.
- When discovery is completed—to save whatever money you have left.

When you make a series of offers, don't become entrenched and continue to make substantially the same offer each time, but rather, use the process to look for an alternative that satisfies both sides. It's possible that each parent has a different agenda, and there may be a creative solution that will give you both what you want.

Avoid Sanctions, Seek Sanctions

If you fail to settle and actually go to trial, it's a safe bet that someone is being unreasonable. The judge knows this, and he or she will try to figure out who it is.

In most states, the judge can order one party to pay the other's attorney's fees and court costs. This *sanction* is intended to punish the paying party for misconduct. The misconduct can include engaging in bad-faith efforts to defeat discovery, or refusing to make genuine efforts to settle. If you make genuine attempts to settle and don't engage in misconduct yourself, you avoid being sanctioned, and increase the chances of the other side getting sanctioned.

Sanctions are serious. Despite your ambivalence towards the other party, most judges will not impose sanctions unless someone's behavior is truly outrageous. A certain amount of antagonism is inherent in adversarial situations, and sanctions are only imposed in the most extreme cases. If you ask for sanctions, be sure of your facts.

Preparing for Trial

If settlement fails and trial is inevitable, there are some simple, basic things you can do to prepare.

As you read through the list, keep in mind that it's still possible you won't have a trial. Any number of people arrive at the courthouse on the day of trial, only to suddenly strike a deal. If that seems wasteful and expensive—given the expense of pretrial activities—it is. But some people simply refuse to believe they're going to court until they actually get there.

However, you can't rely on this, and you must prepare for trial. Here are ways to get ready for your court appearance:

Prepare Evidence
Judges are persuaded by *evidence,* so you'll need yours organized and ready-to-go. Evidence includes witnesses, documents, exhibits, and anything else you plan to present in court.

Witnesses. Witnesses who can testify on your behalf are crucial to making a strong case. Experts are probably experienced at testifying, but teachers, friends, and family members may not be, so your lawyer will need to prepare them. By asking potential witnesses to practice in your lawyer's office, you help them be more effective when testifying, and you get a chance to assess their performance. Because some witnesses can be easily tricked or confused, the opposing attorney could turn their testimony against you, and you may want to drop them. In addition, your lawyer can plan the order for calling the witnesses. Experienced trial attorneys know that witnesses should not just be called in any order, but should be scheduled to testify in a way that builds your case effectively.

Documents. If you have any tangible evidence, such as documents, photographs, audiotapes, or videotapes, you'll need to pull them together. Be aware that you'll need the originals in court—copies are usually not acceptable. For that matter, any evidence you bring may not be admissible until your attorney establishes its *foundation.* Documents you could bring include bank statements, school records, receipts, tax returns, diaries, etc. If you need to play an audio- or videotape, the courtroom may not be properly equipped, and you'll need the necessary equipment.

Exhibits. If you have a reason to use an exhibit, you'll need to create the exhibit ahead of time. Charts, graphs, diagrams—all are useful ways to convey an idea. But keep in mind that anything you glue together will have to be lugged into the courtroom. Charts tall enough for everyone to see across the room get bulky and are a pain to carry for long distances.

A Trial Notebook. You'll want to put all your evidence into a convenient form. Trial attorneys use trial notebooks. A trial notebook can be a notebook, a folder, or anything else you find at the stationery store. Even if you have an attorney, there's no reason why you can't create your own trial notebook to hold the papers you'll need during the trial.

 *Et tu Brute?* Practically speaking, it's a bad idea to force a reluctant witness to testify. He or she can hurt you more than help you.

Prepare Mentally
In addition to pulling the evidence together, you'll need to pull yourself together. That means doing what athletes do before a game—prepare yourself mentally.

Practice with Your Lawyer. If you have to take the witness stand, you'll want to be as confident and knowledgeable as you can. The best way to do that is to practice. You want to practice your own testimony, so you won't forget the points you need to make, and practice answering questions, so you won't be flustered when the opposing attorney interrogates you. An absolute must is to practice how to answer questions. You'll probably be surprised at how little you can say. Both lawyers can cut you off, and when they do, you'll have to stop.

Visit a Courtroom. Surprisingly, trials in real life look just like trials on TV, except there are no commercials. Still, don't rely on reruns of "Matlock" or "LA Law" to prepare for your day in court. Take a trip. Go down to the courthouse. Sit in a courtroom. Watch how the attorneys talk to the judge, and how witnesses testify. Be aware, though, that judges notice people who come into the courtroom, and if you're sitting in the same court as the judge who will be trying your case, he or she may remember you.

Prepare Physically

You also need to prepare physically. A trial is a stressful situation, and you need to be rested, refreshed, and alert. Getting into that condition means following some basic, common sense advice on how to handle stress.

The night before, put out your clothes, arrange your papers, have a good dinner, and then go to bed early. Even if you lie in bed awake, at least you're in bed, and not up and out. Also, write down the courthouse address, the name of the judge, and your lawyer's phone number. Getting lost on the way to court is no fun at all. In the morning, pack a light lunch. Who knows if you'll like what they're serving in the courthouse cafeteria? And finally, leave early. Accidents always happen at inconvenient times, and arriving late to your own trial would be very inconvenient indeed.

Prepare the Children

Finally, in addition to preparing yourself, you need to prepare the children. While the judge may not make a judgment that same day, he might, and the lives of the children could suddenly change. So you'll need to say *something.*

What you say, of course, depends on their age. If they're old enough to be testifying, then they already know what's going on, and you may not need to add anything. On the other hand, if they're younger, they may not necessarily grasp the significance of a trial, so you may be limited to giving a short, simple explanation and reassurance that you will say more later. In either case, since you can't predict what the judge will do, you can't make any guarantees to the children.

All you can do is be honest.

Lawyers' Law Books

If you want to read what lawyers read, contact the American Bar Association and ask for their catalog. Be prepared—some books are low-priced, but others will wipe out your wallet.

American Bar Association
750 North Lake Shore Drive
Chicago, Illinois 606111
(312) 988-5168
www.abanet.org

Recommended Books and Pamphlets
The American Bar Association Family Legal Guide. A BIG, thick, practical guide to family law. Very readable.

Law and the Courts: A Handbook of Courtroom Procedures. Civil procedure explained.

The American Lawyer: When and How to Use One. Clear summary of how to hire a lawyer.

The Child's Attorney: A Guide to Representing Children in Custody, Adoption, and Protection Cases. Strategies and tactics.

Children Held Hostage: Dealing with Programmed and Brainwashed Children. How parents manipulate children.

Grandparent Visitation Disputes: A Legal Resource Manual. Covers judges, evaluations, and becoming a guardian ad litem.

Handling Religious Issues in Custody and Visitation Disputes. Balancing the religious beliefs of the parents and children.

Interstate Child Custody Litigation. The laws of interstate child custody cases.

International Child Abductions: A Guide to Applying the 1988 Hague Convention. Basic information about invoking the Hague Convention. With forms.

Chapter 14
Trial

If you disagree with the other parent, it may be because you disagree about the facts. Or maybe you agree on the facts, but disagree on what you should do about it.

If you agree on the facts, a trial may not be necessary. However, if you fundamentally disagree about the facts, a judge will have to make the decision.

A trial is when each party tells its story to the judge. A trial usually begins when each side makes an opening statement, proceeds as each side presents evidence and calls witnesses, and ends when each side makes a closing statement, followed by a decision by the court.

The litigation may continue, however, if either side decides to appeal the judgment, or if one party files a post-trial motion.

This chapter discusses trial and post-trial litigation.

Types of Trials

There are two types of trials—*judge trials* and *jury trials.*

In a judge trial, or *bench trial,* the judge listens to the evidence, decides what's relevant, and then reaches a decision. In a jury trial, the jury listens to the evidence and reaches a verdict. In family law, virtually all trials are bench trials.

The lack of a jury in a family law trial reduces some of the legal complexities—such as jury instructions—but it also requires the judge to decide what is to be believed and how much weight to give to each facet of the testimony.

 "It would be nice if a wise and kind judge could sit for several hours and listen to you and your spouse rationally discuss the pros and cons of who should get custody, but the truth is that the judge won't have more than a few minutes to decide these most significant issues in you and your children's lives." Patricia Phillips and George Mair, *Divorce: A Woman's Guide to Getting a Fair Share*

Trial Procedure

A trial is conducted in a series of steps, or stages. The order of these steps is designed to give both sides an equal chance to tell their story.

While the *order of battle* is fairly strict, judges often have the flexibility to combine or eliminate certain steps in order to shorten the trial. For example, in some courts, the lawyers make dramatic opening statements, but in others, the judge simply reads the pleadings, and the opening statements are skipped. Conversely, some courts expect closing arguments, while in others, the arguments are bypassed because it's presumed the judge already understands the issues.

However your court handles the trial, there is a standard order to how evidence is presented, and in most cases it is followed. This order is called *trial procedure.*

The Stages of a Trial

A trial consists of the following stages:

The Stages of a Trial

Pretrial Conference
⇩
Opening Statements
⇩
Petitioner's Case
⇩
Respondent's Case
⇩
Closing Arguments
⇩
Judgment

Strictly speaking, a pretrial conference is *pre-trial,* but because it often occurs after the trial preparation is finished and everyone has assembled in court, it's included here.

The formal trial begins with the opening statements, continues through the presentation of the evidence, and ends with the judgment. Sometimes, instead of issuing a judgment, the judge takes the matter *under submission.* If that happens, the formal trial ends, and the decision comes a short time later.

Here is what you can expect when you go to trial.

Pretrial Conference

Before the actual trial begins, the judge and lawyers may meet in a *pretrial conference.* This meeting is to identify all the issues still in dispute, so the judge can limit the evidence to those issues before the court and exclude everything else.

At this meeting, the judge may also set a time limit for the trial. The time limit is important because the lawyers must complete the trial within the time allotted or the judge can declare a *mistrial.*

Trial Brief

In some courts, the lawyers must create a *trial brief* to bring to the pretrial conference. A trial brief is a document that summarizes the issues still in dispute and where you stand on those issues.

The trial brief can include:
- Your present arrangement and present orders.
- The problems you've had since temporary orders were issued.
- The orders you are requesting to solve those problems.

The purpose of the trial brief is to help the judge understand the case, so any documents you attach—such as school reports, charts, or photographs—are useful.

Opening Statements

After the pretrial conference, the formal trial begins. In some courts, this is when the lawyers make their *opening statements.*

The opening statement is a verbal outline about what to prove during the trial. It should identify the issues involved, outline the evidence to be presented, and describe the orders being sought.

Don't be surprised if the opening statements are skipped in bench trials. The judge has already read the pleadings and trial briefs, and opening statements are not always needed.

 Sticker shock. "Litigation can be a black hole right here on Earth, absorbing most of one's time and tens of thousands of one's dollars... As of this writing, in large American cities, simple cases that go to trial consume $10,000 to $20,000 in legal fees and expenses, including travel, witness fees and expenses, phone calls, overnight delivery services, local messenger services, transcripts, and photocopying— lawyers like to charge 20 to 50 cents a page. Some firms even charge for word processing. Not uncommon are cases that take $50,000 to $100,000 in fees and expenses and five or more days of trial." *You Don't Always Need a Lawyer*

Petitioner's Case

After the opening statements are finished, the *petitioner's case-in-chief* begins. This is when the petitioner presents evidence that supports whatever allegations are being made.

The petitioner made the complaint, and must now meet the *burden of proof.* That is, because the petitioner made the initial allegations, he or she must persuade the judge.

In family law, the burden of proof is by a *preponderance of the evidence.* Thus, to win the case, the petitioner must present enough evidence to demonstrate that his or her version of the facts is more believable than the respondent's version of the facts.

When organizing the case-in-chief, trial lawyers know there is a tactical advantage to when facts are revealed. Experienced lawyers will present the evidence to build to a convincing and inescapable conclusion.

 If you can read this... If you cannot speak or understand English, you can hire an interpreter to translate. The interpreter must be court-certified, and will usually cost between $150 and $300 per day for a commonly spoken language. Contact the court clerk to make arrangements.

Evidence

Any information you present to prove your case is called *evidence.* To win the case, you must present enough evidence to convince the judge that you are right.

Physical Evidence
Physical evidence includes anything tangible, such as calendars, diaries, school records, medical records, and so on. For example, physical evidence might include the following:

Diary. You can use a diary to keep track of specific events, such as school activities, other activities, and any contacts you have with the other parent. Often, you can refer to a diary to refresh your memory when testifying.

Portfolio. You might impress the judge by assembling a short portfolio of your positive attributes. Include anything significant, such as awards, diplomas, certificates, etc.

Police Reports. Anyone can walk into a police station and file a report, so the courts recognize a police report for what it is—a one-sided description. Unless the officer was an eyewitness, a police report may have limited value. Even worse, someone who routinely files police reports may appear to be abusing the system.

Photographs, Videotapes, and Audiotapes. In court, photographs are much easier to present than videotapes or audiotapes, but all may impress the judge if used appropriately.

Charts and Graphs. A simple graph can make your point, but you'll need to make it large enough to read across the room. Also, expect the opposing attorney to challenge the data it represents.

Trial notebook. Do what the lawyers do, and organize your written evidence into a trial notebook. This is an 8 1/2" x 11" binder with tabbed sections for each area. By assembling a trial notebook and using it during the trial, you might convince the judge that your information is both reliable and accurate.

Witnesses

You can also introduce evidence through the testimony of *witnesses.* A witness testifies under oath about what they have seen or heard, or gives an opinion about some aspect of the case.

Ordinary Witnesses. An ordinary witness testifies as to his or her personal knowledge. In legal terms, the witness must have firsthand knowledge of an event by having experienced it through one or more of the five senses (sight, hearing, taste, smell, and sound). Normally, except for reimbursement of costs, you can't pay an ordinary witness to testify.

Expert Witnesses. Expert witnesses are people qualified to offer a professional opinion. An expert witness may be asked for a custody recommendation, and the expert's opinion will matter to the judge.

Psychologists and other mental health professionals are considered expert witnesses. Experts are usually paid for their time.

Character Witnesses. Character witnesses are used to demonstrate a parent's skill and involvement with the children. Friends, relatives, clergy—all can testify on your behalf. Because character witnesses are obviously biased, they may have limited value with the judge.

Impeachment Witnesses. An impeachment witness is called to demonstrate that the other parent or one of the witnesses lied. Because credibility is crucial in child custody, an effective impeachment witness can make the judge question the entire testimony of a person shown to be a liar.

Rules of Evidence
Because evidence is so important, there are rules governing what you can introduce and how you can introduce it. These are called the *rules of evidence.*

The rules of evidence help distinguish between information that is important and believable, and information that is unimportant and unbelievable. For a piece of testimony or evidence to be *admitted into evidence,* it must be both *relevant* and *material.* That is, it must relate to the issues involved, and it must be significant enough to matter.

Evidence rules also protect the judge from easily falsified evidence. For example, under the right circumstances, a written document can be very convincing, but it can also be *counterfeit.* That's why—to admit a document into evidence—you will have to show that it is both genuine and accurate. To *authenticate* a written document, you may have to call the author to testify, and for a photograph, you may have to call the photographer.

In family law, judges hear everything and then decide what is admissible. In theory, they're supposed to ignore inadmissible evidence. In reality, it's hard to *unring a bell.* Inadmissible testimony that is highly damaging can't help but influence the judge.

During the trial, many arguments will occur over whether some piece of evidence is relevant and material. Even if the evidence qualifies on other grounds, it still may not be admitted because it's deemed to be *hearsay.*

Your state's rules of evidence can usually be found in the Evidence Code in the *Rules of Civil Procedure.* To find these statutes, check with a law librarian.

Hearsay

Hearsay is repeating what someone else said. For example, if Beth were testifying, and she said, "Steve told me that..." what Steve said—or didn't say—is hearsay. More specifically, hearsay is "a statement, other than one made by the declarant while testifying at the trial or hearing, offered in evidence to prove the truth of the matter asserted." Thus, if Beth were trying to prove something by repeating what Steve said—that's hearsay.

Hearsay testimony is particularly liable to outright lying—or at least gross misrepresentation—because the person who made the statement is not being directly asked, and is not on the witness stand where he or she can be cross-examined. Thus, you can't tell if the statement is true or not.

Hearsay can get complicated, and there are some exceptions that allow hearsay to be admissible—such as *excited utterances* and *statements made against interest*—but generally, hearsay cannot be offered as evidence.

Black's Law Dictionary says, "Hearsay does not derive its value solely from the credit of the witnesses, but rests mainly on the veracity and competency of other persons. The very nature of the evidence shows its weakness, and it is admitted only in specified cases from necessity."

When called to testify, witnesses can be subjected to several rounds of questioning. The order of questioning is:
*   Direct examination.
*   Cross-examination.
*   Redirect examination.
*   Recross-examination.

Direct Examination

A witness called to testify for the first time must take the stand and be sworn in. This means he or she must walk over to the witness stand and answer "Yes" when asked to swear to tell the truth. After that, the witness can be questioned.

Once sworn in, the witness must then tell the truth. If a statement is shown to be a lie, the witness can be charged with *perjury.* In reality, however, people are rarely punished.

The attorney who calls the witness asks questions first. This initial round of questioning is called *direct examination.*

In direct examination, the attorney asks questions in a very specific way. Generally, these are broad, open-ended questions that lead to short, narrative answers. For example:

Direct Examination Testimony

Attorney: "Please tell the court how you get your child ready for school."

Witness: "Well, I always wake him up by seven. Then, he either takes a bath or watches TV while I cook him a good, nutritious breakfast. Usually, he eats..."

Direct testimony is supposed to let the witness explain the situation in his or her own words. The witness may testify to matters of fact—such as the authenticity of a document—or recall events personally witnessed. And an expert witness can state a professional opinion. For example, a psychologist may give an opinion as to which parent should be awarded custody.

A witness called during the case-in-chief must appear credible. If the testimony seems unbelievable, or if the witness criticizes the side who called him, the testimony can be very damaging.

At times, the attorney may ask an inappropriate question, or the witness may say something improper. When that happens, the opposing attorney can *object.* An objection is how the opposing attorney indicates a possible violation of the rules of evidence.

When an objection is raised, the attorneys may briefly argue their position to the judge, who then makes a ruling. If the judge sustains an objection to a question, the witness does not have to answer. If the judge *denies* or *overrules* an objection, the witness does have to answer.

If the judge decides that some testimony is inadmissible, the opposing attorney may make a *motion to strike,* which is a request that the judge delete the testimony from the court record.

Cross-Examination

After direct examination is finished, the opposing attorney is allowed to *cross-examine* the witness.

Cross-examination is used to test the truthfulness of the statements made by the witness during direct examination. In this round of questioning, the opposing attorney tries to undermine the credibility of the witness's testimony.

Because cross-examination is adversarial in nature, the style of the questioning is different. Instead of asking open-ended questions, the attorney asks *leading questions* that call for a simple "Yes" or "No" answer. For example:

Cross-Examination Testimony

Attorney: "Isn't it true that you spanked your child so hard that he had bruises on his bottom?"

Witness: "No."

Cross-examination questions are generally limited to matters that were brought up during direct testimony. However, if the witness is ruled a *hostile witness,* the opposing attorney may be able to broaden the scope of the questioning.

Cross-examination provides much of the drama in a trial. Generally, the opposing attorney asks questions loaded with a distorted interpretation of the facts. The witness must answer, even if it means admitting to something embarrassing or damaging.

To *impeach* the witness, the opposing attorney will try to get the witness to make a statement that:
- Is inconsistent with previous testimony.
- Shows a bias.
- The witness stands to gain financially or in some other way from a particular outcome in the case.

Cross-examination not only reveals dishonest statements made by the witness, but also helps acquire evidence for the other side.

If your best friend testifies, he or she may be declared an *incompetent witness*. That's a witness considered too biased to be objective.

Redirect Examination

After the opposing attorney has finished questioning the witness, the first attorney can return and ask more questions. This *redirect examination* lets the witness add detail to the cross-examination answers. During redirect, the witness can clarify responses and try to recover from any damaging admissions. Because redirect is limited to matters raised in cross, some attorneys may skip it and move on to new evidence.

Think court is crowded? Consider that in one family court, 5,206 domestic cases were filed in a single year.[1] *If the judge actually listened to each case, he would have to decide more than 20 cases a day.*

Recross-Examination

After redirect comes recross-examination, where the opposing attorney once again questions the witness. This back-and-forth continues until the attorneys have fully questioned the witness.

Respondent's Case

When the petitioner's case-in-chief is over, the moving party *rests,* and the *respondent's case-in-chief* begins. This is when the respondent argues his or her version of the facts.

The respondent presents a case just as the petitioner did—by introducing evidence and calling witnesses. As before, the witnesses are subjected to the same rounds of questioning: direct, cross, redirect, and recross-examination. This time, however, the respondent's attorney conducts the direct examination, and the petitioner's attorney does the cross.

In this phase, the respondent not only wants to contradict allegations made by the petitioner, but also to support any counterclaims the petitioner has made.

When the respondent's case-in-chief is finished, the petitioner is allowed to rebut any evidence the respondent introduced. This phase of the trial is called *sur-rebuttal.* And after the sur-rebuttal is done, there can follow a sur-sur-rebuttal. Theoretically, this back-and-forth continues until time runs out.

 If you actually go to trial, don't expect it to last long. One judge estimates that the average family law trial lasts between 3 and 4 hours. *California Divorce Handbook*

How to Appear in Court

Your day in court will be one of the most important days of your life. To win your case, you must appear physically, mentally, and emotionally sound. In fact, your appearance is so crucial that it may persuade the judge even more than the evidence you present.

Here are some practical tips about appearing in court:

First, you want to *dress properly.* In the world of courts, this means dress for business. A good rule of thumb is to imagine that you're going on a job interview. Conservative business attire—coupled with good grooming—conveys the image of a stable role model for your children. Ripped jeans, tank tops, and excessive jewelry conveys the opposite.

Second, you want to *behave properly.* Courtrooms have their own etiquette, and you'll need to conduct yourself accordingly. For example, if the other parent is on the witness stand, and is lying—stay calm. Don't get angry or agitated. This will only make you look like an overwrought, emotional person. If you sit quietly and wait your turn, you'll appear to be both stable and in control. If you need to tell your attorney something, write a short note and slide it across the table.

Third, you want to *be ready.* After arriving at the courthouse early, look on the court calendar or docket to find your courtroom or department. Then, check in with the clerk. If court is in session, wait until the judge takes a break. Tell the clerk you're present, and while you wait for your case to be called—stay close. If things move faster than anticipated, you could be called very quickly.

And fourth, *treat everyone with courtesy.* If you address the judge, call him or her "Your Honor." Call the opposing attorney "Mr." or "Mrs." And remember, you can't talk to the judge or the other attorney privately. Plan to obey the rules that restrict when and how you can talk.

 Politeness pays. The court clerk knows everything about how to move your case along. The clerk can't give you legal advice, but can explain the court rules and procedures. Whatever else you do—be nice. The clerk will tell the judge if you've been rude.

How to Testify in Court

Since child custody involves your fitness as a parent, it's a safe bet that sooner or later you'll have to testify. There's no trick to being an effective witness; all you have to do is answer questions. Family court judges hear conflicting stories every day, and they routinely decide who is telling the truth and who's not.

Here are some tips to help you convey your story in court:

During direct examination you want to show the judge what an honest, credible person you are. You can't tell the story of your life, but you can indicate what you're doing right and what the other parent is doing wrong. You'll only have a little time to talk, so plan to speak in short, comprehensive sentences. Also, consider owning up to whatever you've done wrong. Better to reveal a negative up front than to let the opposing attorney do it on cross-examination. And finally, expect to stick to current events—don't dwell on long-ago slights. What seems important to you may not be to the judge.

During cross-examination you want to avoid being provoked into an angry outburst by the opposing attorney. No matter how insulting the questions are—and they will be insulting—they're only questions, so stay calm and answer honestly. If you can slip in a criticism of the other parent, so much the better. Remember, you're on the defensive during cross, so the less said the better. The opposing attorney is determined to find something wrong with you, so resign yourself to being abused on the witness stand.

If You Settle

Don't be surprised if you never finish trial. Amazingly, many parents arrive in court and even begin a trial, only to suddenly—miraculously— find some middle ground.

Or the judge may read the pleadings, listen to some of the evidence, and then suggest a reasonable outcome. This suggestion, of course, is blatant coercion—but it's very effective. Only the most recalcitrant parent ignores a judge's comments in a bench trial.

If you do reach an agreement, the judge may enter a *consent order.* This order has the same legal effect as a judgment, except that because you agreed to it—*you can't appeal.*

 What was that? If your agreement is read into the court record—pay attention. Once the agreement is entered, it's as good as law. If the words are changed—even slightly—and you don't object, you will be bound by the new orders.

Closing Arguments

After all the evidence has been presented, and both sides have rested, the attorneys may then make *closing arguments.* This is a summation of the main points in each side's case.

When attorneys make closing arguments, they must stick to the issues and evidence presented. Each attorney reviews the evidence favorable to their side and the evidence damaging to the other side, and asks the court to rule in their favor. If custody is disputed, each attorney may state the living arrangements being sought.

As they did at the start of the trial, the moving party goes first and the responding party follows. After the initial go-round, the arguments can go back and forth as each attorney rebuts the other's points. In some courts, closing arguments are deemed unnecessary in bench trials and are skipped altogether.

Post-Trial Memorandum

If the trial was long and complex, each attorney may have to submit a written memorandum to the judge. A *post-trial memorandum* includes a description of the evidence presented, relevant statutes and case law, and the remedy being sought.

Judgment

Finally, it's over. After all the pleadings, depositions, witnesses, testimony, and arguments—it's over. The trial is finished. You have had you day in court, and now the judge must make a decision.

Sometimes the judge will render an immediate verdict—called a *ruling from the bench.* If the judge issues new orders while you are still in court, you are expected to obey the new orders immediately.

More commonly, though, the judge will delay making a decision. If the judge *takes the matter under submission,* he may want to review the trial transcript, review his notes on the witnesses, examine the physical evidence, or consult relevant statutes and case law. When this happens, the judge will send a written decision to the attorneys two weeks to two months later.

Along with the decision, you may receive a document called a *Findings of Facts and Conclusions of Law.* This explains the facts the judge determined were true and the application of law based on those facts. This is a very important paper, and you will need to review it if you are considering an appeal.

You will also receive an order specifying the remedy to be applied. In civil law, the two types of remedies are *monetary damages*—which involve the payment of money—and *equitable remedies*—which concern a person's behavior.

Depending on the case, the judge can order whatever remedy is necessary. For example, in a case of domestic violence, the judge may order compensatory damages, which are payments for loss due to injury, and punitive damages, which are payments designed to punish the wrongdoer.

In addition, the judge may seek to stop future violence by issuing a *prohibitory injunction,* which prevents someone from doing something. If one parent already had a temporary restraining order, the judge may make it a *permanent injunction.*

*"Guilty? Do you realize what that
will do to my resume?"*

Post-Judgment Litigation

When Yogi Berra said, "It ain't over till it's over" he could just as easily have been talking about the legal system instead of baseball. With the trial over and the judgment rendered, you might think the case is over. But it's not. Instead, you begin *post-trial.*

Post-trial is an interesting time, and when child custody is involved, just as much can happen after the trial as before it. For example, you may have to file various *post-trial motions.* These can involve *enforcement,* to order a parent to comply with the existing orders, or a *modification,* to change the orders to fit a changed set of circumstances.

Also, post-trial is when you file an *appeal.* To appeal a case means to ask another court to review the judge's decision. You file an appeal when you disagree with the trial judge and want another court to overturn the judgment. Either side has the right to appeal, but usually only the "losing" party wants to.

 An *appeal* is different from a *modification.* An appeal is made in a different, higher court, and seeks to alter the original judge's ruling. A modification is made in the same trial court, and seeks only to change part of the original order because there are new facts.

Appellate Courts

If you file an appeal, you move your case to a higher court called an *appellate court.* Most states have several layers of appellate courts, starting with an intermediate court, or *court of appeals,* and ending with the highest court, often called the *state supreme court.* When you first appeal, you begin in the court of appeals.

Perhaps the most surprising thing about appellate courts is that they don't retry the case. When you appeal, you don't get a second chance to call your witnesses and make your arguments. Instead, appellate courts exist solely to review the law. The appellate court will not review the facts that lead to the verdict, but rather, decide only if the correct law was applied and the correct legal procedures were followed.

Appellate Decisions

Because appellate courts are strictly concerned with the law, they limit their decisions to the following:

Affirm the Judgment
If the appellate court agrees with the lower court's judgment, it *affirms the judgment.* If you are the *appellant*—the party who filed the appeal—you must then appeal to a higher court or end the case.

Reverse the Judgment
If the appellate court rules that the trial court's decision was wrong, it can *reverse the judgment.* This means the trial court's decision is erased. The court will then either send the case back for retrial, or modify or correct the judgment in some other way.

Remand the Case
The appellate court can also send the case back to the lower court for some other action, such as to correct an error made by the judge. If the case is *remanded,* the trial judge must follow the instructions from the higher court.

Dismiss the Appeal
The appellate court can also *dismiss the appeal* if it has no merit or if the court does not have jurisdiction.

Vacate the Judgment
When the appellate court completely wipes out the judgment of a lower court, it is said to *vacate the judgment.* This often occurs when a higher appellate court—such as a state supreme court—reviews the opinion of a lower appellate court and completely replaces the court's opinion. For legal purposes, vacated judgments cannot be used as *precedent.*

Follow the rules. If you decide to appeal, obey the original court ruling while the appeal is pending. A parent who ignores orders from a lower court can be sanctioned. Even worse, noncompliance can invalidate the appeal altogether. If you cannot obey the trial court's orders, seek an immediate, temporary stay of execution.

Your fifteen minutes. All cases decided in the public court system are a matter of public record, but if you want to keep your private matters private, you can ask for a gag order. When considering a request to seal the court record, the judge determines whether the likely publicity will harm the children.

Grounds for an Appeal

If you get a judgment you don't like, your first reaction may be to rush back into court and file an appeal. But wait. Before you do, you'll need to determine if you have *grounds for an appeal.*

To successfully appeal your case, you must show that the trial judge either made a mistake in interpreting the law, or made a mistake in the trial procedure. And this mistake must have been so significant that it affected the outcome of your case.

That is why you review the *Findings of Facts and Conclusions of Law.* This document explains the judge's legal reasoning and helps you determine whether you have the basis for an appeal.

When You Cannot Appeal
Like everyone else, judges make mistakes, and some judicial errors are allowed. If the judge made a harmless error—one that did not affect the outcome of the trial—the judgment may stand.

Likewise, because the trial court is the *finder of fact,* if the judge chose to believe one parent and not the other, that's usually within a judge's discretion, and is also not the basis for a reversal.

When You Can Appeal
On the other hand, if the mistake was significant enough to harm you, you may have a *reversible error.* Here are some errors a judge might make:

Error in interpreting the law. If the judge didn't apply the correct law, or misinterpreted the law that was applied, you might have the basis for an appeal. Because legislatures routinely write confusing statutes, this happens more than you think.

Error in determining the facts. If the judge made a mistake with the evidence, either by admitting irrelevant facts, or by excluding relevant ones, you might successfully appeal. Generally, you'll need clear and convincing proof of this.

Abuse of discretion. In family law, the judge has plenty of discretion to decide who is telling the truth and who is not, and what is best for the situation. However, the judge must remain within the standards of law, and if he doesn't, you may be able to appeal.

Prejudice. If the judge displays a bias towards you because of your race, gender, age, and so on, you may have grounds for an appeal. To prove this error, you must show that the judge ignored the law and decided the case solely due to prejudice.

Miscalculation. Sometimes the judge just adds up the numbers wrong. For example, when computing child support, the judge may do the math incorrectly. If this type of unintentional error happens, you may be able to file for a modification with the trial court, rather than make an appeal.

 Put the cart before the horse. Believe it or not, you should begin preparing your appeal before the start of your trial. As odd as that sounds, it's based on the fact that your attorney must object to all improper evidence and procedures as they occur. These potential judicial errors are the sole basis for your appeal, and you must get your objections into the record to raise the issues.

How to Appeal

If you believe you have grounds for an appeal, you'll have to file some documents with the court. Once you do, you become the *appellant,* and the other party becomes the *appellee.*

Here are the general steps to appeal your case:

Check the Deadline
The date when your judgment was entered in the court record—called the *entry of judgment*—is critical, because all states have a deadline for how

long you have to appeal. Generally, it's 30 to 60 days. If you miss the deadline, you lose the right to appeal.

File Notice of Appeal

To appeal your case, you must file a *notice of appeal*. This starts the period when you must complete the paperwork. During this time, your attorney must serve notice on the other party that you are appealing, and that party will be able to respond.

If you are appealing an appeal, such as taking a decision from a court of appeals to a supreme court, you may have to file a *Petition for Writ of Certiorari*. This document requests the court to consider your appeal. Higher appellate courts can deny your petition, effectively ending your ability to appeal any further.

Five Reasons Why You Won't Like Your Day in Court

1. *Flaws.* Your weaknesses and weird fetishes will be revealed to everyone.

2. *Backstabbing.* Your best friend may testify against you.

3. *Humiliation.* The opposing attorney will make you look an evil, dysfunctional psychopath.

4. *Surprise.* If your children testify, their answers may shock you.

5. *Karma.* Your past misdeeds may come back to haunt you.

Prepare Briefs

Once you have filed notice, your attorney must prepare and file a brief explaining your reasons for the appeal. Generally, you will have to attach copies of the pleadings and the decision, and arrange for a copy of the transcript to be sent to the appellate court.

Make Oral Arguments

Your attorney may also have to make oral arguments in front of the appellate court. These arguments are usually optional, and if they are made, usually last between 15 and 30 minutes. The justices will have read the briefs, so the time is for asking questions.

Decision and Opinion

After the oral arguments—if they were made—the justices discuss the case and vote on whether to affirm or reverse the trial court's decision. Usually, one justice is assigned to write the opinion that explains the decision. Other justices are free to author their own concurring or dissenting opinions. These opinions are published, and become the basis for future legal decisions.

Trial Tips

The Divorce Handbook: Your Basic Guide to Divorce, James T. Friedman, Random House, $13.00. This excellent book written by a family law specialist offers concise answers to many questions.

---

1 Cases filed during the fiscal year 1991-1992. Source: *Richard A. Curtis, Commissioner,* Los Angeles County Superior Court (Pomona, California)

The Story of Jessica and James

Court

Judge Harold Kaplan was a large-bellied man with a coarse, white beard and gray, stringy hair. At sixty-one, he was waiting for his retirement, a day when he could finally cash in on his years of experience as a family law jurist.

Private judging, or "rent-a-judges," had become very popular in recent years, and Kaplan had watched with envy as his peers on the bench had retired to cushy jobs in the private sector. His turn was coming, he knew, and even before announcing his retirement, he was being courted by the top private dispute resolution firms who routinely sent him thick envelopes espousing the benefits of working as a private judge. Between court sessions, Judge Kaplan often sat in chambers, leafing through the information and carefully weighing the benefits of each firm. It would come soon enough, thought Kaplan, as he glanced at his watch and realized it was time to go to work. He reluctantly put down the brochures and pulled on his robe.

When Judge Kaplan entered the courtroom from the rear, the bailiff called out, "Remain seated and come to order. Court is in session. The Honorable Judge Harold Kaplan presiding."

Immediately, Judge Kaplan sat down and began sifting through the piles of folders on his desk. Mary, his clerk of ten years, had efficiently organized the cases to be heard that morning. He peered at his computer monitor, then opened the first case file on the top of the stack.

"Miller," said the judge.

Ms. Marsh stood up and moved to the counsel table. Mr. Shepard did the same.

"Good morning, your honor. Michelle Marsh, representing the petitioner."

"Paul Shepard, for the respondent."

The judge nodded and the lawyers sat down. Jim and Jessica rose from their seats in the spectator area, crossed to the counsel table, and sat down, too.

Ms. Marsh began. "Your honor, the matter before the court today is to establish temporary orders pending the dissolution of the marriage. It is my understanding that the parties have reached an agreement on the disposition of all marital assets. The only issues to be decided at this time are the custody of the minor child and the amount of support to be paid. My client, Mrs. Miller, has had primary physical custody of the minor child for the last seven months, has provided all of the child's meals, has bought all of his clothes, has taken him to the doctor for shots and tests, has put him to bed at night, and has in every way been the primary caretaker of the child. It is her request that the court maintain the status quo of the child's living arrangement and award her sole legal and sole physical custody, as well as the guideline amount of support."

Mr. Shepard leaned back in his chair. "Your honor, Mr. Miller does not deny that Mrs. Miller has been the primary caretaker of the child since she forcibly removed him from the family home against his will. That's not at issue. We're ready to stipulate that for the last seven months, Mrs. Miller has wiped the boy's nose and fed him pop-tarts for breakfast before unloading him in a daycare center all day long. What Mr. Miller has done is to take care of the child on a number of weekends, and he is now more than ready to care for the child each day the court allows. We're asking for joint legal and joint physical custody, and for Mr. Miller to have the child 50 percent of the time."

Jessica glared at Mr. Shepard. She couldn't believe the things he was saying.

Ms. Marsh quickly stood up. "Your honor, the petitioner did not remove the child from the family home against his will. When the parties separated, they mutually agreed that the child would live with the petitioner, and that to prevent further conflict, Mr. Miller would have visitation rights. Mrs. Miller feeds the child a very healthy breakfast every morning. Also, ensuring that the minor child receives proper medical care requires more than simply 'wiping his nose.' Since the parties separated, Mrs. Miller has taken the child to the doctor on at least three separate occasions for vaccinations and inoculations. Finally, Mrs. Miller brings the child to a daycare center because she must work to support both herself and the child. In the last seven months, the respondent has failed to provide her with even a basic level of support, and she has been forced to rely on her mother for financial assistance."

Mr. Shepard glanced sideways at Ms. Marsh but remained seated. "Of course, Mrs. Miller would not have to put the child in a broken-down daycare facility or run to her mother for money if Mr. Miller had the child half-time. Then, Mrs. Miller could get a real job and undoubtedly earn more than enough to satisfy her opulent lifestyle."

Ms. Marsh stared hard at Judge Kaplan. "As the court is aware,

Mrs. Miller handles insurance forms for a medical office. Her annual income is less than $26,000 a year. This is barely enough for herself, much less the child. Because the parties were married for ten years, Mr. Miller must realize that he may be responsible for spousal support. It is our contention that Mr. Miller seeks to avoid his financial obligations to his former wife and his child by pursuing joint custody—an arrangement that he is completely incapable of assuming."

Jim shook his head. Like Jessica, he had never realized how he would be described by opposing counsel in open court, and it made him angry.

Mr. Shepard spoke up. "Well, your honor, that's what they always say, isn't it? The minute some father wants a little more time with his kid, the mothers all start screaming that it's some kind of manipulative ploy to beat out support. But the facts clearly show that Mr. Miller has substantially cared for the child in the past, can continue to care for the child now, and it would be in the child's best interests to allow him to continue to do so in the future."

"Your honor, I resent opposing counsel making derogatory remarks about women. Mr. Shepard's views are—"

Judge Kaplan interrupted Ms. Marsh. "How much time has the respondent spent actively caring for the child in the prior six months?"

Mr. Shepard crossed his arms. "I believe Mr. Miller has had custody just about every weekend." He looked at Jim for confirmation, but Jim remained frozen, staring straight ahead.

Ms. Marsh jumped in. "In fact, your honor, Mr. Miller has only had visitation with the minor child on about five or six weekends in the prior six months. I certainly wouldn't call that 'every.'"

Mr. Shepard smiled. "Your honor, Mr. Miller wanted more time, but Mrs. Miller was extremely uncooperative and cut him off from seeing the child. He didn't want to make her any angrier than she already was."

Ms. Marsh stood up straight. "That's completely untrue, your honor. Mrs. Miller has let Mr. Miller see the child whenever he's wanted. Mr. Miller is a painter, and he apparently finds it necessary to spend a great deal of time painting. For reasons known only to Mr. Miller, his vocation apparently precludes him from living a normal lifestyle. He often stays up all night, then sleeps the entire next day. He also frequently goes without a bath for a week or longer."

As the lawyers spoke, Judge Kaplan made notes on a legal pad in front of him.

"Mr. Miller does not have a 'bathing problem' as Ms. Marsh alleges. In fact, I'm standing right next to him, and he smells fine to me."

It was Ms. Marsh's turn to smile. "That's not saying much, your honor."

Mr. Shepard shot her a disdainful sneer. "As far as staying up all night, that's a lie. And even if it's true, so what? Many parents work at night. If working a night shift made someone unfit to care for their children, then half the kids in America would have to be put up for adoption."

"We're not talking about America. We're talking about Mr. Miller's highly erratic and unconventional lifestyle. His failure to comply with societal norms makes him unfit to be awarded joint custody. On the other hand, Mrs. Miller works a conventional job with normal hours, has the assistance of her mother for child care responsibilities, and is clearly interested in seeing that the child develop into a normal, healthy, well-adjusted boy."

"Again, your honor. Mr. Miller is as normal as you and me—and certainly more normal than Ms. Marsh."

Ms. Marsh gave Mr. Shepard a cold stare. Judge Kaplan looked up from his desk. "Sir, do you stay up late a lot?"

For a moment, Jim was confused, unaware that the judge was asking him a direct question. Then, he noticed that everyone was staring at him, waiting for an answer. "If I'm trying to get something finished... yeah, I guess, sometimes."

Mr. Shepard dropped his legal pad on the table, tacitly acknowledging defeat. Ms. Marsh smirked.

Judge Kaplan turned to his computer and began typing in numbers. He spoke to the attorneys without looking at them. "Okay. Arguments for support."

Ms. Marsh jumped right in. "Mrs. Miller seeks the guideline amount for both child and spousal support."

"Your honor," said Mr. Shepard. "The court can plainly see that Mr. Miller is a freelance painter who does not earn a regular income. Some years he makes a good living, and some years he doesn't. Applying the guideline amount will result in an unreasonable level of support."

Judge Kaplan flipped through the case file. "From his latest I & E, it looks like he didn't earn anything last year."

Mr. Shepard spoke up. "Exactly my point."

Ms. Marsh broke in. "Due to Mr. Miller's highly erratic earnings, we ask the court to impute his income."

Mr. Shepard spoke up. "For the same reasons it wouldn't be fair for the court to impute too high of an income."

As Judge Kaplan typed numbers into the computer, he glanced at

Mr. Shepard. "Well, he has to pay something. This child needs to be provided for."

Jessica looked up at Ms. Marsh, tapped her on her arm, then whispered something in her ear.

Ms. Marsh turned to the judge. "Mrs. Miller informs me that Mr. Miller has—in the past—regularly earned income of between $25,000 and $30,000 per year."

Jim looked up at Mr. Shepard and vigorously shook his head.

Mr. Shepard turned to the judge. "Oh, come on. The court has the tax returns for the last three years. That's not what they show and Ms. Marsh knows it."

Judge Kaplan finished entering the numbers in the computer, then watched as the program calculated the income and support figures. "The court imputes Mr. Miller's income to be $20,000 per year. Anything else?"

"Your honor," said Ms. Marsh. "There's also the matter of child care expenses. In order to work, Mrs. Miller must place the child in a licensed daycare facility that charges her $300 per month. We ask that Mr. Miller pay half."

Judge Kaplan peered at Mr. Shepard. "Counsel?"

Mr. Shepard shrugged. "We'll stipulate to that, your honor."

Judge Kaplan wrote a few figures on a pad. "Anything else?"

"None, your honor," said Ms. Marsh, and she sat down.

"None," said Mr. Shepard, and he sat down.

At that, Judge Kaplan picked up a sheet of paper and faced the parties. As he spoke, his voice remained flat, as if he was reciting a phrase that he had spoken a thousand times before. "It is the order of this court that sole legal and sole physical custody of the minor child be awarded to petitioner. The respondent is granted twice monthly visitation with the child on alternate weekends beginning this weekend... " Judge Kaplan peered at the printed calendar on his desk. "May 21st. Petitioner will drop off the child with the respondent on Saturday mornings at 8 a. m., and respondent will return the child to the petitioner on Sunday evenings at 6 p.m. Respondent is also awarded visitation with the minor child for a consecutive thirty-day period over the summer, half the Christmas vacation beginning at noon on Christmas day, alternating Thanksgiving holidays in even years, alternating child's birthday in even years, every Father's Day, and every respondent's birthday."

Judge Kaplan turned to look at his computer screen. "Furthermore, it is the order of this court that the respondent pay to the petitioner the sum of $325 each month in child support, $150 each month in child care expenses, and $200 each month in spousal support, for a total of $675 each month. This amount is to be paid on the first day of every month."

Judge Kaplan closed the case file and pushed it towards his clerk. "These orders are to remain in effect until the minor child reaches the age of majority or is emancipated."

Ms. Marsh looked pleased. "Thank you, your honor." She closed her notebook and rose from her chair.

Jessica stood up with her. "I can't thank you enough," she said. She was beaming. Ms. Marsh nodded and smiled back.

"That's it?" asked Jim, stunned at the speed of the proceeding.

"That's it," said Mr. Shepard, as he closed his notebook and stepped back from the counsel table.

"But, what do I do now?" asked Jim

"This weekend play with your kid," said Mr. Shepard. "Excuse me, I have another case."

As Jessica and James walked out of the courtroom, they heard the judge call out, "Christensen," and two more anxious parents rose up and joined lawyers at the counsel table. One lawyer spoke, "Good morning, your honor..."

*   *   *

Alternatives
to Courts
and Lawyers

Chapter 15
Negotiation

When you dispute custody of your children, you don't automatically have to hire a lawyer and start a trial. You can also resolve your disagreement by *negotiating* a settlement.

Negotiation has many advantages—such as lessening the hostilities and saving everyone time and money—but it also has some disadvantages—such as allowing a domineering parent to remain in charge, or letting one parent drag out the dispute indefinitely.

When you prepare to negotiate, you'll have to decide which issues to negotiate and who will do the negotiating—you or a third party.

You'll also have to identify your leverage—bargaining factors that favor your side. And you'll have to choose a negotiating strategy—position-based or interest-based.

Despite your best efforts, the negotiations may fail, and if they do, you'll have to resort to other forms of dispute resolution, including litigation.

This chapter discusses how to resolve your dispute through negotiation.

Settling

If you disagree with the other parent, you don't automatically have to go to court. You can also negotiate a *settlement*.

A settlement is any agreement you work out with the other parent. You can negotiate a settlement before you file a lawsuit, during the pretrial phase, or even during the trial itself!

You don't have to settle everything. You can agree on some issues and leave the rest for a judge to decide. In order for the agreement to be binding, however, you will have to file it with the court, which means a judge will approve or reject it.

Negotiating a settlement is common, with many laws and procedures actually encouraging the parents to negotiate. Lawmakers realize that *private ordering*—where parents work out their own problems—is preferable to judicial regulation.

Advantages of Negotiation

Decreases the Conflict
If you think about it, there may be no better way to increase the conflict than to litigate. By litigating, you are attacking the other parent's rights and position, and forcing them to attack yours. Negotiation, on the other hand, encourages the parents to talk to each other, which allows them to immediately identify and address a problem before it becomes any bigger.

Saves Time and Money
Negotiation lets you quickly and efficiently resolve a disagreement. By negotiating, you don't have to spend endless hours filing motions, waiting for a hearing date, and sitting in court. You also don't have to spend your life savings on legal fees.

Improves the Outcome
If you litigate, you put the final decision in the hands of someone else. If you negotiate, you don't. Negotiation not only gives you more control over the outcome, but also reduces the possibility that an inept third party—such as a poorly trained evaluator, attorney, or judge—will make a bad decision. Negotiation also allows you to get the details right— tailoring the agreement to your specific needs.

Disadvantages of Negotiation

Doesn't Equalize Positions
If one parent wants to sabotage the negotiations by bluffing, threatening, or lying, negotiating will not place the other parent on an equal footing. For negotiation to work, both parents must have equal negotiating skill, equal knowledge, and equal power.

Doesn't Force a Resolution
Since there's no practical time limit to negotiating, a parent who wants to delay can stall almost indefinitely. Negotiation may not be best when the parents are operating under a deadline, and need a definite resolution.

Doesn't Guarantee a Fair Outcome
There's nothing inherent about negotiating that guarantees an agreement will be fair to both sides. Even if attorneys review the agreement, it's possible that a judge would have ruled differently. Also, if you agree but later don't like the agreement—you can't appeal.

Preparing to Negotiate

If you plan to give negotiation a try, you will benefit by *preparing*. The amount of preparation you do depends on the type of negotiation. For a quick chat with the other parent, you may not need to do anything. But if you're planning on elaborate and time-consuming bargaining, you may need to do a lot.

As you prepare to negotiate, you'll need to make several decisions.

Who Will Negotiate?
One of the first questions is *who* will be doing the negotiating—you or a third party, such as an attorney or a friend. If you negotiate for yourself, you can be much more flexible in responding to the other side, and you can save a substantial amount of money—usually on legal fees. That's the good news. The bad news is that you are probably not a skilled negotiator, which means that you won't know how to assess the strengths and weaknesses of your position. You also won't know how to handle the *negotiator's dilemma*—the inescapable conflict between cooperating with the other side to forge an agreement, while competing with them to secure your personal gains.

What Will You Negotiate?
Next, you must select the *issues* to negotiate. While there's a natural tendency to limit the bargaining to a few specific items, inevitably that will leave loose ends that can come back to haunt you. Also, if you hire a third party to handle the negotiations, you'll not only have to tell that person what you specifically want, but also all of the facts that bear upon those issues.

When Will You Negotiate?
Finally, you'll have to decide *when* to negotiate. If you're not ready, or if the other side isn't ready, you won't accomplish anything by beginning the negotiations. Even worse, you may compromise your position by showing your cards too soon. Experienced negotiators know that timing is crucial to success.

 It's easy to get sidetracked when negotiating with the other parent. Anger, hurt, bitterness, revenge—all are feelings that can interfere with negotiations. Your best bet? Stick to one issue and don't talk in front of the children.

Leverage

In addition to making some decisions, you'll also have to assemble information. Because bargaining depends on your ability to pressure the other side into making concessions, you'll need to identify the factors that you can use for *leverage.*

There are many types of leverage, but they generally fall into two categories—*legal* and *psychological.*

Legal Leverage
Legal leverage concerns the legal norms, that is, what would happen to you if the negotiations fail and you go to court. You don't necessarily have to go to court—just the mere possibility of it influences the negotiations. This is called *bargaining in the shadow of the law,* and parents negotiate custody of their children well aware of how courts have ruled in the past. A parent who seeks a traditional or typical custodial arrangement gains a significant *bargaining endowment* that pushes the negotiations in his or her favor.

Psychological Leverage

Psychological leverage has nothing to do with the law, and everything to do with how the parents feel. If one parent is angry or selfish, or the other parent feels guilty, their emotions can dramatically influence the negotiations. It's not unusual for a "burned" ex-spouse to try to punish a former mate by battling over custody. And even if strong emotions aren't involved, the personal preferences of the parents will play a role. For example, if one parent genuinely wants to raise the children and the other doesn't, that will shift the negotiations. In addition, because a judge's decision is never a sure thing, the amount of risk each parent is willing to take is a factor. Some parents will simply be more willing to take their chances in court, while others will be *risk-adverse*—disturbed by the mere possibility of losing.

 "The art of negotiation is the ability to perceive and use these leverage factors to obtain concessions. Since both sides usually have something the other side wants, these factors are traded like chips. The side with more leverage can obtain more concessions in the trading process. The end result of the trades and compromises is the settlement." Eleanor Maccoby and Robert Mnookin, *Dividing the Child*

How to Negotiate

Negotiation can be simple and straightforward, or elaborate and complex. It can stay between the parents, or include third parties. It can take a few moments, or last several months. There's no right or wrong way to negotiate, only what works for you.

If the issue is simple, or if you and the other parent communicate well, first try *talking*. "Why don't I take the kids on Saturday?" "Sure." For many decisions, the simpler the better.

If the issue is more complex, or communication is poor, consider writing a *letter*. In the letter explain the problem and what you propose to do about it. Writing a letter will help you organize your thoughts, and may be a better approach. You can even indicate a response date so the problem isn't ignored. And if the negotiations fail, you'll have the letter as documentation for court.

If the other parent ignores your offer, you can also suggest a face-to-face *meeting.* This can be a private meeting, or it can include third parties— such as lawyers. And if the parent refuses to meet, you will also have evidence of that refusal for court.

In fact, *document* all communications you have with the other parent. And if your lawyer sends or receives letters for you, insist on being given copies.

Finally, if you do reach an agreement, be sure to put it in writing and have everyone sign it. A written record of the agreement will avoid future confusion over what was agreed to.

Five Ways to Deal with the Other Parent

1. *Be reasonable.* Don't expect to get your way more than half the time—if that.

2. *Be flexible.* If you think your kids require flexibility, wait until you start dealing with your ex.

3. *Be kind.* Of course they're not perfect—but you had a child with them anyway.

4. *Be reliable.* Do what you'll say you'll do.

5. *Be quiet.* If you don't have to talk—don't. Less is more.

Negotiating Strategies

However you approach the other parent, you'll be pursuing a *negotiating strategy.* This strategy will dictate what you do and when you do it.

When negotiating, you should know that there are several theories of negotiation. One theory divides strategies into two categories:
- Position-based negotiation.
- Interest-based negotiation.

Position-Based Negotiation

In *position-based negotiation,* you immediately adopt an extreme position and then refuse to budge. As the bargaining proceeds, you demand everything, concede nothing, and threaten retaliation if you don't get your way. To get what you want, you bluff, threaten, lie, posture, and bully your opponent into submission. Position-based negotiation is hardball, where you attack and intimidate your adversary in order to win.

The main advantage of this negotiating style is that it works. The parent who can bargain for children by threatening and stonewalling gains an enormous strategic advantage.

Negotiating Strategies

Position-Based vs.	*Interest-Based*
"win-lose"	"win-win"
hardball	softball
competitive	cooperative
extreme position	mutual interests
threaten, bluff, lie, posture, stonewall	honest, genuine, flexible, constructive
zero-sum	non zero-sum

The main disadvantage is that this style dramatically increases the hostilities. A *scorched earth* approach leaves little of the good will necessary for parents to continue a relationship afterwards.

Position-based negotiation is often adopted by parents who view custody as a *zero-sum game,* where one person's gain must necessarily be the other's loss.

Interest-Based Negotiation

In *interest-based negotiation,* you strive to change a "win-lose" result into a "win-win" outcome. With this strategy, you immediately disclose all relevant information, fully explain your reasons, and then genuinely listen to the other parent as you search for an agreement that satisfies both your interests. This type of negotiation is cooperative, with each side offering constructive suggestions on how to solve the problem.

The main advantage of interest-based negotiation is that it dramatically lowers the conflict, allowing the parents to cooperatively work together in the future.

The main disadvantage is that both parents must genuinely want to participate. If one parent cooperates and the other one doesn't, the cooperative parent is vulnerable to being bullied or coerced by the non-cooperative parent.

Interest-based negotiation is an attempt to turn child custody into a non zero-sum game, where the parents create additional value by cooperative trading. In a sense, this strategy seeks not just to divide up the pie, but to actually make the pie bigger, and then to share the increase.

If Negotiation Fails

If negotiation fails, you have reached an *impasse*. An impasse is when you cannot come to an agreement on a particular issue.

Negotiation can fail for many reasons. Perhaps you approached the negotiations in good faith, but the other parent had a *hidden agenda*—such as wanting to hurt you or to live better at your expense. Or maybe one of you was too emotional to negotiate—letting feelings of insecurity or jealousy get in the way. Or maybe one of you is simply a litigious ex-spouse, viewing any negotiated agreement as a "giving in" or "surrendering" to the other parent.

Whatever the reason, if you still need a resolution, you will have to use another dispute resolution method. These include forms of alternative dispute resolution—such as *mediation, arbitration,* and *conciliation*—and litigation.

 "Contemporary divorce law has increasingly recognized the legitimacy of 'private ordering'—the notion that divorced parents should have broad latitude to negotiate their own financial and custodial arrangements... The judiciary functions primarily not to regulate the lives of divorcing families, but instead to resolve those legal difficulties that divorcing parents cannot work out." Eleanor Maccoby and Robert Mnookin, *Dividing the Child*

Chapter 16
Alternative Dispute Resolution

If you choose to negotiate rather than fight, you don't have to go it alone. There are many forms of assistance available.

Alternative dispute resolution, or ADR, is the name given to a group of techniques that move arguments out of the court system and into the private offices of trained therapists and mediators.

ADR techniques include mediation, which is often used to resolve custody disputes because it encourages the parents to cooperate; arbitration, which is used less frequently because the decision is made by an impartial arbitrator; and conciliation, which is typically used in combination with mediation. Also, you can opt out of the legal system entirely and have custody settled by a private judge, who maybe able to resolve the case more quickly.

This chapter discusses forms of alternative dispute resolution.

ADR

Alternative dispute resolution, or ADR, is a collection of techniques you can use to help you settle your dispute. Unlike traditional litigation—where the parents are pitted against each other as adversaries—in ADR, the parents are generally expected to cooperate to forge an agreement that settles their dispute.

For family courts, ADR techniques represent a way to clear overburdened calendars. For parents, ADR may be the best way to have a say in the final outcome.

The most common forms of ADR are:
*   Mediation.
*   Arbitration.
*   Conciliation.

 "Contested custody proceedings account annually for approximately 7 percent of the more than one million divorces occurring in America." *Divorcing*

Mediation

If you cannot agree on custody of your children, you can try to resolve your dispute through *mediation.*

Mediation, or *assisted negotiation,* is one way for parents to settle their dispute. In *mediation,* the parents meet with a third party, or mediator, who helps them discuss the issues and create a mutually acceptable agreement.

A mediator does not take sides or make a decision for the parents. Instead, the mediator helps both parents find their own solution. If the parents come to an agreement during mediation, the agreement is written up and usually filed with the court—making it an official court order. If the parents do not agree, they can continue with the dispute by reverting to traditional litigation. Of all the forms of ADR, mediation is used most often in custody disputes.

Advantages of Mediation

Mediation offers parents the opportunity to:

Save Time and Money
Compared to full-blown litigation, mediation can save everyone time and money. Gone are the costs and delays associated with the adversarial system—discovery, hearings, motions, and trial. Instead, the parents meet quietly and privately with the mediator to discuss the situation. This informal approach avoids the interminable delays of waiting for an open courtroom, and relegates the lawyers to the limited—and much less expensive role—of an advisor. Mediation lets the parents reach an agreement sooner and keep more of their money.

 "The bottom line is that a fair settlement agreement produced by mediation will save you money. This is the reason that mediation as an alternative form of dispute resolution has become so popular and becomes more so each year." *California Divorce Handbook*

Create a Better Agreement
Mediation can also lead to *better agreements.* When a judge imposes a decision, parents are much less likely to obey it than when the parents create the agreement themselves. This higher rate of compliance results in less conflict afterwards. Also, when parents create the agreement, they can customize it to fit their situation. In reality, most judges will never get all the details right. And finally, when parents make their own agreement, they may be able to find a "win-win" situation where each gets what is felt to be most important.

Learn Problem-Solving Skills
By resolving the dispute through mediation, the parents also learn valuable *problem-solving skills.* When custody is in dispute, the parents do not just resolve the disagreement and move on. In fact, they'll have to interact with each other for many years afterwards. This makes it crucial that the parents learn how to settle future disagreements. Mediation teaches a new model for communication that helps avoid disputes and offers techniques for resolving problems that are disputed.

Disadvantages of Mediation

Unfortunately, mediation isn't for everyone, and it has several disadvantages. Here's the downside:

The Other Parent May Not Cooperate

In mediation you cannot force the other side to participate. If one parent refuses to participate, or if one parent does show up but takes a completely unreasonable position; it won't work. Mediators do not have the power to compel someone to cooperate, and they cannot impose a decision. If the mediation sessions don't result in an agreement, nothing tangible is accomplished.

The Other Parent May Dominate

One of the reasons why parents hire a lawyer is to equalize their relative bargaining positions. If one parent is exceptionally domineering or manipulative, the lawyers can help to offset the imbalance. But when the lawyers are removed—as in mediation—the parents are right back to their former roles. This lets someone who lies or hides information effectively sabotage the negotiations, or bring about a result that would not have occurred otherwise. The lack of extensive pretrial discovery is one reason why mediation costs less, but discovery is also an important check-and-balance in the adversarial system.

The Other Parent May Scare You

In mediation, a parent who has been victimized by prior acts of abuse or violence will lose some protection. Because mediation usually brings the parents together in the same room, a parent who is afraid for his or her own safety may be intimidated and unable to fully participate in the process. Because of this, some states allow the parents to be excused from court-required mediation, while others allow each parent to meet with the mediator privately.

 Mediation withdrawal. Many states allow parents to be excused from mediation if there has been a history of abuse or violence, or if mediation is deemed inappropriate under the circumstances.

What Happens When You Mediate

You typically get involved in mediation when the court orders you to go, or when you and the other parent agree to give it a try. Either way, the process is usually the same.

Preliminary Meeting
Before jumping into the dispute, the mediator often needs a *preliminary meeting* to get everyone organized. In this meeting, the mediator will get the basic information, find out the problems, and dictate the ground rules for the sessions. A good mediator will take control of the process, and not let the discussion disintegrate into endless squabbling and name-calling.

How to Decide If Mediation Is Right For You

1. You are both willing to participate.

2. You are both willing to compromise.

3. You are both able to clearly communicate your goals.

4. Neither of you can dominate the other.

5. Neither of you is too emotional to participate.

Joint Sessions
After the preliminary meeting, the parents usually return to the mediator's office for a series of *joint sessions*. Depending on the mediator, these sessions may last as little as 30 minutes, or as long as two hours. And they may conclude within a few weeks, or stretch out over several months.

In these sessions, the parents discuss the problems. Usually, each parent is allowed to talk without interruption and given a chance to express concerns. Everything is on the table during the meetings, including school involvement, discipline techniques, medical needs, and more. By letting the parents talk, the mediator seeks to help them understand each other and to reach a satisfactory agreement.

Separate Sessions
The parents may also have *separate sessions* with the mediator. These sessions allow each parent to talk privately, and to "sound out" a possible settlement offer without revealing the plan to the other parent. If necessary, the mediator can shuttle back and forth with the offers until an agreement is reached.

Agreement
If the parents can pull together an agreement, the mediator will write it down in some kind of *memorandum.* This document is typically submitted to the judge, who generally approves it and enters it into the court record—making it an official court order. Because this document is so important, many parents ask an attorney to review it prior to signing it.

Court Recommendation
If the parents cannot reach an agreement, they have reached an *impasse* and the process has failed. If the mediation is private, the parents can pursue other approaches—such as litigation. But if the mediation is court-ordered, several things may happen.

In some states, the mediation is confidential, and the parents then proceed with litigation. In other states, the mediator is asked by the judge to make a recommendation, and this recommendation will influence the judge's final decision. In still other states, the mediator can be called to the witness stand and asked to testify about the case. If you are in a court where the mediation is not truly confidential, you are in *muscle mediation,* where the mediator can coerce an agreement if the parents can't agree on their own.

"Consider letting your children participate in at least one of your sessions, if you are not locked in battle. It will allay their fears about what is going on and will give them a chance to speak, be heard, and thereby gain a sense of control over their lives. My children were surprised at the orderliness of mediation. They had envisioned a long table where we sparred verbally with mediators trying to control us. They were surprised about the small room, the informal setting, and the fact that the mediator was in charge." Vicki Lansky's *Divorce Book for Parents*

Using Lawyers in Mediation

When you go to mediation, you may want the final agreement to be as close as possible to what a court would order. The problem is, most people don't know what that is. In the heat of negotiations, one parent may demand something totally outrageous, and the other parent won't even know it.

That's why—even though you go to mediation—you still need a lawyer. Your lawyer won't be in the mediation room with you, but can act as an advisor by answering questions and reviewing any agreements before you sign them.

By hiring a lawyer, you not only protect your legal rights, but you'll learn the parameters of a reasonable agreement. This will help you negotiate with the other parent while still keeping your agreement close to the likely outcome in court.

Choosing a Mediator

Whoever mediates your dispute is important. Because you and the other parent cannot agree on custody, you must look to a mediator for help in reaching an agreement. This makes the skills and abilities of the mediator crucial to your success.

If your state requires mediation, you may end up with a *court-appointed mediator.* If your state does not require mediation, or if you choose to move your dispute away from court, you can hire a private mediator to help you.

Court-Appointed Mediators

Court-appointed mediators sometimes work right in the courthouse, and you may be able to see one by just walking down the hall. These mediators typically are limited to giving you only a few hours of time, and to only mediating the most basic issues of custody and visitation. Because court-appointed mediators rarely charge more than a small fee, you can save a lot of money with them. Unfortunately, in some states, the mediator may be asked to make a recommendation, which will put pressure on the parents to reach an agreement during the sessions.

Court-appointed mediators often charge a minimum amount—around $35 per hour. Private mediators charge more and often base their fees on their professional background. For example, a therapist or counselor may cost $75 to $100 per hour, while an attorney might bill at $150 to $250 per hour.

Private Mediators
Private mediators are not limited to helping you with just the basic agreement. You can hire a private mediator who will spend as long as you need on your dispute, and who will see you at your convenience. Also, a private mediator is not going to be asked by the court to make a custody recommendation, so your mediation sessions will stay private.

When you hire a mediator, you will have many choices. Therapists or other mental health professionals will often deal better with the emotional aspects, while attorneys or former judges will usually know current family law. If you can't find one person who does both, you can hire an attorney-therapist team.

Mediation in a Nutshell

Choosing a Divorce Mediator, Diane Neumann, Owlet, $16.95. Written by the past president of the *Academy of Family Mediators,* this book explains how mediation works, the types of disputes that are appropriate for mediation, and how to find the right mediator.

The Divorce Mediation Handbook, Paula James, Jossey-Bass, $16.00. This well-organized book explains the entire process of mediation, beginning with the decision to engage in mediation, and ending with the completed agreement. The author is a family law attorney who has mediated more than 500 divorces.

A Guide to Divorce Mediation, Gary J. Friedman, Jack Himmelstein, Workman Publishing, $12.97. Friedman, a former trial attorney, illustrates the mediation process by showing how 11 different couples fared when they chose mediation over litigation.

Arbitration

Another type of alternative dispute resolution is called *arbitration.*

Arbitration is when you submit your dispute to a third party for a resolution. The *arbitrator* listens to each parent, listens to the witnesses, reviews the evidence, and then makes a decision. In arbitration, you present your case just as if you had gone to trial, and the arbitrator makes a ruling just as if a judge had decided.

Arbitration has several advantages, chief among them that it's often less costly and much faster than a formal court proceeding. Unfortunately, arbitration still requires the parents to present their case, which means spending additional time and money. And for arbitration to be useful, both sides must agree beforehand not to appeal the decision—which is not always best.

For these reasons and more, arbitration is unusual in custody disputes.

Conciliation

The final common form of ADR is called *conciliation.* Conciliation is very similar to mediation, and in some courts, there may not be any meaningful difference between the two.

Generally, conciliation is when the parents meet separately with a *conciliator,* who tries to help them to reach an agreement. Depending on the court, the conciliator may first meet with the attorneys, then with each parent separately. In some courts, the conciliator may also speak with the children. After talking with everyone, the conciliator will call them all back for a summation of the problem and a review of various ways to resolve the dispute.

As with mediation, if you reach an agreement in the conciliator's office, the conciliator will write it up and ask both parties to sign it. This agreement will go to the judge, who will likely enter it into the court record—making it an official court order.

The main advantage of conciliation is that it's low-key. If an agreement is reached, you save enormous expense and the emotional strain of a full-blown trial. And if it doesn't work, you can still proceed to mediation.

Alternative Dispute Resolution

Academy of Family Mediators
1500 South Highway 100, Suite 355
Golden Valley, MN 55416
(612) 525-8670
www.igc.apc.org/afm
The Academy of Family Mediators is a nonprofit organization that
provides referrals to mediators in your area. They train and establish
criteria for mediator education, and have about 3,000 members.
They publish the journal: *Mediation Quarterly* and some videotapes,
including *Mediation: It's Up To You.*

American Arbitration Association
140 West 51st Street
New York, NY 10020
(212) 484-4000
www.adr.org
The *American Arbitration Association* makes referrals to professional
arbitrators in your area. They will send a pamphlet with the
addresses of the several dozen regional offices around the country.

Association of Family and Conciliation Courts
329 West Wilson Street
Madison, WI 53703
(608) 251-4001
The AFCC makes referrals to mediators, counselors, and evaluators in
your area. They have over 1600 members. They also publish the
journal *Family and Conciliation Courts Review.*

Society of Professionals in Dispute Resolution
815 15th Street NW
Suite 530
Washington DC 20005
(202) 783-7277
A national association of ADR service providers, the Society makes
referrals to ADR providers in your area. SPIDR has local chapters in
every state.

Private Courts

If other forms of ADR don't work for you, you have yet one more option—
private judging.

You can hire a private judge, or "rent-a-judge," to do the same thing a
public court judge does. The "courtroom" may be a real courtroom, or a
conference room in an office building. And the judge who listens to your
case may be a retired judge with plenty of experience in hearing the same
kind of case you have.

If you hire a private judge, you can wait until it's time for trial, or start
with the initial pleadings. Hired judges can rule on pleadings, motions,
discovery, and more. And if you disagree with the decision you can even
appeal to the public courts.

To move your case into a private court, both sides have to agree. Usually,
the attorney for one side suggests the idea, and the other party concurs.
You can agree to split the cost, or one side can volunteer to cover the
fees.

 Choosing a private judge can save each side thousands of
dollars. For example, if each parent pays half, a three-hour
hearing can cost as little as $600.

Advantages of Private Courts

You may choose to bypass the public court system for reasons such as the
following:

To Save Stress
The legal community has a saying, "Justice delayed is justice denied."
Nowhere is that more true than with child custody. If the dispute drags on
for three or four years—whatever the original point—the damage to the
children will far outweigh the gain. In contrast to the regular court system
where it may be years before trial, in a private court the judge can hear
the case quickly, make a decision, and everyone can move on in their
lives.

To Save Money

This ability to decide a case quickly offers more than emotional savings—it offers real *financial savings,* as well. In the public courts, the parties will typically have to pay for their experts to appear on short notice—a very expensive option. Also, in the public courts, the trial may be stopped as other cases intrude on the judge's time, forcing the litigants to miss more work days to return to court. And finally, a public court trial will involve time-consuming legal procedure, slowing the case down and making the parties pay higher legal fees. None of this is true in a private court. The parties will have an early and well-anticipated trial date. The judge will give his or her full attention to the case without interruption, and the parties can simplify the procedure, thus creating a shortened, abbreviated trial.

"A rent-a-judge is a retired judge who sits by agreement of the parties and is given, for that case, all the powers of an active judge. Unlike an active judge, the retired judge is compensated by the parties at a rate of at least $200 per hour with no overhead attached."
California Divorce Handbook

To Keep It Private

You may also want to take your case to a private court to do just that—*keep it private.* Because public court trials are normally open to the public, the decisions of the judge become part of the public record—available to anyone who wants to read it. This has certain advantages, such as protecting the public by revealing the biases of a given judge, but it also exposes the most intimate details of your personal life. By taking your dispute to a private court, you can maintain confidentiality.

To Get a Better Judge

If you've ever been in front of a judge before, you probably know there are good judges and there are bad judges. In many court systems, family law is not a sought-after assignment, and the judge who hears your case may be the most *inexperienced* judge around. This can lead to a legal mistake that may force one of the parents to undertake a costly and time-consuming appeal—not to mention the potential harm to the children. In a private court, the judge must be approved by both sides, so you can research his or her public record to ensure that the judge is unbiased and has plenty of experience with cases similar to yours.

Disadvantages of Private Courts

There are also disadvantages to private courts, such as the following:

You Will Need a Lawyer
Because a private trial is still a trial, many of the rules of evidence and civil procedure remain the same. This means you will probably still need a lawyer to represent you.

You Will Lose Leverage
If your goal is to pressure the other parent—either by threatening to expose secrets, or by engaging in endless litigation—then a private court is not for you. When you take your dispute to a hired judge, you lose the ability to force the other parent into a favorable settlement. In fact, it could be argued that private courts are only useful when both parents are acting in good faith and genuinely want to resolve the dispute fairly. If your goals are anything else, a private court may not be helpful.

You Are Buying Justice
And finally, many opponents of private courts argue that they only widen the split between rich and poor, allowing the wealthy to secure justice quickly, while relegating the poor to an overburdened public court system. If you can afford a private judge, this may not seem like a disadvantage, but some insist that private courts drain quality judges from the public court system and deprive the public from the valuable precedent which helps evolve contemporary law.

 "Private judging creates a situation where the wealthy can avoid the burdens of the public courts and purchase speedy and, for them, relatively affordable justice... The unspoken message [is] that while justice is blind and available to all, it is readily accessible only at a certain monetary price." Justice Irving R. Kaufman

Where to Rent a Judge

Finding a private judge is not hard. These two nationwide companies may send a judge to your city, or conversely, you can travel to the closest city where they have an office.

Judicial Arbitration and Mediation Services/Endispute, Inc.
www.jams-endispute.com
JAMS is a large, well-known ADR service that employs over 300 retired judges. JAMS has offices in 26 cities and nine states. Judges charge $350 per hour. JAMS reports that over 90% of its disputes are resolved.

Judicate of Philadelphia
Judicate is another large, nationwide ADR firm, employing more than 600 former judges in 49 states. Judicate says it specializes in short nonjury trials—single sessions of three hours or less. Each party pays $240 for a one-hour session, or $540 for a three-hour session.

Chapter 17
Representing Yourself

When you hire a lawyer, you're hiring someone who knows the law. Your lawyer knows which laws apply to you, and has the skills to represent you in court.

But family law—like all law—is based on common sense. If you have the time and the desire, you can acquire enough basic knowledge to represent yourself.

Representing yourself—or being a pro per litigant—allows you to save substantially on lawyer's fees. Unfortunately, you'll also have to learn the court rules and procedures, and you may make errors that cost you much more than if you had hired a lawyer in the first place.

If you decide to represent yourself, you can seek out many resources for help, including legal typing services, divorce assistance centers, and self-help law books. You can even hire an attorney as a legal coach--that is, someone who gives you advice, but who doesn't represent you in court.

This chapters discusses the pros and cons of being a pro per.

Pro Per

If you have to interact with the legal system, either because you need to file some legal papers or because you must to go to court, you're not required to have a lawyer represent you. You can also represent yourself.

If you represent yourself in a legal proceeding, you are often called a *pro per* or *pro se.* Both are Latin phrases meaning "for yourself."

Pro per litigants can do everything a lawyer can do, including:
- Write and prepare legal documents.
- Investigate prior judicial decisions.
- Conduct discovery.
- Negotiate settlements.
- Argue a case at trial.

Representing yourself in a legal matter is a statutory right, and many people choose to do so. The right to self-represent, however, does not extend to representing others. Only licensed attorneys have the right to represent someone else.

 Many people represent themselves. How many? One Florida judge estimates that approximately 70% of the litigants who appear before him are pro pers. A California judge estimates that half to three-quarters of the litigants he sees are pro pers. [1]

Advantages to Representing Yourself

There are many reasons why you might want to represent yourself. These include:

To Save Money
A main reason to self-represent is to *save money.* In family law—which is to say civil law—a party is not automatically entitled to an attorney if he or she can't afford one. Thus, for many lower and middle-income families, access to the legal system is limited.

For example, when you're seeking a minor adjustment to child support, paying an attorney to file a modification may simply not be worth it. The gain in monthly support would be less than the cost of the attorney to secure the increase.

And even a parent who can afford an attorney may not want one. Some people hold the view that courts are primarily a place for lawyers to make money. For those individuals, going pro per offers *psychological satisfaction.*

The savings do not end with the first ruling, either. Because child custody often represents an ongoing conflict, the parent who self-represents stands to save even more over the long run.

When You Should Consider Representing Yourself

1. You have a simple matter to bring before the court.

2. You can get legal assistance.

3. You can communicate with the other parent.

4. You're dealing with a small amount of money.

5. A mistake won't hurt you in a substantial way.

To Make the Decisions

Another reason to represent yourself is to retain control over the *decision making.* Ultimately you—and not the attorney—have to live with the court orders. When you allow others to make the decisions for you, you lose your ability to influence the outcome.

Also, since every family is unique, you're the only one who can truly say what is best for your children. Sometimes the professionals—no matter how well-intentioned—can't understand your situation. In those cases, it may be best to take charge of your own affairs.

And finally, when you make your own decisions, you're more likely to have a *good outcome.* That is, pro pers are more likely to comply with the court orders, are less likely to relitigate, and often have less post-divorce conflict.

To Keep It from Escalating
When you hire an attorney, you're hiring an advocate to act on your behalf. It's quite likely the attorney will file accusatory motions, adopt a harsh negotiating stance, and threaten litigation at every turn. Attorneys are mercenaries in an adversary system, and those are the tools they have to work with.

If the parents are bargaining from dramatically different positions, hiring lawyers can help balance the equation. On the other hand, when it comes to family law, this confrontational approach has been criticized. When lawyers become involved, formerly pliable parents may become entrenched, hardened into extreme and polarized positions.

After the court battles are over, and the lawyers have gone home, parents still have to deal with each other.

When lawyers become involved, a simple case involving one issue can suddenly blossom into full-scale litigation. When one parent gets a lawyer, the other parent responds, and soon a case needing only a few simple forms to be filled out turns into a litigation nightmare.

By representing yourself, it's possible to lessen the adversarial nature of the proceedings, and leave yourself room to *do business* with the other parent afterwards.

Disadvantages to Representing Yourself

There are also many reasons why you might not want to represent yourself. Here are some things you might do that could make matters worse:

Make Legal Mistakes
The fact is, a lawyer is someone who has usually completed four years of college, three years of law school, and passed a bar exam. During that time, he or she was trained to analyze complex legal problems and handle intricate legal work. You weren't. If you represent yourself, you're much more likely to make a mistake—possibly a serious one.

Also, keep in mind that many court procedures are steeped in arcane, obscure rituals initially derived from another country. While common sense usually prevails in the long run, there's no guarantee that a simple procedural error won't cost you much more than if you had hired an attorney in the first place.

And finally, realize that lawyers must stand behind their work. Not only do attorneys carry *malpractice insurance,* but most states have a *client security fund* that may reimburse you. If you represent yourself and make a mistake—you have no recourse.

"The man who has himself for a lawyer, has a fool for a client." —Abraham Lincoln

Make Negotiating Mistakes

Since most cases settle, it's a pretty sure bet yours will too. If you try to negotiate for yourself, you'll be hampered not only by your lack of *knowledge* about what you're entitled to, but also by your lack of *skill* at obtaining that result.

For some parents, this lack of knowledge leaves them vulnerable, open to being coerced into giving up their rights to a savvy or dominating ex-spouse. For others, it means just the opposite—they become outrageously unreasonable and demand an arrangement that no judge in his right mind would approve. Also, a parent who goes pro per is much less likely to recognize a fair settlement offer when the other party makes one.

And, of course, when you don't know how to negotiate, you don't know what's important to the judge. When you represent yourself, you're much more likely to blurt out the wrong thing, fatally damaging your case even before you begin.

"Encourage your spouse to obtain competent counsel. It is almost impossible to settle a case with someone who lacks legal advice. Cases settle when both sides conclude that a settlement gives each side about what each would obtain if the case were decided by a judge." Judge Stewart, *California Divorce Handbook*

Create Problems for Court Personnel

A final reason why you may not want to represent yourself goes to the very heart of our system of justice. The adversary system assumes that each side to a dispute has roughly equal expertise. But if you represent yourself, and the other side doesn't, you may end up causing some real problems for the court personnel you deal with.

First, by representing yourself, you place the judge in a difficult position. On the one hand, he may want to help you. For the truth to come out, evidence must be presented, and the rules of evidence are tricky. On the other hand, the judge must avoid taking sides. This quandary is awkward, and some judges will respond by holding the pro per to a lesser standard than the opposing lawyer, while others will respond by getting annoyed with the pro per to the point of ruling against that person.

The attorney involved also faces a dilemma. *Professional codes* require aggressive pursuit of the client's interests, yet allow only limited contact with the other party. If you represent yourself, the attorney is restrained in his or her ability to negotiate a settlement. And if you hire an attorney in some capacity as a legal coach, that attorney is still vulnerable to malpractice claims, even if she only provides information on part of the case.

And finally, the filing clerks and court clerks who know all the details about court procedures have neither the time—nor are they trained—to handle endless questions from pro pers.

 "There is no doubt that a family law calendar full of pro pers is a whole lot more difficult for a judge than one in which the parties are all represented by attorneys. Pro pers frequently don't understand the law, so hearings drag on as the judge struggles to keep them on point. Necessary evidence isn't brought to court so sometimes a decision must be made without facts that might have turned the case around. The judge's attempt to lend a hand to a litigant struggling with a difficult legal point will frequently cause the other party to charge favoritism. The door in the back of the courtroom gets kicked on the way out more than it deserves." Judge Roderic Duncan, Alameda County Superior Court

What Happens When You Represent Yourself

If you're thinking about representing yourself, you should know how it may affect your case.

In 1991, the American Bar Association conducted a study of 273 litigants who completed their divorce cases in Maricopa County, Arizona. The results were reported in *Self-Representation in Divorce Cases.*[2]

Type of Cases
Of all the couples who divorced during the study, almost 90% involved one side who self-represented, and 52% involved both sides self-representing. The authors examined these cases, and found that—as a general rule—when someone self-represented, the legal issues in the case were often less complex and the litigants were usually more cooperative. However, when attorneys took over, the legal issues in the case were often more complex, and the parties were more adversarial.

Agreement
As reported in the study, when at least one side self-represented—and custody, visitation, or support was an issue—the parents were more likely to reach an agreement outside of court. The authors decided that when a parent chose to represent themselves, it may have meant the couple was able to agree on custody before the pleadings were filed.

Expense
Also as reported, when one of the parties self-represented, the case was likely to end sooner, and the litigants were likely to spend less money. The reverse was also true—when lawyers were involved, the case usually took longer, and the litigants spent more. The authors concluded that this was to be expected, since attorneys were more likely to be involved in the more difficult cases.

Temporary Orders
As the study revealed, the attorneys were likely to request temporary orders, but none of the pro pers made such a request.

Litigation
During the study, when attorneys represented the parties, the case was more likely to result in a written agreement, or barring that—to go to trial.

However, when someone self-represented, the case was more likely to be resolved through a default judgment.

Custody Decisions
Interestingly enough, when comparing child custody decisions, the study discovered there were *no meaningful differences* between cases involving self-representation and cases involving attorney representation. This would seem to fly in the face of common wisdom, but—at least for the litigants in the study—choosing to self-represent did not seem to influence the final custody arrangement.

What Happens When You Represent Yourself

	If you represent yourself...	If an attorney represents you...
Agreement	More likely	Less likely
Time	End sooner	Last longer
Cost	Spend less	Spend more
Temporary Orders	Less likely	More Likely
Litigation	Trial less likely	Trial more likely
Custody	No difference	No difference
Satisfaction	72% would do it again	79% would do it again

Satisfaction
And finally, attorney-represented litigants said they were "significantly" more satisfied with their final result than were the self-represented litigants. To explain the result, the authors noted that a number of self-represented cases were one-sided, where one party went pro per but the other hired an attorney. As a group, pro pers that had to face attorneys were much less happy with the outcome.

Still, at the conclusion of their cases, 72% of the self-represented litigants said they would do it again, and 79% of the attorney-represented litigants felt the same.

How to Represent Yourself

If you decide to represent yourself, you'll be entering a brave new world with many new rules and customs.

Some of the rules may seem significant, such as the admonition to only serve legal papers on your opponent's attorney. Other rules may seem minor, such as having to use *pleading paper,* or having to attach a *blue-back* to everything. No matter what, though, you must adhere to the rules, or you'll end up spending even more time and money to correct your mistakes.

That said, there is more to going to court than simply obeying the rules. As a pro per, you'll get a chance to present your case, and when you do, you can speak in your own words. You're not a lawyer, and no one   · expects otherwise. Plain speaking and common-sense reasoning are fine when writing motions or talking in court.

You don't have to go to law school to know what is right.

If you decide to represent yourself, you'll need to know the mundane, prosaic details of procedure such as filing fees, service of process, and so on. You can often find this information in a desk reference. Legal secretaries, paralegals, and law librarians know where to find one. In California, try *The Paralegal's Handbook.*

Getting Help

As a pro per, you can get help from many sources, including:

The Court Clerks

If you need help with legal documents, consider asking the people who handle them every day—the *court clerks.* Court clerks know all about the procedural details, such as which form to use and how to get copies of documents.

Self-Help Law Books

If you represent yourself, you'll need to buy some self-help law books. Nolo Press carries the best-written books available.

Nolo Press
950 Parker St.
Berkeley, CA 94710
(800) 992-6656
www.nolo.com

Recommended Books
Child Custody: Building Agreements That Work, Mimi Lyster. An enormously useful book for creating a highly detailed parenting plan.

Family Law Dictionary, Leonard and Elias. An A-to-Z guide to the enormous complications of family law.

Nolo's Pocket Guide To Family Law, Leonard and Elias. A solid book that covers every issue imaginable in family law.

Practical Divorce Solutions, Charles Sherman. An informal guide to the practical problems of divorce.

Divorce & Money: Everything You Need To Know About Dividing Property, Woodhouse and Felton-Collins, with Blakeman. Excellent book on the money side of divorce.

How To Do Your Own Divorce In..., Charles Sherman. A fill-in-the-forms book. This book is the essence of self-help.

Represent Yourself In Court: How To Prepare And Try A Winning Case, Bergman and Berman-Barrett. Court procedure 101.

Legal Research: How To Find And Understand The Law, Elias and Levinkind. It explains the law library, and you'll need it.

But before rushing down to the courthouse, realize that some clerks may get annoyed by your questions. They're trying to handle everyone who needs help, and you're slowing them down. That's why—to get your questions answered—you may have to turn to other sources.

Self-Help Law Books

Some *self-help law books* have the correct legal forms and instructions on how to fill them out. You can use the forms to prepare pleadings and other kinds of documents. If your legal needs are simple—such as preparing a simple modification—than using a self-help book can save you money. But if your needs are more complex, or if complications arise, then you'll need to get more help.

Paralegals

If you're struggling with the legal forms, and a self-help book doesn't cut it, you can seek out a *paralegal*. Typically, paralegals provide help with preparing your documents so that the documents are accepted by the court. These professionals cost much less than attorneys, but—as with attorneys—there are good ones and bad ones. You'll have to check out a few to find one with acceptable credentials.

Law Library

When you're ready to go beyond a self-help law book, you can find just about everything you need in a *law library*. Law libraries contain the rules of evidence and procedure, court cases, statutes, and much, much more. So much more, in fact, that you can get lost in one. If you do stop by a law library, be sure to ask the librarian for help.

Lawyers

Finally, of course, you can hire a *lawyer.* You don't always need to turn your whole life over to a lawyer; instead, you can choose to retain one as a *legal coach*—someone who provides you with basic information and direction—but who leaves you in charge. Having a legal coach is a

 The American Bar Association estimates that "government-funded legal services plus private and pro bono services satisfy only 20.5% of the total legal needs of those Americans whose income falls below the poverty line." [3]

Do-It-Yourself Web Sites

Courtmate Systems, Inc.
www.ccaonline.com/courtmate
Makers of the *Future Single Parent Plan,* which helps you document
all events surrounding your custody case.

Divorce Forms and Laws
www.divorce-forms.com/prod.html
Offers summaries of divorce laws and legal forms for persons desiring
to file for divorce without an attorney.

Divorce Helpline
www.divorcehelp.com
If you live in California, the *Divorce Helpline* can handle your legal
needs. For everyone else, the site has a directory to self-help services.

Low-Cost Legal Divorce Center
www.divorceme.com
Specializing in matters of divorce with local and national child
support services.

National Divorce and Bankruptcy Center
www.cyberstation.net/~paralegal/divorce.htm
Nation wide services to assist in divorce and bankruptcy.

---

1 *Judge Ted Coleman,* Family Court Division, FL, and Judge Roderic Duncan,
Alameda County Superior Court, CA.
2 *Self-Representation in Divorce Cases, A Report Prepared for the Standing
Committee on the Delivery of Legal Services,* January, 1993
3 *1989 Pilot Assessment of the Unmet Legal Needs of the Poor and of the Public
Generally,* American Bar Association, 1989

The Story of Jessica and James

Aftermath

When Jessica returned home from the court hearing, she was ecstatic. The judge had given her everything she had wanted—and more. The minute she opened the door to her apartment, she knew she couldn't stand to stay home and cook dinner that night, so she picked up Julian and took him out to the best restaurant she could afford. All through dinner, as Julian played with his food or made faces at the other patrons, Jessica laughed out loud, giddy at the excitement of a new day in her life, and relieved that the years of conflict were finally over.

When Jim returned home, he was crushed. In one all-too-brief moment of time, a judge had taken Julian away from him. He was now reduced to being a visitor, a father restricted to playing with his son rather than raising him. Jim didn't know how he could live with the orders, and for the next few days, he holed up in his house until the food ran out.

Things might have stayed that way, but summer quickly came, and with it the time when Jim was to keep Julian for thirty days. As the moment grew near, Jim became excited by the prospect of having real time with Julian, and rushed around the house, carefully cleaning up the accumulated dust he had long ignored.

When Jessica first dropped Julian off, Jim was afraid that the switch in homes might upset him, but Julian ran right into the house and began jumping on the bed. Jim knew he was happy to be home.

* * *

A few nights later, while Jim was cooking dinner, Julian turned off the TV and came into the kitchen.

"Want to help me make dinner?" asked Jim.

"No way," said Julian.

"Okay. But I'm having all the fun and you're not."

"That's okay. Go ahead."

Julian sat on a kitchen chair and began playing with his Lego. He watched his father mix up the ingredients in their dinner. "Mommy doesn't do it that way," he said.

"I guess that means I'm not Mommy!" said Jim, and he made a wacky face at Julian.

Julian laughed, "You're funny, Daddy." Then he grew serious. "Daddy?"

"What?"

"How come Mommy doesn't live here?"

"You know why. We talked about it."

"I remember."

"Well, nothing's changed."

"Daddy?'

"What?

"You want to know what Mommy said?"

"What?" asked Jim, putting the cooking spoon down and lowering the heat on their dinner.

"She said that I could come here as much as I wanted."

"Really?" Jim asked. He walked over to the kitchen table and pulled up a chair. "She said that? Really?"

"Yep." said Julian. "She's not mad at you anymore."

"She's not?"

"Nope."

"Hmmm," said Jim. "That's interesting. I would say that's very, very interesting." He made a gurgling sound in his throat, and Julian laughed again.

"You know what? She said that if you wrote her a letter, she would be nice."

"Really?"

"Yep," said Julian. "She might even come home."

Jim looked hard at Julian. "She didn't say that. Did she? Really?"

"Yep," said Julian again, nodding his head. He got out of his chair and stood next to his father. "I'll help you write it."

Jim burst out laughing. "Are you crazy? You don't even know how to write!"

Julian's gaze remained steady. "I'll tell you the words and you write them down."

Jim stared into his son's eyes. "Tell you what. This is between me and Mommy. I'll write the letter. Okay?"

"Okay," said Julian, and he went back to the T V, his mission accomplished.

Jim sat at the kitchen table, thinking about what had happened. Then he leaned back and smiled. In that moment, sitting at the kitchen table, he loved his son more than anything else in the entire world.

*   *   *

When Jessica came home and saw the letter from Jim, she was surprised. Jim was not much of a letter writer, and his attitude towards her hadn't exactly improved since the court hearing. Still, she was curious, and opened it right away.

Dear Jessica,

Once you have a child with someone, they will be the other parent forever. We will always be connected through Julian. I know we haven't always agreed, but that's in the past. Our future is in front of us. From here, we can take two roads. One is the road of being apart and alone, and the other is the road of being together. We were in love once. We had a child. For Julian's sake, let's take the second road.

Love always,
Jim

Jessica stood by the door and read the letter, then read it again. She knew what Jim wanted, even if he didn't come right out and say it. He wanted to get back together. No, she thought, it would never work. It had taken her years to break free, and now he wanted to ruin everything! She grew mad that he would want that. She tossed the letter aside and started making dinner, but no matter how hard she tried, she couldn't stop thinking about it. Finally, she picked up the phone and called her friend Monica.

"Hello?" answered Monica.

"It's me," said Jessica. "You'll never guess what happened."

"What?"

"Jim sent me a letter."

"Really?" asked Monica, suddenly intrigued. "What did he say?"

Jessica read the letter to her, and when she was finished, asked, "What do you think?"

"How rude!" said Monica, clearly irritated. "Does he imagine you're going to turn your whole life upside down just to please him?"

"He's just trying to be nice."

"He's still pushing you around."

"He said he's thinking of Julian."

"He's thinking of himself. He'll never change."

Jessica paused. "Maybe."

"I'm right," said Monica confidently. "You're much better off without him."

"I guess," said Jessica. "But it couldn't hurt to be nice to him. I mean, he is Julian's father."

"That's right. And has he been paying his child support?"

Jessica paused again. "He's gotten a little behind. But he doesn't have the money right now. Really. He's promised to make it up to me."

Jessica could hear Monica's disapproval come right through the phone. "Sure he will. Look, I have to go. Call me later, all right?"

"All right," said Jessica.

After Jessica hung up the phone, she sat down and put her head on her hands. She had a lot to think about.

✱   ✱   ✱

When it was time to return Julian, Jim was excited. Since he had mailed the letter a week earlier, he had been filled with hope. Surely Jessica still felt something towards him, and he knew that if he could just get past whatever it was that was making her angry, they could work it out. Why couldn't they be friends? Why couldn't they share their child and get along? And maybe, possibly, why couldn't they get back together? Was that totally inconceivable? After all, all that stood in his way was a flimsy piece of paper from the court. Driving Julian over to Jessica's apartment, Jim couldn't help but be optimistic.

Jim rang the doorbell, and Jessica immediately answered. Julian leapt right into her arms, and she gave him an enormous hug. Jim watched, a smile on his face.

"How are you? Did you have a good time at your Daddy's?"

"It was fine, Mommy." Julian allowed himself to be hugged by his mother, then rushed into her apartment.

Jim and Jessica looked at each other. "Well," said Jim. "Here he is, safe and sound."

"Okay," said Jessica. And she started to close her door.

"Wait," said Jim. "Did you get my letter?"

"Yes," said Jessica.

"And?" asked Jim.

"Jimmy," said Jessica looking away. "I don't know what you want from me."

"I just thought..." Jim's voice trailed off. "You know."

"I don't see how it can work it out."

"Don't you want to try?"

"If we could get along, then why did we get a divorce?" asked Jessica. Then she stepped inside and shut the door.

Jim stared at the door, then turned and went home.

✳   ✳   ✳

Legal
Problems

Chapter 18

Mistreatment of Children: Abuse, Neglect, and False Accusations

Domestic violence, child abuse, and child neglect touch the lives of many children each year. These children are found in all families, in all parts of the country, and at all income levels.

An adult who suspects a child has been abused must report the problem to a child protective agency or the police. A caseworker will then investigate by gathering physical evidence and interviewing the child. Though many reports are genuine, when custody is in dispute, there are also many false accusations.

This chapter discusses the mistreatment of children.

Child Abuse

When an adult hurts a child, it is called *child abuse.* Child abuse and child neglect cover many forms of injury and cruelty to children, including physical harm, emotional harm, and neglect.

Parents have a responsibility to protect their children. Not only are parents prohibited from hurting their children, but they must ensure that other adults don't hurt them either. This includes being responsible for the behavior of other family members, baby-sitters, and anyone else with access to the children.

Types of Child Abuse

There are many types of child abuse and neglect. They include:

Physical Abuse
Physical abuse is physically hurting a child. Beating, burning, bruising, throwing, or kicking a child are all examples of physical abuse. When a parent punishes a child by spanking, it may be considered physical abuse if the child is injured, even if the injury is only temporary.

Sexual Abuse
Sexual abuse is when an adult molests or otherwise uses a child for sexual pleasure. Examples of sexual mistreatment include fondling, anal or oral intercourse, and vaginal or anal penetrations. Sexual abuse can also include placing the child in inappropriate situations, such as exploiting the child in prostitution or pornography.

Emotional Abuse
Emotional abuse is subjecting a child to extreme humiliation that deprives the child of dignity and self-esteem. Examples of emotional abuse include humiliating the child in front of family and friends, isolating the child for long periods of time, and using language that causes the child emotional harm.

Neglect
Child neglect occurs when an adult fails to meet the basic needs of the child. *Physical neglect* involves failing to provide the minimum food, clothing, and shelter needed by the child. *Medical neglect* involves failing to provide the basic medical, dental, and psychiatric care needed

by the child. *Educational neglect* concerns the failure to educate the child according to the state's educational laws. And *developmental neglect* concerns the failure to provide the basic nurturing and cognitive stimulation needed by the child.

Endangerment
Endangerment involves reckless behavior by an adult that causes—or could cause—harm to the child. An example of physical endangerment includes leaving a young child alone in an area where dangerous items are within reach.

Abandonment
Abandonment involves leaving a child alone or with someone else in such a way as to indicate that you are abdicating parental responsibility. For example, leaving a child in a dumpster and walking away would certainly qualify as abandonment.

 "Many states, faced with civil lawsuits, criminal prosecutions, and mounting public outrage over abuse cases... have in the past decade regularly toughened their codes. They've also squeezed out caseworker discretion by sharpening definitions of abuse and standardizing the decision-making process." *Los Angeles Times*

The Reality of Child Abuse

Identifying the exact number of children abused each year is difficult because many reports turn out to be false.

For example, in Los Angeles, an estimated 25,000 families—or about 50,000 children—are reported *each month* to the Department of Children's Services as possible abuse cases.[1] About one-third of those cases are closed within ten days because the allegations are unfounded or cannot be proven, and only 3% actually go to court.

Nationally, one survey estimated that approximately 3,000,000 abuse and neglect reports are made each year, but only one-third are substantiated after an investigation.[2]

Also, abuse allegations seem to go hand-in-hand with custody disputes. As one researcher found, when custody is in dispute, over 83% of abuse and neglect allegations turn out to be false.[3]

Still, despite the high number of false reports, many, many children are abused or neglected each year. And the number of reports is climbing. From 1976 to 1993, the number of child abuse accusations rose an astonishing 333%, and the number of sexual abuse accusations increased by over 1,400%![4]

Reporting Child Abuse

All states have laws that require suspected child abuse to be reported. Usually, these reports are made to an agency called the *Department of Children and Family Services (DCFS)*, or *Child Protective Services (CPS)*, or something similar. If the police are notified, they may investigate, or contact the agency.

Who Has to Report
Depending on your state, virtually everyone who works with children may be required to report suspected abuse. This includes:
- Doctors.
- Nurses.
- Teachers.
- Day Care Workers.
- Social Workers.
- Police.
- Sheriff.

These *mandated reporters* are usually protected from being sued by the family, and in some states, the reporter's identity is kept secret. In addition, many states have *abuse hotlines* so that neighbors and family members can make reports.

 "Nationwide, police make about 12% of all reports received by child protective agencies. This percentage is about the same as that for such other professional groups such as medical (11%), education (12%), and social services (12%)."[5]

What to Report

Generally, you do not need absolute proof of child maltreatment to make a report. Usually, you only need *reasonable suspicion* or a *reasonable cause to believe* that abuse has occurred.

This suspicion may be based on *direct evidence* or *circumstantial evidence*. Direct evidence includes your own observations of a parent's abusive behavior or the child relating some harmful behavior by an adult. Circumstantial evidence includes suspicious injuries to the child, or signs of apparent mistreatment by looking at the condition of the child.

While you don't need incontrovertible proof, you can't simply make accusations based on some vague "gut feeling" either. Generally, you must have objective evidence to support your claim.

 "Everyone's on the defensive. They're afraid that if they don't make a report, they'll be deemed criminals if they inadvertently put a child back in the hands of a real abuser." Dr. Richard A. Gardner, Professor of Child Psychiatry, Columbia University

Failure to Report

To encourage reports, many states sanction mandated reporters for *failure to report*. In some states, failure to report is a misdemeanor with a possible fine and imprisonment, but in others, the penalties are virtually nonexistent. In addition, failing to report can often lead to a civil lawsuit, and indeed, many police officers, doctors, teachers, and even family members have been sued for not protecting the child.

Child Abuse Database

In some states, when a report is made, it is logged into a *child abuse database*. The database, or *registry*, keeps track of everyone suspected of child abuse, even if it turns out to be false.

This list of suspected abusers helps authorities know who has been accused before. The database may also be used by certain employers when making a background check—for example, in screening an applicant for a child care position.

"The fact is, we have some nice, good, well-meaning people on the central registry. Nice, good people don't always do what's right. For most of them, it's never going to happen again. But we do find some people repeat. That's why we have a registry. So we can know of the second or third incident." Eric Sage, Chief of the Bureau of Support Services, Iowa Department of Human Services

Unfortunately, once you are logged into the database, it's not easy to get out. A parent who has been the target of an unfounded accusation may be listed for a few months, a few years, or even for life.

Investigating Child Abuse Accusations

It's not easy to investigate child abuse. The officials who do it complain that the process is confusing and frustrating. On the one hand, they must gather enough evidence to determine if the charge has a factual foundation—that is, if it's true—but on the other, they must avoid traumatizing the child even more.

As well as anybody, these officials know that "a child's world revolves around the family, and no matter how dysfunctional that family may be, it is usually the only one the child has ever known." That's why the case is often handled by social workers, rather than law enforcement personnel.

Child Protective Service Agencies
In many states, child protective services caseworkers are responsible for investigating child abuse. These workers interview the family, inspect the home, and may make "suggestions" on how to correct the problem. If the parents do not accept their suggestions, the caseworkers often have the authority to force them. For example, they may be able to require the parents to undergo counseling. If more serious measures are required, the caseworkers can compel the parents to submit to a lie detector test, or they may even be able to deny access to the children.

The Police
While child protective agencies often call on the police for help, usually the police only get involved in more serious cases, such as those involving injuries or sexual abuse.

Typically, police get involved when:
- A parent is uncooperative, or is threatening a caseworker.
- The charge is serious enough to warrant the parent being arrested.
- The child is in immediate danger and must be placed in protective custody.
- An emergency occurs after hours, and an immediate response is needed.

Because the police have the legal authority to protect citizens (including children), they are best equipped to deal with a dangerous or threatening parent. Absent a court order, only the police can forcibly enter a home, remove a child, and place that child in protective custody.

Physical Evidence

When abuse has occurred, *physical evidence* often exists. Police and caseworkers will search for this evidence and carefully document it. They may take pictures, have the child x-rayed, or make written descriptions.

 "About 1 million cases [a year] are substantiated, most with a finding of some credible evidence. In about 40% of those million cases, sexual and physical abuse can be shown by such means as x-rays, radiology reports, or rape tests." [6]

Suspicious Injuries
Suspicious injuries are injuries suggesting physical abuse. These are not injuries that result from normal childhood playing—such as bumping or falling down. Rather, they are injuries with the distinctive characteristics of physical abuse. Investigators look for these indicators:

Type of injury. Some injuries are almost impossible for children to do to themselves, such as a fracture to the upper thigh in a toddler. Other injuries are almost always inflicted by others, such as abdominal injuries.

Shape of injury. Many assaults on a child leave telltale marks. For example, there may be choke marks around the neck, or injury from a belt buckle, coat hanger, or hot iron, which leave distinctive signs of abuse.

Location of injury. Children often bang into things and injure their hands, elbows, knees, and shins. But they rarely hurt their thighs, upper arms, buttocks, and genital and rectal areas.

Number of injuries. A child who has many injuries, some new and some old, is unlikely to be merely an accident-prone child. Multiple injuries often indicate abuse.

Family Abuse

These heart-wrenching books were written by the survivor of what has been described as "the worst child abuse case in California."

A Child Called "It": An Abused Child's Journey from Victim to Victor, David J. Pelzer, Health Communications, $9.95.

The Lost Boy: A Foster Child's Search for the Love of a Family, David J. Pelzer, Health Communications, $10.95.

Corporal Punishment
Parents are allowed to punish their children, and some injuries may be the result of *corporal punishment.* For example, a parent is usually allowed to spank a child's bottom with an open hand. Some states even allow the use of a hairbrush or belt.

But if the punishment is excessive, it may be abuse. To distinguish between reasonable and excessive, the official must consider the child's age and misconduct, the parent's purpose, and the degree of harm. It is not abuse if the injury is a true accident where the parent could not have foreseen the consequences.

Other Physical Evidence
Besides injuries to the child, *other physical evidence* may exist. For example, if a child was beaten or burned, the instrument that was apparently used—such as a belt, stick, iron, or cigarette lighter—may be considered evidence. In sexual abuse cases, the child's clothes may be ripped or stained, and may contain blood, semen, or pubic hair. In child neglect cases, the home may contain drugs, firearms, or poisons accessible to the child.

Interviewing the Children

When a child abuse accusation is made, the child will almost always be *interviewed*.

Generally, the investigating official will attempt to interview the child in private, away from the parents. The interviewer will ask vague, open-ended questions, such as "Can you tell me what happened?" or "I can see you're upset, and I'd like to know about it." The child is allowed to answer in his or her own words, and the interviewer is trained not to react with shock or disapproval. The interviewer is also taught not to suggest answers to the child.

The purpose of the interview is to gather information. Even very young children are considered reliable enough to explain what happened. In fact, children are often considered the best source of information regarding possible mistreatment.

If the child gives information that requires some action to be taken, and the child is old enough, the interviewer may explain the situation. The child may also be assured that he or she is not to blame for what has happened, or for what may happen to the parents.

Child Describes Abuse

When a child makes a statement that indicates abuse, the investigator must decide if the child is telling the truth. Some hold that *children never lie,* and unless there is a reason to discount the child's statement, it must be believed. Others point out that—like adults—children lie, exaggerate, and fantasize. For example, an older child may claim abuse to escape an intolerable home situation. To evaluate the statement, the investigator will look for *indicators,* such as convincing details and descriptions.

 If you feel pressure building to the point where you want to lash out at your child, try these tips from *Parents Anonymous:* take 10 deep breaths, phone a friend, take a hot bath, or put on some music.

Child Denies Abuse

Similarly, when a child denies abuse, but there is reason to believe it has occurred, the investigator must determine if the child is telling the truth. To some people, this a catch-22 situation—denial of abuse indicates abuse. But others know that children may be threatened or bribed by their parents, or may fear retaliation if they reveal the abuse. To discover what happened, the investigator will compare the child's injuries with the explanation. For example, if the child claims he got into a fight with a playmate, or fell down some stairs, the injuries should fit the accident.

When court-appointed mental-health professionals interview a child, they frequently qualify their conclusions because they can't say for sure what really happened. Often, they conclude their reports with phrases such as "I can't say for certain that a molestation occurred, but some event happened to put the child in turmoil."

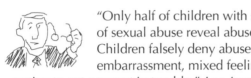

"Only half of children with specific physical findings of sexual abuse reveal abuse when questioned. Children falsely deny abuse for many reasons: embarrassment, mixed feelings for the offender, not wanting to get a parent in trouble." *Los Angeles Times*

Interviewing the Parents

In addition, the investigator may interview the parents. The parents will be asked to provide an explanation for the injury, and if they cannot give a satisfactory answer, they may be suspected of child abuse.

When listening to the parent, the investigator will consider if the explanation is consistent with the injury, such as when a parent says a child suffered terrible burns when she stepped into a tub of hot water. They will also evaluate the situation to see if excessive or inappropriate force was used, such as when a parent describes disciplining the child, but claims it was necessary to punch the child in the head.

While many injuries do not automatically establish abuse, investigators are likely to err on the side of caution. Moreover, even if a parent is believed, there are times when an investigator may feel that the child needs protection, such as when a parent is indifferent to the injury.

Protective Custody

All forms of abuse and neglect hurt children, but some types do not pose an immediate threat. Rather, they harm the children through long-term exposure. In those cases, the child is often left in the home, and the family is given time to correct the problem.

But in extreme cases, the police have authority to remove the child from the home and place them in *protective custody.* The police may remove a child when:

- The child has been beaten, poisoned, or burned.
- The child has been tortured or viciously punished.
- The child has been sexually abused.
- The parents cannot provide for the child's basic needs.
- The parents may flee with the child.
- The child is in immediate danger because of conditions in the home.

Depending on the laws of the state, there are three ways a child may be placed in protective custody:

Parental Consent
In many states, the *consent* of the parents is often sought before removing the child from the home. Caseworkers know that forcing some parents to cooperate may only hinder their long-term efforts to correct the situation. Some parents respond to an intrusion into the family by becoming defensive and combative. Other parents, however, might agree to relinquish the child as a welcome relief from the ever-present burden of child-raising.

Prior Court Order
If the parents do not cooperate, the child can also be taken into protective custody through a *court order.* These cases may represent parents who have had time to correct the situation, but have been unwilling to do so. Having a court review a potential removal helps ensure it is the correct decision.

Emergency Removal
And finally, if the parents do not cooperate, and if the child is in such immediate danger that there is no time to get a court order, the police can make an *emergency removal.* Emergency removals are literally life-and-

death decisions, and generally happen only when the child will be harmed during the short amount of time it takes for the caseworker to be notified and respond. If a child is removed in this way, all states require a hearing within a short time—usually 48-72 hours.

Arrests

Although child protective agencies focus on maintaining the family, when abuse has occurred, the police may *arrest* the abuser.

Before they arrest someone, the police must have *probable cause*. This means the officer must have a reasonable belief that a crime was committed and that the suspect did it. Since all forms of abuse are crimes, once abuse is substantiated, arresting a parent becomes a possibility.

However, a parent is normally arrested only when the officer believes that doing so is the only way to protect the child, or if the parent interferes when the officer tries to take the child into protective custody.

Better safe than sorry. When an officer or caseworker places a child in protective custody, they are given immunity from civil liability. But if they don't remove the child, they may be liable and possibly sued by family members.

Hearings

Once it's established that child abuse has occurred, a *court hearing* will be held to resolve the issue.

The purpose of the hearing—and any subsequent trial—is to either correct the problem that led to the abuse so the family successfully reunited, or to terminate all parental rights.

If a voluntary plan can be worked out, the family will be supervised by the agency, and may be subject to future oversight. If the parents lose their rights, the legal bonds are cut, and the child is free to be adopted. Alternatively, the child may be placed in the home of a relative, a foster home, or an institution.

Shelter from Violence and Abuse

National Coalition Against Domestic Violence
P.O. Box 18749
Denver, CO 80218
(303) 839-1852
(800) 333-SAFE
www.webmerchants.com/ncadv/default.htm
NCADV is a national referral center for shelters for battered women.
They can refer you to a shelter, or send you an information kit on
domestic violence. They publish a quarterly newsletter: *National
Coalition Against Domestic Violence-Voice.*

National Council on Child Abuse and Family Violence
1155 Connecticut Ave. NW
Suite 300
Washington, DC 20036
(202) 429-6695
(800) 222-2000
This organization works to disseminate information on family
violence. They will send you information or a brochure. The toll-
free number provides referrals for community services.

AMEND
777 Grant St.
Suite 600
Denver, CO 80203
(303) 832-6363
An organization that provides therapy for batterers and training
programs for schools. They also publish: *Battering: An AMEND
Manual for Helpers.*

Batterers Anonymous
8485 Tamarind
Suite D
Fontana, CA 92335
(714) 355-1100
This organization rehabilitates parents by requiring them to attend
weekly meetings so they will better handle their stress.

False Accusations

When child custody is in dispute, it's not unusual for false accusations to be made. Specifically, sexual abuse allegations are such a common weapon that they have their own name—*sexual allegations in divorce.*

Accusations are often made without substantiating evidence, and against parents who have no history of suspicious behavior. They may be pure fabrications—such as stories that are completely concocted—or they may be based on recovered memory—such as when an older child "remembers" an event from her past.

While the timing of such an accusation make it suspect, some argue that the period of the family splitting apart is a natural time for repressed examples of dysfunction to come out. Others, of course, insist that the accusations are a ploy to gain an advantage in the dispute.

 Sue me. You can sue the other parent for accusing you falsely, but don't expect to win. As Kim Hart, director of the *National Child Abuse Defense and Resource Center* says, "You have to prove malice, and that's almost impossible."

Why Parents Make False Accusations

Parents have many reasons to make false accusations, including:

Getting Revenge
Clearly, some people are motivated by *revenge.* An angry parent looking to "get even," or a jealous parent seeking to sabotage the child's relationship with the other parent need look no further than a false allegation. Abuse accusations—whether true or not—effectively destroy the reputation of the accused. The charges often bring a stigma that can alienate parents from friends, coworkers, and family. And because the accused is generally assumed to be *guilty until proven innocent,* the damage is done when the charges are made—whether or not they turn out to be true.

Gaining a Tactical Advantage

Another reason to make a false accusation is that it automatically gives the accuser a *tactical advantage.* Under some circumstances, the accusation itself may be enough to cut off the other parent's contact with the children until the investigation is finished. And that could be months—or even a year. This gives the accuser a powerful weapon to use—one that can bring attention, sympathy, and maybe even victory—all without even having to prove that he or she is telling the truth.

Starting a Criminal Investigation

And finally, an abuse accusation forces the other parent to endure a *criminal investigation.* This probably means spending money on a lawyer to defend against the charges. Because prosecutors often have much greater resources than parents, a hard-working, middle-class parent may be financially devastated by the legal defense needed to defend against such a charge.

 Why do parents make false accusations? "It's simple, fast, and guaranteed to achieve the desired result. In one fell swoop, she can get her husband completely out of her and her children's lives and assure herself complete custodial control. And in one fell swoop, she can completely destroy the man's life, and any semblance of a normal relationship between him and his children." Anne P. Mitchell, attorney, San Jose, California.

What to Do If You Are Accused

If you are accused of abusing your children, the first time you hear about it may be *after* your children are interviewed by caseworkers. That means there is already a case building against you.

As attorney Melvin Belli says, "First, get yourself one hell of a good child-custody lawyer." It may seem obvious, but you'll need immediate expert *legal advice* on how to protect yourself during the investigation. And if the attorney you hire recommends that you plead guilty—but you are innocent—get another lawyer.

When You Are Accused

Guilty Until Proven Innocent, Kimberly A. Hart, National Child
Abuse Defense and Resource Center, $25.00. This excellent book
has very specific, very detailed information for those accused of child
abuse. Written by the director of *The National Child Abuse Defense
and Resource Center,* it provides useful, day-to-day information that
is required reading for anyone fighting a false accusation.

Second, ask the judge to *appoint an attorney for your child.* This attorney
can help move the case to a conclusion so you won't be left dangling for
months with the charge hanging over your head.

Third, *cooperate fully* with the police and caseworkers. Show up for
appointments, answer all questions honestly, and admit to any contact
you've had with your children. If you get defensive or argumentative, you
don't help your case.

Fourth, *demand a polygraph* (lie detector) test. While the results are not
admissible in court, if you pass the test, it will help convince some people
you are innocent. If the police won't schedule a polygraph for you, you
can arrange your own, but be sure the examiner you hire has a reputation
for competence and neutrality. Also, consider demanding that the other
parent submit to a polygraph. If the parent refuses to take the test or fails
it, that will bolster your case.

Fifth, consider hiring a *mental health professional.* When caseworkers
evaluate an abuse accusation, they rely on "indicators" such as
nightmares, bed-wetting, and thumb-sucking. The problem is, these

---

A picture is worth a thousand words. If you are
falsely accused, ask a neighbor or friend to "make a
documentary record of your child's removal. Use a
video camera, a still camera, an audiotape recorder,
or a journal to chronicle the events. In court a judge will find the
conduct of police or social workers, and your child's reaction to
being removed, useful in rendering a decision." *Parents Magazine*

---

behaviors are common, and there's a good chance that a perfectly normal child could be seen as an abuse victim. While it can be difficult, you may be able to find a psychologist willing to refute the charges.

And finally, insist on a *hearing.* If you've been cut off from your child, and it has been more than 90 days, ask to hold a hearing to resolve the issue and to reestablish your access to the child. In some states, however, if the police or child protective agency is still investigating, the judge must defer until their work is complete.

Answering False Accusations

National Child Abuse Defense & Resource Center
P.O. Box 638
Holland, OH 43528
(419) 865-0513
Strategic advice and referrals for parents falsely accused. The NCADRC also maintains a library of case law.

Victims of Child Abuse Laws (VOCAL)
7485 E. Kenyon Ave.
Denver, CO 80237
(303) 233-5321
Nonprofit organization that helps people who have been falsely accused. Makes referrals and will send a brochure.

---

1 *Los Angeles Times,* August 16, 1995
2 *The National Committee for the Prevention of Child Abuse,* 1993.
3 *Dr. Melvin Greyer,* Family Law Project of the University of Michigan
4 *The National Committee for the Prevention of Child Abuse,* 1993
5 *Child Abuse: A Police Guide,* Douglas J. Besharov, Police Foundation and the American Bar Association, 1987
6 *The National Committee for the Prevention of Child Abuse,* 1993

Chapter 19

Access to Children: Kidnapping, Custodial Interference, and Moveaways

If you've ever seen pictures of children on milk cartons, you've seen children who are missing or who have been *kidnapped.*

A kidnapped child is often caught in a custody tug-of-war. Some parents take the children as a prelude to an interstate custody fight. Other parents remove the children from the country.

If the children are not kidnapped, but the other parent won't let you see them, that is *custodial interference.*

This chapter discusses problems arising from access to children.

Parental Kidnapping

Parental kidnapping is when one parent takes the children and refuses to return them to the other parent. This is also called *child-snatching*.

While either parent could theoretically kidnap the children, typically the noncustodial parent abducts the children in order to thwart a custody order. The kidnapping parent then moves with the children in order to block access by the other parent.

The Reality of Parental Kidnapping

No one really knows how many family abductions occur each year. Statistics quoted by different sources vary widely and often favor a particular view.

One study, released by the *United States Department of Justice,* estimates that there were more than 350,000 abductions in one year. Here's what the study found:

The Reality of Parental Kidnapping[1]

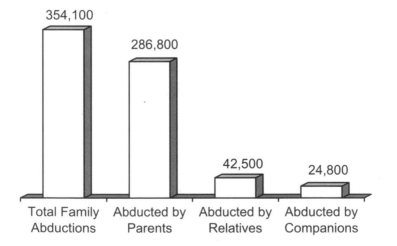

These figures were based on cases that required active intervention by police and social agencies, and did not distinguish between true parental kidnapping and other problems, such as custodial interference.

Statistics can also be misleading when trying to determine how many children are recovered. The *Justice Department* found that many of the children were returned within seven days, with only 10% still missing a month later. On the other hand, one national organization, *Child Find of America,* estimates that only "one in three missing children who are abducted by a parent are eventually found or returned." Or, to put it another way, they predict that fully 66% of the children who are kidnapped will disappear for good.

Also, according to the *State Department,* the vast majority of family abductions result in the child staying within the United States. As reported in the *Los Angeles Times,* in one year, "there were [only] 1,200 active custody cases involving an American child abroad."[2]

Why Parents Kidnap

While parents have many justifications for kidnapping their children, their reasons often fall into three categories:

Disagreement with the Custody Order
Sometimes a parent who loses custody may feel they didn't get a reasonable or fair hearing in court. This parent may feel like a second-class citizen in their children's lives, and is convinced that he or she has a "natural right" to the children that supersedes what any court says. Such a parent may decide to "overrule" a custody order by kidnapping the children in order to enforce the "correct" custody decision

Fear of Harm to the Children
Some parents may kidnap their children to protect them from the other parent. They may believe that the other parent is a bad parent with an erratic or unacceptable lifestyle, or that the other parent is abusing or endangering the children. Physical, sexual, and even psychological abuse are all reasons that have been used to justify a kidnapping, even when there the court has investigated the accusations and is unconvinced.

Revenge Against the Other Parent
To paraphrase a common quote, child custody involves "good people acting their worst." Some parents may kidnap the children simply to get even. As a justification for a kidnapping, revenge has nothing to do with what is best for the children, and everything to do with how the parent feels.

Anticipating a Kidnapping

As the famed attorney Melvin Belli said, "The best way to deal with child-snatching is to prevent it from ever happening at all." This means anticipating the possibility that your former mate will kidnap the children and taking steps to prevent it.

First, consider the *time* when a kidnapping is most likely to occur. Because of the stress and uncertainty of custody proceedings, many abductions occur right before or right after a custody decision.

Second, take a good *look* at the other parent. Has he or she threatened to snatch the children? If so, take it seriously. Or if the other parent has the profile of a probable kidnapper—be cautious.

Here are the traits to look for in the other parent:
- History of violence or child abuse.
- No stable community ties.
- Poor employment history.
- Poor finances or trying to escape creditors.
- Has job skills useful in other states or knows someone who will provide financial support.

Third, before the other parent disappears, assemble all the *identifying information* you can. This includes driver's license number, social security number, bank account numbers, credit card numbers, etc.

Fourth, if you think it can happen—*tell somebody.* You can ask teachers, school bus drivers, and other people to be alert for suspicious people.

Keeping Children Safe

Raising Safe Kids in an Unsafe World, Jan Wagner, Avon Books, $11.00. The author boils down child safety into 30 simple lessons in a bright and easily readable book.

When Parents Kidnap, Geoffrey L. Greif, Rebecca L. Hegar (Contributor), Free Press, $27.95. Contains detailed case histories of parental kidnappings, including the effect on the "left behind" parent and the long-term psychological impact on everyone involved.

Your lawyer can request an order barring the other parent from taking the children out of state, and the *Passport Office* can withhold issuing passports for the children unless a valid custody order is included.

Fifth, *prepare your children* by making sure they've memorized your phone number, including the area code. They will also need to know how to call you collect, or you can give them a telephone credit card.

And finally, *eliminate the reason* for a parental kidnapping by allowing the other parent to remain connected to the children. An involved parent has less reason to snatch the children.

Five Warning Signs of a Kidnapping

1. The other parent threatens to kidnap the children.

2. The other parent just lost custody.

3. The other parent is paranoid or unstable.

4. The other parent has easily transferable job skills that allow him or her to work in another state or country.

5. The children are between the ages of three and nine—the most likely age for an abduction.

What to Do If Your Children Are Kidnapped

If your children are kidnapped, the first few hours are critical.

First, *call the police.* They will need to see a notarized or certified copy of your current custody orders. If the children are still in the state, the district attorney or state attorney general can get involved. If the children have been abducted to another state, the FBI can be notified.

Then, *call your lawyer,* who can obtain a felony warrant against the kidnapper and initiate a contempt proceeding, which lets you recover your costs and fees. Also, your lawyer can request that the *Federal Parent Locator Service* be used to track down a parent in hiding.

After that, *call everyone else,* including your ex-spouse's family members, friends, neighbors, and employer. Some may reveal nothing, but others might give you a lead to the whereabouts of your children.

If you still haven't located your children, *call the media.* You can notify newspapers, television stations, and radio stations about your plight. You can also print up posters with your children's names, photos, and description. If you call a missing children's organization, such as *Child Find of America,* they can register you in their database.

And finally, consider hiring a *private investigator.* This can cost you tens of thousands of dollars—or more—but may be your only hope of finding your children. An investigator can track a kidnapper through mail, bank records, and even the transfer of school records.

 Fighting fire with fire. If your children have been kidnapped and you know where they are, consider the consequences before kidnapping them back. For one thing, retaliation can keep the chain of abductions going. For another, a kidnapping involves physical dangers to the children. And finally, kidnapping is against the law.

Kidnapping Laws

Once you find the children, your problems may not be over. If the other parent has taken them to another state and initiated a custody proceeding in that state, you must then deal with *jurisdiction.*

The fact is, child custody is determined by state laws, and each state may decide it differently. That means a parent can lose custody of the children in one state, kidnap them to a different state, and seek a modification there.

To avoid this kind of interstate legal dispute, two laws have been passed. They are:
• The Uniform Child Custody Jurisdiction Act.
• The Parental Kidnapping Prevention Act.

Uniform Child Custody Jurisdiction Act

The *Uniform Child Custody Jurisdiction Act* is a uniform law that has been adopted by all 50 states and the District of Columbia. This law removes one incentive for parental kidnapping by determining which court has jurisdiction.

The UCCJA makes one court—and one court only—responsible for the child. Under the law, the case can only be heard by the court where the child and family have the closest connection. Specifically, for the case to be tried in a given jurisdiction, it has to meet one of the following tests, in order of priority:

- *Home State.* If the child has lived in the state for the past six months, or was in the state for six months but was recently removed, that state is considered the home state and the court can hear the case.

- *Best Interests.* If the child has significant connections to others in the state, or it is in the best interests of the child to remain in the state, the court can hear the case.

- *Abandonment.* If the child has been abandoned, or was mistreated or abused elsewhere, the court may hear the case.

- *No Other State.* Finally, if no other state meets one of the tests or if another state does but chooses not to hear the case, the court can hear the case.

When the UCCJA is followed, interstate conflicts are avoided. Before hearing a case, the judge must look to see if another state has already made a decision, or if there is a case pending, or if another state has a higher authority. Only if the court has the superior claim to jurisdiction can the case be heard.

But the UCCJA went further and required that custody orders made in one state be enforced in other states. By giving *full faith and credit* to custody decisions, judges must enforce custody decrees made in other states. This means the original court retains jurisdiction unless the parents and child "no longer have appreciable ties with that court, or that court declines to exercise its jurisdiction."

Thus, if a parent kidnaps the children and runs off to another state, and then in the new state seeks custody, the court will decline to hear the case, the original judgment will stand, and the court will enforce it.

 Under the UCCJA, "A parent who has wrongfully removed or retained a child in order to create a home state or significant connections will be denied custody."

Parental Kidnapping Prevention Act

In 1980, the *Parental Kidnapping Prevention Act (PKPA)* was enacted. This federal law also requires states to recognize and enforce custody decisions made in other states.

The PKPA specifically requires courts in one state to enforce judgments made by courts in other states unless:
- The original court didn't have jurisdiction.
- The original court declines to exercise jurisdiction.
- There's an emergency—such as abuse, neglect, or abandonment— and the court must intervene to protect the child.

While the UCCJA established guidelines for deciding initial jurisdiction, the PKPA set guidelines for deciding continuing jurisdiction. The act also authorized the use of the *Federal Parent Locator Service* to locate kidnappers.

The *Federal Parent Locator Service (FPLS)* is a national computer system used primarily to find parents who need to pay child support. Both the federal government and many states operate parent locator services.

These computer systems locate parents by tracing tax refunds, unemployment checks, DMV record transfers, and so on. You cannot file a request with the FPLS directly, but must go through an official, such as the district attorney.

 In one year, the Federal Parent Locator Service received 2,307,274 requests for locating a parent.[3]

International Kidnappings

An even more disturbing problem occurs if children are kidnapped to another country. A parent who takes children to a foreign country effectively bypasses American kidnapping laws.

To address some of the enormous difficulties in international child abductions, the U.S. passed a law called *The International Child Abduction Remedies Act.* This federal statute enabled the U.S. to follow procedures set up in the *Hague Convention on Civil Aspects of International Child Abduction.*

The Hague treaty is an international agreement among countries to provide for the return of kidnapped children. It ensures that custody rights in one country are respected in another country.

Unfortunately, not all countries have adopted the treaty. As reported in the *Los Angeles Times,* "Only 37 countries have signed an international accord on custody issues. In the Middle East, only Israel is party to the accord. The upshot is that custody orders issued by U.S. courts can be meaningless overseas."[4]

While the Hague treaty helped to discourage parental abductions, children are still routinely kidnapped to West Germany, Mexico, Italy, Japan, and the Middle East. If the country is not a Hague signatory, "the United States can do little to help parents caught in a custody battle."

But the reverse is not true. When children from other countries are kidnapped to the U.S., courts must recognize and enforce a custody decree made in another country, unless it is shown that the child is in danger.

 For assistance when a child is abducted to another country, or when a child from another country is abducted to the U.S., contact the U.S. State Department Office of Citizen and Consular Services.

When Parents Kidnap

National Center for Missing and Exploited Children
2101 Wilson Boulevard
Suite 550
Arlington, VA 22201
(800) 843-5678
www.missingkids.org
Helps parents and law enforcement officers locate missing children.
Call the toll-free hotline for sightings. Publishes: *Parental
Kidnapping: How to Prevent an Abduction* and *What to Do if Your
Child is Abducted.*

Child Find of America
P.O. Box 277
New Paltz, NY 12561
(800) I-AM-LOST
A national organization that locates missing children by publicizing
their disappearance. Also sponsors a mediation program to prevent
abductions. Both parents and children can call the toll-free number.

Missing Children HELP Center
410 Ware Blvd.
Suite 400
Tampa, FL 33619
(813) 623-5437
(800) USA-KIDS
This organization maintains a database of the procedures followed in
each state for locating missing children. Call the toll-free hotline to
report a missing child.

Adam Walsh Child Resource Center
11911 U.S. Hwy. 1
Suite 301
North Palm Beach, FL 33408
(407) 775-7191
Provides referrals and support services for families of missing
children.

Custodial Interference

Custodial interference is when one parent interferes with the other parent's access to the children.

Custodial interference differs from parental kidnapping in that the children are usually not abducted. Instead, it often involves a more minor dispute over access—one parent wants to see the children, and the other parent won't allow it.

Custodial interference isn't always a case of "You can't see the kids!" It may also occur when one parent *impedes communication* by ripping up letters or cutting off phone calls. Or it may occur when one parent *delays the exchange* by telling the other parent to wait outside until the children are ready, and then taking an hour to get them ready.

Whatever form the obstruction takes, if a parent's physical custody is interfered with, it is considered custodial interference.

Reasons for Denying Contact

Parents have many reasons for blocking access. Some may be acceptable to a judge, and some may not. Here are some categories:

Anger at the Other Parent
Children make easy pawns in a custody war, and some parents may use them as weapons. One obvious example is when the noncustodial parent stops paying child support, and the custodial parent retaliates by denying visitation. Another motivation is jealousy, such as when one parent has remarried, and the other parent is jealous of the new mate.

Children Are Endangered
Another reason to block access is when a parent endangers the children. For example, if one parent arrives to pick up the children and has been drinking heavily or using drugs, the other parent may refuse to turn over the children. Threats to the children include the possibility that the parent may kidnap them, or is likely to abuse or molest them. Protecting the children is often considered a good-cause defense for custodial interference.

Children Won't Go
If the children are old enough—that is, usually teenagers—another reason
for custodial interference is that the children don't want to go. If the
children are not old enough to decide for themselves, a parent must make
a good faith effort to comply with the court orders, even if the children
object.

> *Visitation rights.* "A parent not granted custody of the
> child is entitled to reasonable visitation rights unless the
> court finds, after a hearing, that visitation would
> endanger seriously the child's physical, mental, moral,
> or emotional health." UMDA § 407

How to Enforce Your Custodial Rights

If the other parent won't let you see your children, you'll have to *enforce
your custodial rights.* While there is no single way to do that, you'll
probably have to hire a lawyer and go to court.

Realize, however, that while the other parent must cooperate by allowing
you to see your children, if your custody order only specifies "reasonable"
visitation, and you are the noncustodial parent, it may be difficult to prove
your access was impeded. The lack of specific visitation times in vague
custody orders works against noncustodial parents.

Nevertheless, if your access to the children has been hindered, and a valid
court order is in place, the simplest solution is to ask the judge to find the
other parent in *contempt of court.* If he or she is found guilty of civil
contempt, the judge can impose a fine, or even a jail sentence.

In some extreme cases, custodial interference may also be a reason for
switching custody. In theory, this response isn't designed just to "punish"
the recalcitrant parent, but rather, to solve the access problem by
awarding custody to the more cooperative parent.

And finally, if visitation has been consistently sabotaged, the judge can
suspend child support. This is a highly individual decision, with some
judges using it when necessary, while others would never even consider

it. In general, the interference must have been both deliberate and persistent enough to warrant the punishment.

> *Daily journal.* If your access to the children has been blocked, be sure to keep a daily log of events. This evidence will come in handy in court.

Failing to Visit

There is, of course, another side to all this, and that's when the noncustodial parent *fails to visit* the children.

As a legal matter, failing to visit may be a violation of a court order and could be considered contempt of court. As a practical matter, failing to visit rarely is as important to the judge as, say, paying child support. Parents who pay their bills but don't see their children are often safe from legal repercussions.

However, if one parent fails to visit, and that action costs the other parent money—the judge may order that the injured party be compensated.

© 1994 AL ROSS

*"I can't remember the names of my ex-wives.
I just call them plaintiff."*

Moveaways

A final problem that involves access to the children occurs when the custodial parent wants to *move away.*

Moveaways are not uncommon after parents have separated or divorced. The custodial parent may want to move to start a new job, or to follow a new mate, or to be closer to family.

But when the custodial parent wants to move far away, and the noncustodial parent has substantial visitation, the result is that much of the visitation time with the children is lost. The increased distance effectively shuts out the noncustodial parent from being involved in the children's day-to-day lives.

This makes moveaways a difficult issue to resolve. A moveaway pits the right of the custodial parent to move against the right of the noncustodial parent to see the children.

Moveaway Laws

To prevent parents from simply picking up and moving with their children, many courts routinely include a notice requirement in the court orders.

For example, some courts require the custodial parent to give 30 or 45 days' written notice before making a move. Other courts include restraining orders preventing the custodial parent from moving unless the court gives permission. And still other courts require that the noncustodial parent agree before a custodial parent can move.

If you agree about the move, you need only file an amendment with the court. But if there is a dispute, the court has to make the decision.

Because there are no firm guidelines for moveaways, courts must evaluate each case individually. Typically, they consider:
- If the move is in the child's best interests.
- If there are pragmatic reasons for the move.
- How the move will affect the child's relationship with the noncustodial parent.

Allow Move

Generally, a court is more likely to allow a move if it is shown to be in the child's best interests. The judge will decide if the move is being made in *good faith* and will lead to enhanced job opportunities for the custodial parent or to an improved family relationship.

If the move is allowed, the judge may divide the increased costs for visiting between the parents, or—more likely—require the custodial parent to pay the entire amount. In addition, the judge may revise the schedule to give the noncustodial parent more time with the children during holidays and summer.

Prohibit Move

However, if the judge believes the custodial parent is acting in *bad faith* and is trying to sabotage the noncustodial parent's time with the children, the move may be prevented. Since adults have a right to travel, the court cannot stop the parent from moving, but can switch custody if that happens. The reasoning is that a change of residence is grounds for the change in custody.

 Moving day. In Daghir v. Daghir, the custodial parent tried to move without having a compelling reason. The court blocked the move, stating, "A custodial parent may be properly called upon to make certain sacrifices to ensure the right of the child to the benefits of visitation with the noncustodial parent." An opposite result occurred In re Marriage of Lower, when the custodial parent was allowed to move because, "While there is much to be said for the maintenance of visitation rights by the noncustodial parent, the interests of the custodial parent and child may be overriding."

1 *"Survey of Missing, Abducted, Runaway, and Thrownaway Children in America,"* First Report, Executive Summary (U.S. Justice Department, Office of Juvenile Justice, May 1990)

2 *Los Angeles Times,* November 13, 1994

3 *Child Support Enforcement Fifteenth Annual Report to Congress, 1986-1990.*

4 *Los Angeles Times,* November 13, 1994, and Thursday, September 19, 1996

Chapter 20
Support for Children: Establishing Paternity and Collecting Child Support

Ask anyone involved with *child support,* and you're bound to hear about problems.

Either the amount paid isn't enough, or the amount paid is too much. Either enforcement is too lenient, or enforcement is too strict. And either everyone is a deadbeat, or you can't get blood from a stone.

The fact is, child support is a flawed and imperfect mechanism for transferring money between separated or divorced parents. Establishing paternity, moving across state lines, earning below ability—all become obstacles a parent must overcome to get that monthly check.

This chapter discusses how to enforce a child support order.

The Reality of Child Support Collections

While statistics can be misleading, there is one circumstance that virtually everyone agrees on—many parents with custody of their children don't receive child support.

Though a great deal has been written about *deadbeat parents*—parents who are ordered to pay but fail to comply—astonishingly, this is not the biggest reason why many custodial parents don't receive support.

According to the *Census Bureau,* in one year there were 11.5 million single parent families, but only 6.2 million—or 54%—had a support award.[1] That means that almost half the custodial parents didn't collect child support because *no one* was ordered to pay them.

When the *Office of Child Support Enforcement* investigated the problem, here's what they found:

Why Parents Don't Have a Child Support Order[2]

Did not want an award	21.9%
Did not pursue an award	19.3%
Paternity could not be established	16.5%
Parent unable to pay	14.5%
Parent could not be located	13.6%
Other settlement	8.6%
Final agreement pending	5.6%
	100%

Didn't Want Child Support
As it turns out, 41% of the parents didn't have an order because they didn't want or pursue one. When asked why, some said they were afraid of the other parent and wanted to minimize his or her involvement with the children. Others said they didn't know where the noncustodial parent was, and didn't want to look.

Couldn't Get a Child Support Order
But when parents did seek an award, many found it difficult to get. In a number of families, the noncustodial parent disappeared and couldn't be located. And many never-married single mothers, had to establish paternity—but couldn't do so.

The ties that bind. Once child support is ordered, it remains a debt until it is paid. It cannot be erased by a bankruptcy or subsequent modification. And the court can tack on all reasonable costs incurred in collecting the support as well as penalties on top of that!

Couldn't Enforce a Child Support Order

And of course, even when custodial parents did establish an award, there was no guarantee they would get paid. When the *Census Bureau* surveyed child support collections, they found that only 51% of the parents received full payments, 24% received partial payments, and 25% received no payments at all.3

To explain the gap, some have suggested that the support is too high, and the paying parents simply don't earn enough. Others have suggested that the gap is due to more personal reasons, such as a desire for revenge or retaliation.

Whatever the cause, it's clear that a custodial parent faces many obstacles to collecting child support.

The times are a' changing. As reported in *Time Magazine*, "Fourteen percent of 'deadbeat dads' are actually moms." 4

How to Collect Child Support

Collecting child support is not automatic. Just because you have custody of the children, don't expect the payments to automatically flow in. There are many obstacles to collecting child support, and you may have to overcome some—or all—of them to get that check.

To collect child support, you must:
- Locate the other parent.
- Establish paternity (if the other parent is the father).
- Establish the support order.
- Enforce the support order.

Finding a Parent

For many custodial parents, the first obstacle to collecting child support is simply to locate the noncustodial parent. In order to establish paternity, obtain a support order, and enforce that order, the receiving parent must find the paying parent. In addition, the noncustodial parent's income and assets must be identified.

Parent Locator Services

In every state there is a *child support enforcement agency.* These agencies access federal and state parent locator services to track down missing parents.

The parent locator services find missing parents by doing computer searches through the records of a variety of government agencies, including the following:
- Social Security Administration
- Department of Motor Vehicles
- Department of Corrections
- Department of Health and Human Services
- Bureau of Employment
- Internal Revenue Service
- Veterans Administration

In addition, state parent locator services can look for missing parents by examining voter registration rolls, tax and property rolls, records of utility connections, and so on.

Because it's pretty difficult to exist without leaving some kind of paper trail, parent locator services are very successful. The *Office of Child Support Enforcement* reports that parent locator services successfully find a missing parent 70-80% of the time.

Using the Parent Locator Service

To access the parent locator service, you'll need to submit a request to the child support enforcement agency. You can either have your attorney do it, or you can complete the application yourself. In some states, you can request that the District Attorney do it. Depending on your situation, it may cost as little as $25.

When you submit the request, you'll need to supply the agency with information about the missing parent. At the minimum, they will need the parent's name and social security number. If you don't know the social security number, it can often be found on tax returns, bank account statements, credit applications, hospital records, police records, and so on.

In addition, any other information you provide the agency can only help. If you know the missing parent's birthdate, current employer, or even creditors, that will improve your chances.

While there may be some differences in time limits, by law, every child support agency must conduct the search shortly after you file the application, usually within 20 to 70 days. Because many parents remain in the same state after splitting up, the first search will be through the state parent locator. If the state search is unsuccessful, another state may be searched, or the federal parent locator may be accessed.

 "If the noncustodial parent works, drives a car, pays taxes, receives any kind of government compensation or benefits or has engaged in any one of a number of activities from registering for the draft to going to jail, there's an excellent chance of [the parent locator service] finding him." Marianne Takas, *Child Support: A Complete, Up-to-Date Guide to Collecting Child Support*

Other Ways to Find a Parent

Of course, there is another way to find a missing parent—look for that person yourself. As a practical matter, there is nothing stopping you from doing your own investigation, and indeed, it's possible you may be successful where others are not. Here are some standard investigative techniques:

Documentation. You may be able to find the other parent simply by poring over every scrap of paper you can find. Look carefully at tax returns, medical records, loan applications, licenses, etc. Unless you waited years before starting to look, something is bound to be current. *Networking.* You can talk to past employers and business associates, as well as parents, relatives, friends, and even former neighbors for clues to the whereabouts of the missing parent. Also, check clubs, organizations, or unions he or she belonged to.

Public Records. You're allowed to search the following public records: records of the state for titles to property, voter registration rolls, and even the Department of Motor Vehicles. In addition, you can do an address verification through the post office.

Establishing Paternity

If you were not married when the child was born, another obstacle to collecting child support may be to *establish paternity.* Establishing paternity is when a court decides who the father is.

Paternity disputes typically arise when a mother seeks child support or some other benefits, and the man denies that he is the father. These disputes can also arise when a man wants certain legal rights with the child, and the mother denies that he is the father.

Once paternity is established, the man is formally deemed to be the father, and the child gains many of the rights and benefits that he or she would have had if the parents had been married.

 "California spent more than $30 million in fiscal year 1993-94 to establish paternity for 90,000 California children born to unmarried women."[5]

Why You Should Establish Paternity
Perhaps the single biggest reason to establish paternity is that it's necessary to get a *child support order.* Even if the father can't afford to support the child now, once the obligation is in place, the child becomes entitled to receive support until adulthood.

Also, once paternity is established, the child is eligible to receive the father's *medical and life insurance.* Medical coverage is expensive, and the father may be ordered to carry the child under his policy. In addition, the child will have access to the father's medical records, and can learn any relevant medical history.

Establishing paternity also gives the child the *right of inheritance.* If the father dies, the child will be able to make claims against his estate, and possibly become eligible to receive social security, veterans benefits, retirement benefits, and so on.

From a father's point of view, establishing paternity is necessary if the mother denies that he is the father, and he wants to pursue his right to *custody and visitation.* Once paternity is established, he can pursue custody as if he had been married when the child was born.

And finally, establishing paternity allows the child to *know who the father is.* Paternity is crucially important for the child, whose very identity is uncertain when the biological parents are unknown. Knowing both the father and mother allows the child to learn about his or her heritage, and offers the chance to have a connection to both "sides" of the family.

$ Till death do we part. If the child support order is properly written, it will remain as a claim against the estate of a paying parent who suddenly dies. In addition, the paying parent may be required to carry life insurance with the children named as beneficiaries.

How to Establish Paternity
There are several approaches to establishing paternity. The easiest—and by far the simplest—is for the father to *voluntarily acknowledge* that he is the father. A father can sign a written admission of paternity, under oath, which is filed with the court. This makes him the *acknowledged father* of the child.

In many states, fathers are asked to sign *paternity acknowledgment forms* while the mother is still in the hospital. Depending on the state, these forms may or may not be legally binding, but they do provide critical information about the potential father if he subsequently disappears.

If either the man or the woman denies that the man is the father, either one may start a *paternity suit.* A paternity suit is a lawsuit that decides who the child's father is. While some states impose a time limit, many allow a paternity suit to begin any time before the child reaches adulthood.

In a paternity suit, the court attempts to determine if the man is the father of the child. Science being what it is, that usually boils down to *blood and genetic tests.* If either side to the suit requests it, all parties must submit to testing.

There are several kinds of tests available, ranging from simple blood tests that compare the blood types of the father and the child, all the way up to elaborate DNA screening that checks as many as ninety different genetic markers. While no test is infallible, the DNA results are considered to be as much as 99.9% reliable. Needless to say, this statistical probability mightily impresses judges and juries, and makes it very difficult—though not impossible—to refute.

While blood and genetic testing cannot absolutely prove that a man is the father, they can absolutely prove that he is not the father. This is one reason why a wrongly accused man will demand a test—to clear his name. Also, if the mother had sex with several men at the time of the baby's conception, she might ask all candidates to submit to testing.

Because tests are not perfect, there is room for other evidence in a paternity suit. Generally, the court will listen to any evidence that establishes a link between the father and child, such as:
- *Physical evidence:* Pictures, gifts, and letters the father sent to the child.
- *Testimony:* The dates and times the father and mother had sex; if the father ever described the child as "his" to other people.
- *Documentation:* The father's signature on the birth certificate; the father adding the child's name to his insurance policies.

Interestingly enough, in many states, if the parents were married when the child was conceived, there is a presumption that the husband is the father unless proven otherwise. And in a few states, the husband is presumed to be the father no matter what the tests prove!

 Approximately 90% of fathers attend the birth of their children, regardless of whether the parents are married or ever intend to get married.[6]

Child Support Laws

Title IV-D of the Social Security Act in 1975
The first in a series of laws aimed at reducing the number of single parents on welfare. Title IV-D (4-D) created a federal agency—the Office of Child Support Enforcement (OCE)—and required all states to establish state offices.

The Child Support Enforcement Amendments of 1984
These amendments to Title IV-D required states to develop formula-based guidelines for setting child support. Following these guidelines was not mandatory.

Family Support Act of 1988 (FSA)
The Family Support Act, which went into effect in January 1994, made formula-based guidelines mandatory, and required that all new child support orders include an automatic wage attachment.

Child Support Recovery Act of 1992
This act made it a federal crime to fail to pay child support for a child who lives in another state.

Uniform Reciprocal Enforcement of Support Act (URESA)
A uniform law passed by all 50 states that makes it easier to collect child support from a parent who lives in a different state. Under this law, the receiving parent files in the home state, and a court in the second state tries the matter.

Revised Uniform Reciprocal Enforcement of Support Act (RURESA)
A revised version of URESA. Between URESA and RURESA, there is essentially a national procedure for establishing and enforcing child support across state lines.

Uniform Interstate Family Support Act (UIFSA)
A uniform law that is currently being enacted in all states. UIFSA strengthens enforcement across state lines by preventing the second state (of residence) from altering the amount of support ordered by the home state.

Enforcing a Child Support Order

Finally. You've found the noncustodial parent, you've established paternity (if you are the mother), and you've successfully secured a court order requiring child support be paid to you. Your problems are over. Not!

If you are the receiving parent, not only are your problems not over, but you may find that it's more difficult to *enforce* the support order than it was to get it in the first place.

That's because a paying parent who is self-employed, unemployed, works in another state, works for cash, or moves around a lot, may be able to throw up all sorts of roadblocks between you and your support check.

Fortunately, there are many resources available to help you enforce a court order. Some resources, such as the IV-D agency, won't cost you a thing. Others, such as work done by a private collection agency, will cost you a percentage of the funds collected.

No matter what, though, the ultimate responsibility for enforcing the court order is yours. If you are not receiving your child support and you don't do anything about it, no one else will, either.

Enforcement Methods

Here are some tools to help enforce a valid child support order:

Wage Assignments
A paying parent who is steadily employed or has some source of regular income will be subject to a *wage assignment*. A wage assignment, or *wage withholding*, is when the monthly child support is automatically withheld from the paying parent's paycheck by the employer. The employer then sends the money to the receiving parent, or forwards it to the court clerk or IV-D agency, who then sends it to the receiving parent. Depending on the state, a wage assignment will either be automatically ordered or must be requested.

A wage assignment works best when the paying parent is employed by someone else and doesn't change jobs frequently, or when the parent receives regular income from sources such as a pension, retirement fund, trust, social security, disability, or annuity payout. If a paying parent is self-employed, unemployed, or changes jobs frequently, a wage assignment may not be effective. In all states, the maximum amount that can be withheld is set by the Consumer Credit Act—55% to 65% of the person's income.

Diversion of Government Benefits
If the paying parent is unemployed, you can *attach his or her benefits*. This procedure allows you to deduct the child support payment from unemployment compensation, worker's compensation, or other benefits, and have it sent directly to you.

Delinquency Notices
If the paying parent is self-employed or works irregularly, you may decide to send *monthly billing statements*. That way, if the parent falls behind, you can send delinquency notices. With some self-employed parents, this may be all that is needed.

Posting Bonds or Depositing Funds
Another way to collect from self-employed parents is to require that the paying parent *post a bond* or *deposit funds* into a security account. This money is used to guarantee the child support payments. If the paying parent falls behind, the receiving parent can withdraw from the fund, and the paying parent has to replenish it. Or, the judge can order the entire bond forfeited if payments are missed. The amount that can be posted varies, but it may be up to two years of support.

Credit Checks
If the paying parent is earning income under the table, such as receiving payments in cash, or has placed assets in someone else's name, you can request the IV-D agency perform a credit check. To find hidden assets and income, look for:
- Commissions and bonuses.
- Excessive deductions.
- Bank accounts, stocks, or bonds.
- Elaborate real estate, cars, boats, or motorcycles.
- Extravagant jewelry, art, or coin collections.

Also, self-employed, under the table earners may list fraudulent loans to the business or maintain inordinately high retained earnings.

Wage Garnishments

If the paying parent owes back support, you have a whole host of methods to collect the money. One choice, a *wage garnishment,* works just like a wage assignment. That is, the amount is deducted from the paying parent's paycheck and is then sent to the receiving parent. For this method to work, the paying parent must have a steady source of income. Garnishments are available for any money-based legal judgment.

Property Liens

If the paying parent owes back support, you can also place a *lien* on personal property. A lien is a claim that gives you the right to be paid first when the property is sold. The lien is not an actual source of cash, but rather, it's an order preventing the owner from selling, transferring, or borrowing against the property until the debt is paid or the lien is removed. Liens can be made against homes, land, jewelry, coin and art collections, boats, motorcycles, and much more. However, in many states, you cannot place a lien on a primary residence.

If the paying parent has funds in a bank account, you can impound the money, or you can seek an order to withhold and deliver, which places the assets with the court. If the paying parent owns a company, the company can be placed in receivership, with the trustee ensuring that the child support is paid.

Tax Refund Diversion

Another popular approach to collecting back child support is to *divert the income tax refund* of the paying parent. The state tax agency or Internal Revenue Service can attach the parent's refund and send the money to the IV-D agency, who then forwards it to the receiving parent. If this happens, the paying parent will be notified and given a chance to contest it. If the paying parent has filed a joint return and some of the money belongs to the new spouse, the new mate can seek a portion of the money under the injured spouse provisions. If the claim is honored, and you have already received the money, you will have to give it back.

Receiving parents can also request the *IRS Full Collection Service* to satisfy back support. This invokes the full power of the IRS to seize property, attach assets, and close businesses. This tactic may be best when the paying parent is self-employed, lives in another state, and owes at least $5,000.

Civil Contempt

When a parent owes back support, you can request a *contempt of court* hearing. At the hearing, the parent will be ordered to explain why the support is past due. If he or she could not pay due to a loss of work or lack of money, that person cannot be found in contempt. But if the parent was able to pay but chose not to, the judge can declare him or her in contempt.

Civil contempt is serious, and a parent found guilty of contempt can be punished in many ways. The judge can order extra child support payments to make up the difference, require that a bond be posted, or even send the parent to jail until back payments are made. If the delinquent parent doesn't show up for the hearing at all, the judge can issue an *arrest warrant.*

Five Reasons Why Parents Don't Pay Child Support

1. Want to "get even" because visitation was frustrated or denied.

2. Believe the other parent should support the children.

3. Want the other parent to get a job.

4. Convinced the children don't need the money.

5. Don't like to be ordered to do anything.

Criminal Nonsupport

An even more serious tactic is to file *criminal nonsupport* charges against the paying parent. Criminal prosecution for nonsupport means the paying parent is accused of criminally neglecting the child by failing to pay support. Depending upon the state, it may be a misdemeanor or a felony.

When a district attorney files charges of criminal nonsupport, a warrant is issued, who is arrested and arraigned. The parent has the right to a jury trial, where the evidence can be refuted. If the parent is found guilty or pleads guilty or no contest, he or she may be offered probation, or may be put in jail for a year or more.

Criminal nonsupport works well against debtor parents who are self-employed and who flee across state lines. Many states will extradite a parent if the laws of the state make non-payment of court-ordered child support a felony.

 Civil vs. criminal. If the contempt is civil, the person is being punished for not doing what the court wants. Generally, he will have a chance to comply with the court orders to avoid punishment. But if the contempt is criminal, the perosn is being punished to prevent a repetition of certain behavior, and he may be jailed on the spot.

License Blocking
Other methods to enforce a child support order include *license blocking,* which revokes or prevents the renewal of the driver's license, business license, or professional license of the paying parent. This can method succeed when the paying parent has a profession that requires a license, such as a doctor, dentist, attorney, hairdresser, and so on.

Report to Credit Bureaus
Child support delinquencies are now routinely reported to *credit bureaus,* which reduces the paying parent's credit rating and ability to borrow. By law, the IV-D agency must report any delinquency over $1,000 to the credit bureaus, but it can report lesser amounts, as well.

Report to "Most Wanted" Lists
In some states, a receiving parent who reports the delinquency to the IV-D agency can anticipate a publicly announced "most wanted" list mentioning the delinquent parent. These lists are an attempt to shame delinquent parents into paying up.

Private Collection Agency
And finally, if all else fails, a receiving parent can hire a *private collection agency.* These private services use the same procedures as any other collection service, such as dunning letters, phone calls, etc. Often, they work for a percentage of the amount collected, which may range from 20% to 40%.

A cold day in hell. If you do not receive your child support, you will be standing in a long line of persons waiting for that check. In one year, the Census Bureau estimated that 10 million parents owed approximately $39 billion in child support. The *Los Angeles Times* reported that in Los Angeles County alone, the Bureau of Family Operations opens approximately 9,000 cases per month and had a current caseload exceeding 615,000.

Collecting Across State Lines

Paying parents who move across state lines create special problems. That's because the responsibility for enforcing a child support order rests with the state, and each state has its own court system, rules, and laws.

However, federal and uniform laws have been passed that require states to cooperate when it comes to child support enforcement. Here are three methods for interstate enforcement:

Interstate Wage Withholding
If you know where the paying parent works, *interstate wage withholding* may be the simplest solution. The advantage of this method is that it bypasses involved court hearings and prevents a court where the paying parent lives from reducing the payments. To start this action, you normally ask your local IV-D agency, and they forward three certified copies of the court order, the withholding order, and information about the paying parent to the IV-D office where the paying parent lives. As with other wage assignments, this method works best when the paying parent receives a regular paycheck.

URESA and RURESA
The *Uniform Reciprocal Enforcement of Support Act (URESA)* and its revised version, the *Revised Uniform Reciprocal Enforcement of Support Act (RURESA)*, are two tools to enforce a child support order between states. Because similar versions of these laws have been enacted in all 50 states, there is a consistent approach to enforcement across the nation.

The laws do not decide support, rather, they set up procedures for different courts in different states to coordinate with each other. The laws make it easier for a receiving parent in one state to collect support from a paying parent in a different state.

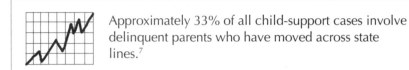

Approximately 33% of all child-support cases involve delinquent parents who have moved across state lines.[7]

Under these laws, you can *register your order,* which means you have a court order and want a court in a different state to enforce it, or you can initiate a *two-state proceeding.* In a two-state proceeding, you file your suit where you live, and if the court finds probable cause, they transfer it to a court where the paying parent lives. Once the case has been transferred, it is litigated according to the rules of the second state.

The two-state proceeding lets a parent litigate in a different state without having to go there. It allows for support orders to be modified across state lines, and in some cases, to be created.

Foreign Certificate
Finally, a *foreign certificate* can be registered in the court that has jurisdiction. This method is faster than URESA, but it opens the door for custody and visitation hearings. To register a foreign certificate, you send three certified copies of the order, plus all other documentation, to the court where the paying parent lives. Once you notify the court, they begin enforcement proceedings.

Hasta la vista, baaaby. If the paying parent has left the country, you may still be able to collect your support. "Many state CSE agencies have agreements with foreign countries to recognize child support judgments made in either country. You will need the same kind of information as is required for enforcement in this country and as much specific address information as you can find. If the non-custodial parent works for an American company, wage withholding might work even if the country he lives in does not have any agreement to enforce an American State's order." *Handbook on Child Support Enforcement,* OCSE

How to Improve Your Chances of Collecting Child Support

When it comes to child support, there are other ways to increase your odds of getting that check. Here are some suggestions.

Have a Joint Custody Agreement
Simply stated, the single best tactic to improving your chances of collecting child support is to have a joint custody agreement. Here's why:

Fathers Who Pay Child Support

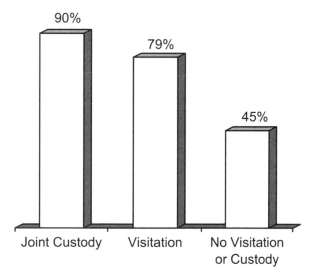

Notice that fathers with joint custody were much more likely to pay than other fathers—especially fathers with no visitation at all.

It's not hard to imagine why. When parents have joint custody, each maintains a separate relationship with the children, and both parents are encouraged to act responsibly. But if custody is restricted and visitation reduced, the parent who is cut off— the father or mother—is *discouraged* from accepting responsibility.

However, if joint custody won't work for you, consider some other strategies to improve your chances of collecting child support.

"Several [studies] indicate that there is a strong relationship between compliance and contact between fathers and their children. I believe strongly that if fathers stay involved emotionally with their children, they will also be economically responsible."
Constance Ahrons, *The Good Divorce*

Obtain and Keep Current a Wage Assignment Order

When the paying parent earns regular wages, a wage assignment makes the support payments as painless as possible. Virtually every other alternative only increases the potential for noncompliance. If the paying parent changes jobs, you must send the order to the new employer.

Be Your Own Detective

You know the other parent best, so it's your job to keep track of the details, such as where he or she works, vehicles that are purchased or sold, an increase in wages, any changes in residence, etc.

Work within the System

The IV-D offices are staffed by civil servants, and when you work with them, you must work with their rules and regulations. No matter how frustrated you get, yelling at a caseworker won't help. Also, writing letters to your Congressman or Senator will only get you a standard reply letter. Try focusing your complaint on key state officials, such as the governor, director of the IV-D agency, and members of the state legislature. Send a brief, factual letter to these people, and you may get help.

The big picture. "Remember what the big picture is to you. You want to create a situation in which the path of least resistance for the IV-D program to take is to treat you fairly and decently. Do not get sidetracked into a tirade about how horrible the IV-D program is in general. If you want to form a crusade to reform the IV-D program, do it. But do it after it no longer matters whether key persons think you are reasonable or not. People who were patient, reasonable and fair and who got the sympathetic attention of key people in state government got justice." Bruce Walker, *The Single Parent*

Collecting Child Support

U.S. Department of Health and Human Services
Office of Child Support Enforcement
370 L'Enfant Promenade, S.W.
Washington, DC 20447
(202) 401-9373
www.acf.dhhs.gov/programs/cse
Every state has a *Child Support Enforcement Agency.* Also called a
IV-D office, these agencies help parents establish and enforce child
support orders. The federal office issues policies while the state
offices actually run the program. The state offices can:

- *Find an Absent Parent.* The agency has many resources to find
  absent parents, such as the *Parent Locator Service* that looks
  through IRS records, DMV records, etc.

- *Establish Paternity.* The agency can help a mother legally
  identify the father by establishing paternity. If the father doesn't
  acknowledge paternity, the office can arrange for blood tests.

- *Establish the Support Obligation.* If a parent needs to secure or
  modify a child support order, the agency attorneys can represent
  the parent in court.

- *Enforce a Child Support Order.* Once a valid order is in place,
  the caseworkers can help parents enforce the order by arranging
  for wage attachments, diversion of income tax refunds, posting
  of cash bonds, etc.

Association for Children for Enforcement of Support (ACES)
2260 Upton Avenue
Toledo, OH 43606
(800) 537-7072
An organization that provides information about child support
enforcement and how to collect current and back support. ACES has
chapters in 49 states serving 25,000 members. Publishes *How to
Collect Child Support.*

Child Support Enforcement
www.supportkids.com
Dedicated to collecting past-due child support for custodial parents.

1 U.S. Bureau of the Census, Current Population Reports

2 Office of Child Support Enforcement, U.S. Department of Health and Human Services, June 1993

3 U.S. Bureau of the Census, Current Population Reports (full citation is in Chapter 21)

4 *Time Magazine,* June 19, 1995

5 *Los Angeles Times,* August 6, 1996

6 U.S. Department of Health and Human Services, Administration for Children and Families

7 *Los Angeles Times,* May 14, 1995

Child
Support

Chapter 21
The Laws of Child Support

When one parent has primary responsibility for the children, the other parent is expected to pay *child support.* Child support is the money one parent pays the other to help care for the children.

Usually, the noncustodial parent pays the custodial parent. That's because—while both parents are responsible for their children—the custodial parent is meeting the obligation through the act of custody. The noncustodial parent meets the obligation by paying child support.

When setting the amount of child support to pay, the two parents can agree on their own. If they don't agree, the amount will be set by a judge, who will specify it in a court order.

Child support orders can arise out of a number of circumstances, including: divorce, legal separation, annulment action, and a paternity action.

This chapter discusses how child support orders are created.

Types of Child Support

There are several types of child support:

Temporary Child Support
When parents first separate or file for divorce, the judge may order that one parent pay *temporary* child support. The amount set will be based on some preliminary information available to the judge, and may be raised or lowered when the divorce is complete.

Permanent Child Support
When a final court order is issued that includes child support, the support is called *permanent child support.* This means that the obligation remains until some specific event occurs. Calling this permanent may be misleading, because any orders regarding the child—including support—can be changed if circumstances change.

Family Support
Some states allow parents to combine alimony and child support into one payment called family support. Unlike child support, family support is taxable income to the receiving parent and a deduction for the paying parent. When the paying parent earns much more than the receiving parent, paying family support can save money in taxes. Family support, however, cannot be enforced with the same tools as child support.

Child Support Guidelines

When deciding how much support should be paid, judges must use *child support guidelines.* These are minimum amounts that are either listed in tables or are calculated by applying a mathematical formula.

The guidelines are not set by judges, but rather, by lawmakers in each state who create the family laws. Lawmakers use standard tables or formulas in order to be fair and impose the same child support award on parents in similar economic circumstances.

After determining the guideline amount, the judge can then add (or sometimes subtract) money based on several other factors. These other factors account for specific and unusual circumstances, such as special needs of the child, special hardships of the parents, and so on.

The guideline amounts are also called the *presumed correct* figure. This is the amount presumed to be the correct amount of support, and a judge can award less only if there are special circumstances. If less is awarded, the reasons must be stated on the record.

> Child support has no effect on your federal income tax return. The payments are not taxable income to the receiving parent and are not a deduction for the paying parent.

While child support guidelines are the same within a state, they can vary considerably from state to state. That's because the lawmakers in each state are free to choose what's important when setting child support.

Some states think that only the net income of the two parents is important, while other states consider the additional income of a new mate if either parent has remarried or has begun living with someone. And still other states consider how much time each parent spends with the child.

However child support is decided, the goal remains the same.

The goal of child support is to provide for the economic needs of the child without overburdening the paying parent, who may be unable to make the payments if the amount is too high.

How the Guideline Amounts Are Determined

The guideline amounts are not chosen arbitrarily, but are designed to meet the costs of raising children at various standards of living. Generally, the guideline amounts are based on:

Needs of the Child
Child support payments are an attempt to meet the minimum economic *needs of the child.* The guideline amounts only cover the minimum expenses of raising a child—basically food, clothing, and shelter. Because children almost always need much more, all states allow additional expenses to be considered when setting child support.

Parent's Ability to Pay

Each parent must support the children according to his or her *ability to pay*. Ability to pay is usually what a parent earns—gross income less some allowable expenses.

Allowable expenses vary from state to state. Some states only allow mandatory expenses to be subtracted from gross income. Mandatory expenses include: income taxes, FICA, SDI, health insurance, and required union dues. Expenses that are not mandatory are excluded because—if they were included—a parent might artificially reduce income by taking numerous deductions, and then pay less support.

A number of states also allow a deduction for support paid for children from another relationship. This allows all children to be treated equally, so that each has an equal claim to the parent's earnings. Also, many states allow a child care expense deduction for a custodial parent who pays for child care expenses in order to work or attend school.

 Ability to pay is different from ability to earn. Ability to pay is based on your net income. Ability to earn is what a judge thinks you are capable of earning, whether you're actually earning it or not. This can happen when a parent works less than 40 hours, or when he or she quits work and refuses to find another job. If this economic misconduct occurs, a judge may set support based on a parent's potential to earn rather than actual earnings.

Standard of Living

When parents divorce, they must create two homes where there was one. Two homes cost more, which usually means a decrease in the standard of living. A goal of child support is to *maintain and balance the standard of living of the child.*

Maintain the standard of living. Had the parents stayed together, the child would have enjoyed a certain standard of living. Child support guidelines try to maintain the child's former standard of living, while at the same time realistically reflecting the increased costs of maintaining two households.

Balance the standard of living. When one parent earns much more than the other, the child may go back and forth between two homes of vastly different economic circumstances. *Child support can be used to transfer wealth from the higher-earning parent to the lower-earning parent.*

When the standard of living of the lower-earning parent is improved, the child is then sharing in the standard of living of both parents. This is an explicit goal of child support. And it's also, by the way, the reason why a parent can spend child support on things not directly related to the child—such as buying new furniture. By definition, the custodial parent and the child have to share the same standard of living. Thus, benefits to the parent cannot easily be separated from benefits to the child.

When a Judge Can Depart from the Guideline

In divorce, parents give up certain rights over their children and the judge takes over. This *judicial authority* allows the judge to:

Depart from the Presumed Correct Figure
Judges have the last word on child support, so a judge can always depart from the guideline. To depart from the presumed correct amount, a judge must find that it is unjust or inappropriate due to *special circumstances* in the particular case.

There are specific factors a judge can consider, and—as stated earlier—if a judge awards less than the guideline amount, he or she must state the facts that justify the departure.

 In *California Divorce Handbook,* Judge Stewart estimates that the guideline amount is awarded over 90% of the time.

Overrule the Agreement between the Parents
Because the court has final authority over all child support decisions, the judge can *overrule* any agreement between the parents. This safeguard prevents a parent from bargaining away the right to receive child support. If an agreement does not provide for the support of the children, the judge may approve it anyway if the custodial parent has sufficient resources to support the children.

While judges have the authority to reject an agreement between the parents, that doesn't mean they will. Judges recognize that an agreement is the result of bargaining, and may resist disturbing the arrangement unless there is clear evidence that the best interests of the child are not being served.

Paying Child Support

After the amount to be paid is set, the next question is how the support will be paid. This is not an easy question to answer, since many parents fail to pay some or all of their child support.

 In one year, of all parents who were awarded child support, 51% received full payment, 24% received partial payment, and 25% received no payment at all.[1]

If a parent owes back child support, there are many ways to collect the money. The following methods, however, are for routine, on-time payment:

Sending a Check to the Receiving Parent
In some states, the paying parent can send a monthly check to the receiving parent. This method is best suited when the paying parent has been paying support, and has a record of full, on-time payments. Because federal law requires all new or modified support orders to include a wage assignment, parents who choose this method will have to ask the court to *stay the service* of the wage assignment.

Wage Assignment
Also called *wage withholding,* a wage assignment is when the child support is automatically deducted from the paycheck of the paying parent and sent to the receiving parent. Wage assignments are appropriate when the paying parent earns a salary or has another regular source of income, such as payments from a pension, annuity, retirement fund, or disability. Basically, for a wage assignment to work, there must be a payment

administrator on whom to serve the wage assignment. Wage assignments do not work when the paying parent is self-employed or does not receive regular income.

Wage assignments are automatically initiated on new or modified orders. Typically, the court sends a copy of the orders to the paying parent's employer, who will wait ten days before deducting any money from the parent's paycheck, giving the parent time to contest the assignment.

Since wage assignments are automatic, if the parents don't want one, they must ask the judge to *stay the service* on the employer. This is a subjective decision, and some judges will be more agreeable than others.

A *wage assignment* stays in effect until the paying parent's employment ends, the support obligation ends or is modified, or the parent succeeds with a motion to quash the assignment.

Paying an Officer of the Court

A third way to pay child support is for the paying parent to send a check to an officer of the court—usually the *court clerk* or a *court trustee*. When the officer receives the check, a payment is sent to the receiving parent. Some states allow payments to be sent to the child enforcement agency or some other state agency. An advantage to this method is that if the paying parent misses some payments, collection procedures begin automatically.

This method is the best approach when the paying parent is self-employed or doesn't receive regular income.

Other Payment Elements

In addition to deciding how support will be paid, parents may add the following elements to an agreement:

Insurance

If something happens to the paying parent, the children's support will be at risk. To secure future payments, support orders may require an irrevocable *life insurance* policy on the paying parent, with the children as the beneficiaries.

Security Deposit

Another way to secure support is to require the paying parent to deposit money into a *security account.* When the paying parent misses some payments, the receiving parent withdraws money from the fund, and the paying parent has to replenish it. The security deposit can be equal to one to two years of support.

Late Payment Fees

Late fees are useful when the support is paid directly—not through wage withholding. Late fees are justified if the support is being used to pay creditors who themselves charge late fees for missed payments.

 When child support orders are being drafted, try to synchronize the receipt of the money with the bills you'll be paying. If you can't influence when the checks arrive, try asking your creditors to change the dates when they get paid.

COLA Clause

COLA, or *Cost of Living Adjustment,* is a clause used to automatically increase child support when the cost of living increases. Generally, this increase is based on some common index, such as the Consumer Price Index. The advantage of a COLA clause is that—as inflation reduces the buying power of child support—the receiving parent gets an increase without returning to court.

When Child Support Ends

Generally, child support ends when your child reaches the *age of majority* or when certain circumstances occur. Child support may end earlier if:

- You gain custody.
- A court orders your child support to end.
- A court declares your child emancipated.
- Your child gets married.
- Your child joins the military.
- Your child moves out of the house to live independently.
- Your child is adopted.
- Your child dies.

However, child support can end later when certain things happen. Child support may end later if:

- Your state requires you to support your child until he or she completes high school or turns 19, whichever comes first.
- Your state requires you to support your child until he or she completes college or turns 21 or 23, whichever comes first.
- Your child is disabled.
- You agree to continue paying support (for whatever reason).

Five Ways to Prevent Child Support Payment Problems

1. Have payments sent to an officer of the court.

2. Include a late-payment fee.

3. Require a security deposit.

4. Include a Cost of Living Adjustment (COLA) clause.

5. Keep wage assignments up to date.

Also, child support may earlier if your child becomes *emancipated*. Emancipation is when a child demonstrates freedom from parental control. For a child to become emancipated, the court must order it. This usually happens because a significant act occurred, such as the child getting married, joining the military, or moving away from the custodial parent and becoming self-supporting. Parents cannot simply declare their children emancipated, but must bring a special proceeding to have the child declared emancipated.

Child support may end later if you live in a state that requires you to assist your child through further schooling. For example, in Massachusetts, divorced parents may be required to continue child support until the child turns 23 so long as the child remains in college. Also, a court may require a parent to continue paying support if the child is physically or mentally disabled.

1 U.S. Bureau of the Census, Current Population Reports, series P-60, no. 173, *"Child Support and Alimony: 1989"*

Chapter 22
The Reality of Child Support

While the goals of child support are to provide support for the child, the reality of child support is quite different.

As you navigate the rocky road of child support, be prepared for what really happens after child support orders are issued.

First of all, child support is almost always awarded to mothers. There are many reasons for this, and it's changing, but for now, the mother is the parent most likely to get child support.

Second, even though child support is usually awarded to the mother, that doesn't mean that all mothers actually get their check. Only about half of all mothers get a full payment on time, and about one quarter receive nothing at all.

Third, despite efforts to increase awards, the average amount received is less than half of what it costs to actually raise a child.

And finally, partially because support is so little, single mothers have total income dramatically less than any other family group.

This section addresses the reality of child support: who gets paid, how much they get, and how much more they need.

Who Gets Child Support Awards

Child support is almost always awarded to the mother because of *custody* and *income.*

Custody
When custody is decided, the mother is much more likely to be the custodial parent. This outcome is vital in determining support because the guidelines used to set the *presumed correct* amount assume that support will be awarded to the custodial parent.

Here are the results of one study of divorced families:

Custody Arrangements[1]

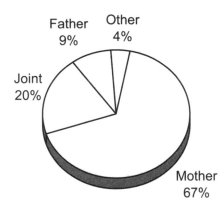

In their study, Maccoby and Mnookin found that mothers had sole or primary custody about 67% of the time, fathers had sole or primary custody about 9% of the time, the parents shared custody about 20% of the time, and the rest had a different arrangement.

Income
Generally, the higher-earning parent pays child support to the lower-earning parent. This usually means fathers pay mothers, because—as Maccoby and Mnookin found—fathers typically earn almost twice as much as mothers. Disparity in income is so important in deciding who pays and how much that it can lead to a lower-earning noncustodial parent paying child support to a higher-earning custodial parent, or a custodial parent paying child support to a noncustodial parent!

By the way, even though the mother is the parent most likely to get a support award, that doesn't mean that all mothers get one. According to the Census Bureau, in one year, only 81% of the mothers who wanted a child support award actually received one.[2]

But even when mothers receive a child support award, it still doesn't guarantee they will get paid...

What Percentage They Collect

As many parents have already found out: getting an award is one thing, getting a check is something else.

As the Census Bureau has reported, only about half of all mothers who are owed child support received the full amount. The other mothers received less than they were owed—or nothing at all. Here's an illustration:

Child Support Collections[3]

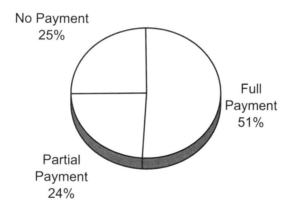

No Payment 25%

Full Payment 51%

Partial Payment 24%

This is the statistic, by the way, that generates all the headlines about *deadbeat dads.* As the Census Bureau reported, in one year, mothers received only 68.7% of the money they were due.

Many people have offered reasons for this, and many have offered suggestions about how to improve it. What seems likely is that the problem won't be going away for a long time.[4] *If you are a receiving parent, be aware that your odds of receiving your full child support check are only about 50-50.*

What Amount They Collect

Even when mothers receive their child support check, the amount is not very much. Again, according to the Census Bureau, the average amount received by all mothers was $2,995.

That's not very much, but what is more important is that the average figure disguises a critical distinction:

If the mother never married the children's father, she received much less support than if she divorced the children's father.

Annual Child Support Receipts[5]

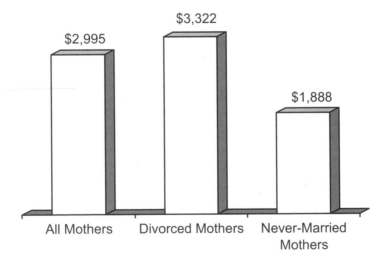

This is particularly bad news for never-married mothers. According to Census Bureau data, never-married mothers received an average of $1,434 *less* per year than divorced mothers.

Now, take a look at what it costs to raise a child...

This subject generates endless books and articles. Some recent books: *Fatherless America,* by David Blankenhorn, *Growing Up With a Single Parent,* by Sara McLanahan and Gary Sandefur, and *Marriage, Divorce, Remarriage,* by Andrew J. Cherlin.

What It Costs to Raise a Child

If you've been dragged into a Toys R Us recently, you know that it costs a ton to raise a child. But the government has actually calculated an average per year. Here's the chart:

Annual Costs to Raise a Child[6]

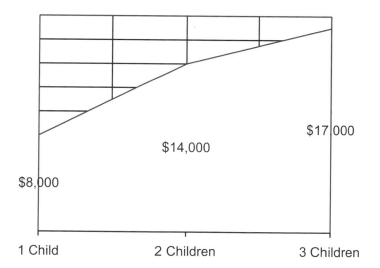

$17,000

$14,000

$8,000

1 Child   2 Children   3 Children

Interestingly enough, these estimates are probably *low,* as they only represent the direct costs of raising a child. They exclude such hidden costs as taking time off work to care for the children when they're sick, or working at a lower-paying job so that you can be with them more, and so on. And they completely omit the single biggest expense that most parents face—college!

Now, combine the cost of raising the children with the average child support received, and you get...

The Child Support Gap

The *child support gap* is the difference between what the children cost, and what the parent receives.

The Child Support Gap

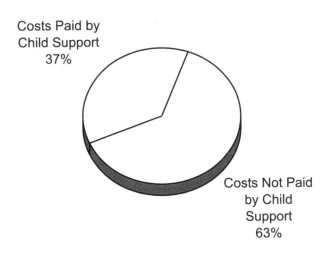

Costs Paid by
Child Support
37%

Costs Not Paid
by Child
Support
63%

As you can see, for the average parent, child support just doesn't make it. In fact, typical mothers receive only 37% of what it costs to raise one child, and the percentage goes way, way down when there are more children.

By the way, it should be noted that this figure is highly simplified, since custodial parents can take advantage of the head of household filing status, the dependency exemptions for the children, and other child care tax credits to help reduce the child support gap. Still, don't be unduly surprised to discover that the child costs much more than the child support pays.

For many receiving parents, this means that they will simply live on less; much less—as it turns out— than any other family group.

Single Parent Family Income

Single mothers earn dramatically less than any other family group.

Specifically, the Census Bureau calculated that all other family groups had greater total income than single mothers. In some cases—much more. For example, married couples brought in $28,168 a year more than single mothers, and even single women managed to collect $7,494 a year more than single mothers!

Annual Family Income[7]

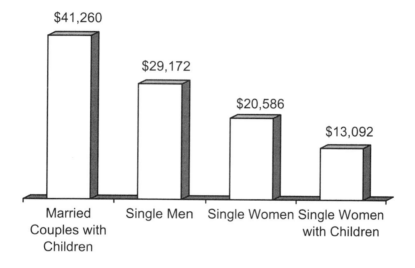

Why is this? Again, there's no shortage of people suggesting reasons. In one classic book, Lenore J. Weitzman in *The Divorce Revolution* argued that "...on the average, divorced women and the minor children in their households experience a 73 percent decline in their standard of living in the first year after divorce. Their former husbands, in contrast, experience a 42 percent rise in their standard of living."

Years later, Andrew J. Cherlin in *Marriage, Divorce, Remarriage,* updated those numbers with this response "...separated and divorced women suffered an average drop of about 30 percent in their standard of living in the year following a marital break-up. Men, in contrast, experienced a rise of 10 to 15 percent..."

Whichever sets of numbers you believe, it seems likely that—after divorce—the living standard of women and children declines.

---

1 *Dividing the Child,* Eleanor Maccoby and Robert Mnookin.
2 U.S. Bureau of the Census, Current Population Reports, series P-60, no. 173, *"Child Support and Alimony: 1989"* The primary reason given why the mothers couldn't get an award was that they were unable to locate the father.
3 Ibid.
4 One theory that seeks to explain the lack of compliance considers the status of fathers. By including large numbers of incarcerated men who owe child support, as well as the homeless and indigent, it's possible to conclude that most able-bodied fathers are already paying support. For mothers who don't receive support, it may be because the father is in jail, destitute, or dead.
5 U.S. Bureau of the Census, Current Population Reports, series P-60, no. 173, *"Child Support and Alimony: 1989"*
6 U.S. Department of Agriculture, Family Economics Research Group, *"Expenditures on a Child by Husband-Wife Families: 1990"* You should know that these estimates were for a two-parent middle-income family, but it seems reasonable to use them for all families—two-parent or not.
7 U.S. Bureau of the Census, Consumer Income, series P-60, no. 174, *"Money Income of Households, Families, and Persons in the United States: 1990"*

Chapter 23
Calculating Child Support

When it comes time to calculate child support, judges have some pretty difficult questions to answer.

How much does it cost to raise a child? How much of the noncustodial parent's income should be made available to the children? How should visitation time be accounted for? What about income from a new mate, or additional expenses from subsequent children?

There are no easy answers to these questions, yet family courts have to resolve them every day. That's why—in response to federal laws—all states now calculate child support based on standard guidelines derived from a mathematical table or formula.

This chapter describes how child support is determined.

What Financial Information the Court Needs

When parents go to court for child support, they must first supply their financial information. Generally, this means completing forms that ask for income and expense information. Along with the forms, the parents may have to attach copies of various pay stubs, tax returns, financial statements, loan applications, and so on.

These *financial statements* allow the judge to construct an accurate picture of each parent's finances.

Income

Because child support is based on the parent's *ability to pay,* the court must know the income of each parent. In some states, this means gross income, and in others, it means adjusted gross or net income. Whether it is *before-* or *after-tax* income is an important element in the calculations.

Gross Income	Every dollar you received…
- Expenses	Minus some expenses allowed by the court…
Adjusted Gross	Is your AGI
– Deductions	Minus more deductions allowed by the court…
Net Income	Is your net income

Gross Income

Gross income is everything you receive. This includes wages, interest, capital gains, and so on. Gross income usually does not include court-ordered support to children from a previous relationship, and certain public assistance payments. If your state uses gross income as the base for calculating child support, no deductions are allowed prior to calculation of the guideline amount. Only a few states base support on gross income.

Adjusted Gross Income

If the income base in your child support formula calls for *adjusted gross,* you can usually deduct certain expenses. Depending on your state, these expenses may include court-ordered support for children from a previous relationship, as well as health insurance for current children. Many states base support on adjusted gross.

Net Income

If your state calculates support on *net income,* you can deduct certain other expenses from your gross income. Though it varies by state, deductions are usually the mandatory payments you must make, such as:

- Federal and state withholding.
- FICA.
- SDI.
- Mandatory union dues.
- Mandatory retirement contributions.

In addition, a number of states allow you to deduct support to children from a previous relationship.

 *Disposable income* to a judge may be different from *net income* to a banker. That's because a judge is not interested in whether you can repay a car loan, he wants to know your ability to pay child support.

Imputing Income

If there is reason to believe that a parent is intentionally unemployed or underemployed, the judge can calculate the parent's *potential income* and set child support accordingly. When a judge calculates theoretical income, it is called *imputing income.*

The need to impute income can derive from a number of circumstances, such as when a parent with a history of steady employment suddenly loses a job and does not return to work, insisting that he or she cannot find another job. Or a parent with a history of steadily increasing wages may suddenly go to work for a different company at lower pay, insisting that he or she cannot return to their former level of earnings.

Whatever the reason, whether it is deemed *willful suppression of income,* or *failure to earn to capacity,* all states allow the judge to consider a parent's capacity to earn—rather than actual earnings—when setting child support.

Of course, some parents are quick to suggest that their former spouse is earning below ability. However, others point out that a parent is under no legal obligation to maximize economic wealth. Indeed, they suggest that rising and falling wages reflect the natural career movement that all adults experience—whether married or not.

If imputed income becomes an issue in the child support calculations, the judge will have to weigh many more factors, including the number of hours the parent works, prevailing wages in the area, recent work history, and even the parent's personal assets—such as a car, real estate, etc.

 Judges know how much you're supposed to have withheld from your paycheck. If you jack up your withholding to make it look like you earn less, the judge will simply recompute your proper withholding.

Expenses

In addition to the parent's ability to pay, the judge needs to know the expenses involved in raising the child. These include direct expenditures on the child, and in some cases, may include expenses of the parent. Expenses fall into two groups:

Children's Expenses
In setting child support, the judge wants to provide for the child. To do that, he must know all the child-related expenses. Here's a checklist of typical expenses:
- *Insurance:* health and dental premiums.
- *Medical:* uninsured health care costs.
- *Child Care:* day care, after school care, baby-sitting.
- *Education:* tuition, room and board, books, tutors, activity fees.
- *Extracurricular:* sports lessons, uniforms and equipment, hobbies.

Parent's Expenses

As appealing as it may seem, there is little to gain by going into court and telling the judge about your bills. In truth, many of the parent's expenses are not relevant in setting child support. For your expenses to be considered, they must establish your standard of living or support a *finding of special circumstances.* Some expenses that may be relevant include:

- *Housing:* rent or mortgage, utilities, telephone, repairs.
- *Food:* groceries, meals outside the home.
- *Transportation:* gas, repairs, parking, public transportation.
- *Insurance:* life, health, dental, disability, homeowner's, auto.
- *Medical:* uninsured health care costs.
- *Debts:* credit cards, charge accounts, auto loans, personal loans.
- *Other:* clothing, entertainment, gifts, memberships.

Determining the Guideline Amount

Once the financial information is in front of the judge, he or she will determine the guideline amount. Since there is no *national* child support formula, it is done differently in each state.

Some states use formulas, others use tables. Some consider the earnings of both parents, others include only the income of the noncustodial parent. Some use net income, others use gross or adjusted gross.

The only thing that all states have in common is that they provide a mathematical formula for calculating base child support, and they all allow for adjustments due to special circumstances.

Here are the basic models of child support guidelines:

Income Shares Model

The most common model for calculating child support is called the *income shares model.* In this method, the income of the two parents is first added together—giving a total family income. Then, the judge either uses a table or a formula to determine how much of this money should be spent on the child. Finally, the support is calculated by splitting the amount owed in proportion to each parent's income. Typically, the noncustodial parent pays his or her share to the custodial parent.

This model is based on the belief that children should not suffer when their parents break up. It requires both parents to share in the cost of supporting their children. It also incorporates a sliding scale that decreases the percentage of family income spent as total income increases. This prevents children of high-earning parents from receiving much more money than they could possibly use.

Example of Income Shares

Here's an example of a child support calculation based on the income shares model.

Suppose a mother has primary custody of her two small children. She earns $1,000 per month, and the father earns $3,000 per month. To keep it simple, all these amounts are net amounts, and there are no other factors (such as the percentage of visitation time). In a typical state, here's what might happen:

First, the judge adds the parents' incomes together:

	Mom's Earnings	$1,000
	Dad's Earnings	+$3,000
	Combined Earnings	$4,000

Then, the judge consults a large chart or inputs the numbers into a computer program. This helps determine the total amount of support:

	1 child	2 children	3 children	4 children	5+ children
$2,000	427	662	831	936	1,020
$2,500	526	816	1,023	1,152	1,255
$3,000	561	872	1,092	1,232	1,340
$3,500	575	894	1,119	1,264	1,375
$4,000	609	946	1,185	1,336	1,455
$4,500	677	1,050	1,314	1,484	1,615
$5,000	738	1,148	1,437	1,616	1,765

In the example, the total child support is $946 per month.

Next, the judge calculates each parent's share of the total family income:

Then, the total support is split between the two parents in proportion to their income:

Finally, the judge orders the father to pay 75%—or $709.50 per month— to the mother. Because the mother has custody, she's assumed to be already paying her share.

This is the method used in a majority of the states, but it is by no means universal. There are several other child support models in use.

Percent of Income Model

A second method for calculating child support is the *percent of income model.* In this model, child support is based on either a fixed or varying percent of the noncustodial parent's income. This method assumes that the custodial parent is already providing for the child by virtue of having custody, and that the noncustodial parent should contribute financially.

The *fixed percent of income model* calculates child support as a fixed percentage of the noncustodial parent's income. Thus, a noncustodial parent with two children will pay a standard percent—say 25%—of his or her income in child support, no matter how much is earned. Some states use the parent's gross income in the calculations, others use adjusted gross or net income.

The *varying percent of income model* works the same way as the fixed percent, except the percent changes based on the income of the noncustodial parent.

Thus, a noncustodial parent who earns more will pay more in child support, but the overall percent of income diverted to child support will decrease.

Example of Percent of Income

Here's an example of a child support calculation based on the fixed percent of income model.

In this model, the only two factors that are considered are the income of the noncustodial parent and the number of children. In this case, there are two children, the mother is the custodial parent, and the father earns $3,000 per month. Here's how the child support might be computed:

First, the judge looks up the percent from the child support guidelines:

Children	% of net income
1	20%
2	(25%)
3	32%
4	40%
5	45%
6+	50%

Then, the judge applies that percent to the noncustodial parent's income:

Dad's income	$3,000
% of income	x 25%
Child support	($750)

Finally, the judge orders the father to pay $750 per month in child support.

By excluding the income of the custodial parent, this model makes it easier to calculate support, but it also ignores whether the custodial parent is contributing anything towards the care of his or her children.

Melson Delaware Model

A final child support model is called the *Melson Delaware formula.* This model considers many more factors than the other models, and thus is more complicated.

Basically, the model computes the basic amount of support needed by the child. Then, the support obligation is divided between the parents based on ability to pay. Next, a standard of living allowance is applied, and finally, child-care expenses are added to the amount to be paid.

While this model is much more comprehensive than the others, it is also more difficult to implement. Only a few states currently use this model.

> To get a copy of your state's child support guidelines, you have several choices. The easiest is to make an appointment with a family lawyer. Generally, they offer an initial consultation for $50 or less. Other choices include calling the district attorney, the local child support enforcement office, or the court clerk. They should all have the same information.

Problems with Child Support Models

No generalized table or formula can possibly account for the differences in child-rearing between households, which leads many skeptics to criticize the shortcomings of the current models.

For example, many guidelines are based on a set of assumptions. While these assumptions reflect the majority of parents that come before the court, they don't reflect everyone, and in some cases, the assumptions will be wrong and the guidelines will recommend an inappropriate amount.

Here are a few typical assumptions built into some guidelines:

"Traditional" Custody
Often, the custodial parent has physical custody of the children about 80% of the time, and the noncustodial parent has visitation 20% of the time. This 80-20 split means that the custodial parent is shouldering most of the costs of raising the children. However, when parents devise a different schedule, say a 50-50 or 60-40 division of the children's time, some guidelines don't account for the more equitable sharing of the child rearing costs.

Income Differential
Because many custodial parents earn less than many noncustodial parents, some guidelines assume that the custodial parent earns about 25% less. This assumption is embedded in the amounts the guidelines recommend as presumed correct. When it's not true—such as when the custodial parent earns more than the noncustodial parent—the guidelines will be inappropriate.

High and Low Income
Very low or very high wage earners have something in common—they make it difficult to set child support by a mathematical formula. That's because either they cannot pay for the most basic costs of raising children, or they can pay so much the children can't possibly use all the money.

*"He never forgets our anniversary now
that I'm paying him child support."*

Standard of Living

Many guidelines seek to maintain the child's standard of living at pre-divorce levels. Unfortunately, this ignores the reality of divorce in that two households must be supported where there formerly was one. This results in less income overall, forcing the families to lower their standard of living. Unfortunately, some guidelines do not consider that, forcing the parents to maintain previously higher levels.

Noncustodial Costs

And finally, because the guidelines focus on the parent's income—and not the actual costs of raising the children—expenses incurred by the noncustodial parent are often overlooked. This may include a bed, clothes, toys, books, games, etc., that children require when they "visit."

 Dependency exemption. Generally, only the custodial parent can claim exemptions for the children. However, that parent can transfer the exemptions to the noncustodial parent so that both parents can share the tax savings.

Departing from the Guideline Amount

After determining the guideline amount, the judge can then adjust it up or down. To do this, he or she must find that the award is *unjust or inappropriate due to special circumstances* in the particular case.

The factors that can be considered for a finding of special circumstances vary by state. In addition, some states have *mandatory add-ons* that must be shared by both parents.

Factors That May Affect Child Support

Most factors that influence child support either increase or decrease it, depending on which parent is affected. Factors that increase support involve additional expenses for raising the children, or make more income available to the paying parent. Factors that decrease support reflect decreases in the cost of raising the children, or increase the income to the receiving parent.

Here are some typical factors that influence the guidelines:

Medical Expenses

Most group health plans require you to pay a small deductible or copayment, but if the children have allergies, asthma, or other chronic conditions, the costs can really begin to climb. If the receiving parent pays—or anticipates paying—the children's unreimbursed health care costs, the judge can increase the award. Alternatively, if the paying parent pays those costs, the judge can decrease the award. Quite often, the judge will order the cost of health care not covered by insurance to be paid equally or prorated based on income.

 How likely is it the judge will depart from the guideline amount? Not very. In *California Divorce Handbook,* Judge Stewart reasoned that for a judge to deviate from the guideline he "...must state in writing or on the record the facts and circumstances underlying the rebuttal factor, the value of the factor, and the length of time the factor will be in effect." Practically speaking, this is not feasible in many overworked courts, because "The time it will take to make all the findings necessary to justify such a factor will seem like a lifetime to a busy judge."

Medical Insurance

Whichever parent pays the premiums for the children's health insurance can get the savings. If the receiving parent pays, child support can be increased. If the paying parent pays, child support can be lowered. All states require the paying parent to include the children under his or her health and dental plan—if a plan is available through work or at a low cost. If insurance isn't available that way, either parent can buy the insurance, and the cost may be divided between them.

Life Insurance

In order to provide security for the children, the paying parent may be ordered to maintain a life insurance policy naming the children as irrevocable beneficiaries until the child support order ceases. The paying parent may get a reduction in child support to pay for the premiums for this policy, or—if the receiving parent has to pay for the policy—he or she may get an increase in support.

Children from Previous Relationships

Parents have a duty to support all of their children. Thus, if a receiving parent pays support to children from a previous relationship, he or she has less available for their own household, and the judge may increase the support. Likewise, if the paying parent supports children from a previous relationship, child support may be lowered. These payments must be required (payments from stepparents are generally considered voluntary), and are limited to the amount dictated by the guidelines.

Children from Subsequent Relationships

However, if the children are from a subsequent relationship—that is, the parent had them after support was established—it may not have the same effect. That's because most guidelines do not explicitly address this issue, leaving it up to judges to use their discretion. In real life, some judges have been sympathetic and accounted for the extra children in the support award, while others have been extremely unsympathetic and insisted that the children have little or no effect on the support.

New Mate

In some states, if a new mate enters the picture, child support can be adjusted. That's because a new mate usually—though not always—adds income to the household of the parent involved. Thus, if the receiving parent has a new mate, the judge can decrease the amount of support. Alternatively, if the paying parent has a new mate, more money is available for the children, and the judge can increase the award. The amount of the new mate's income that can be taken into account varies. Some judges may decide that all of the new mate's income is available to the parent, while others may decide that as little as 25% of the income should be considered. And, of course, still other judges will decide that none of it is available.

"Non-Traditional" Custody

Some states include the percentage of time with the child in their support calculations. This means that an award can be raised or lowered based on how much time the parent spends with the child. For example, if the receiving parent has the child 80% of the time, and the paying parent has the child 20% of the time, a typical award may be for $500. But if the parents change the schedule, giving the receiving parent the child 60% of the time, and the paying parent 40% of the time, child support can be decreased. This reflects the reality that the more time a parent spends caring for the child, the more he or she is likely to spend. To calculate percentage of time with the child, the parents may simply have to add up all the hours in an entire year each parent spends with the child.

 "The guidelines do seem to be working. Support awards are higher and more equitable, and the entire process takes less court time. In addition, more cases are settled and those that are litigated are often narrowed in scope." *When Your Ex Won't Pay,* Nancy Palmer and Ana Tangel-Rodriguez

Hardship
If the receiving parent suffers an extreme financial hardship due to uninsured catastrophic losses, the judge can increase the child support award. Likewise, if the paying parent suffers a financial hardship due to catastrophic losses, the judge can decrease the child support award.

High Income
If the paying parent earns a great deal of money, the formula may indicate an amount greater than what the children realistically need. If that's the case, the judge can lower the amount of support to a more reasonable amount. High income is subjective, but generally, if the paying parent earns more than $200,000 a year, the guideline will certainly indicate more support than is needed. That's because most schedules begin to lose their usefulness when one parent's earnings reach high levels.

Low Income
The opposite of high income is low income. If the paying parent would be left with too little to live on, child support may be lowered. This is the "don't kill the goose that lays the golden egg" argument. Low income is subjective, but generally, if the paying parent keeps less than 40% of net income after paying child support, he or she no longer has an incentive to continue working.

Child Care
Child care costs include both day care and after-school care. In some states, the costs are automatically prorated, while in others, accounting for this expense is entirely at the discretion of the judge. Typically, the receiving parent must pay child care costs in order to work or go to

school, and the judge will increase the support in kind. Interestingly, child care is one of the few costs that actually decreases as the children grow older.

Travel Costs
This comes up when one parent moves far away, and the children have to start taking long trips by plane, train, or car. If the receiving parent pays the travel costs for visitation, the judge can increase child support. If the paying parent pays visitation costs, support can be lowered. By the way, in some states it doesn't matter who moved away—the judge isn't allowed to give that issue weight when resolving the matter. More likely, though, the move-away parent ends up paying for the cost of transportation if there is no other agreement between the two parents.

Job Expenses
If the paying parent must maintain a car or special work clothes for his or her job, the judge may lower the child support award.

School
School costs typically include tuition, fees, books, room and board, and so on. If the receiving parent pays these costs, he or she can seek to have child support increased. Alternatively, a paying parent who pays these costs can ask to have child support lowered.

Children's Income
In a few states, if the children have independent income, the paying parent may be able to lower the amount of child support.

Bargain Housing
When the receiving parent remains in the family residence and pays a much lower mortgage than what rent would be, the judge can lower child support. The reason is that the receiving parent is getting a financial break, and thus has more income available for the children.

Other
Finally, if an expense doesn't fit another other category, but the judge believes it's appropriate, the judge can adjust the award. Costs in this category might include summer camp, religious training, and so on. The parent who pays the costs may be entitled to an adjustment in the child support.

Counting Your Support

Child Support Survival Guide, Bonnie M. White, Douglas Pipes, Career Press, $12.99. This book is an excellent guide to understanding how child support works and how to deal effectively with the federal *Child Support Enforcement (CSE)* agencies.

Divorce and Money, Violet Woodhouse, Victoria F. Collins, Robin Leonard, M.C. Blakeman, Nolo Press, $26.95. This excellent book on the money side of divorce includes extremely detailed discussions of marital property, retirement benefits, insurance, taxes, business assets, debts, and spousal and child support.

The Dollars and Sense of Divorce, Judith Briles, Carol Ann Wilson, Dearborn Financial Publishing, $17.95. An informative guide to divorce issues, including dividing property, retirement plans, etc. It includes a list of helpful organizations.

Don't Settle For Less, Beverly Pekala, Doubleday, $12.95. Written by a lawyer who advocates women's rights, this book offers a step-by-step explanation of how women can keep from being economically victimized by divorce and custody settlements.

How to Collect Child Support, Geraldine Jensen with Katina Z. Jones, The Association for Children for Enforcement of Support, Inc. (ACES), Longmeadow Press, $7.95. An accurate and very easy-to-follow guide to enforcing support orders.

The Single Parent's Money Guide, Emily W. Card, Macmillan, $14.95. Written by a lawyer and a single parent, this book explains alimony and child support, insurance coverage, budgeting for medical emergencies, and other financial decisions.

When Your Ex Won't Pay, Nancy S. Palmer and Ana Tangel-Rodriguez, Pinon Press, $12.00. Co-written by the Chair of the Florida Family Law Bar, this book explains the laws and various methods for collecting support.

Chapter 24

Calculating Child Support: Worksheet

Want to calculate your child support? Here's what you need for a quick estimate.

The following worksheet will approximate the amount of child support likely to be awarded. Remember, there is no national child support formula. Not only do different states use different formulas, but judges can deviate from the formula—so the resulting calculation is a rough estimate only.

To complete the worksheet, you'll need the following information for both parents:

- Pay stubs.
- Last year's tax return.
- Adjustment expenses.

If you don't have this information handy, you can still complete the worksheet. Just keep in mind that the more accurately you guess, the more reliable the estimate will be.

Step 1. Preliminary Information

Some of this information isn't strictly necessary, but completing it will
help you get all your information in one place (which you'll need to do
for court anyway).

Number of children. The number of children eligible for child support.
This may be different from the number of dependents you claim on your
tax return.

Tax filing status. Your choices are: single, head of household, married
filing jointly, married filing separately, or widow(er).

Number of dependents. The number of people you claim as dependents,
adding one for yourself.

Percentage of time with the children. The annual percentage of time each
parent spends with the children. If you have more than one child, and the
schedule is different for each child, use an average of the total time.

Step 2. Monthly Income

In this section you determine your *net monthly income.* Your net monthly
income is your gross monthly income minus your deductions.

Everything in the worksheet will be based on monthly averages, so if
you're not paid monthly (or if your income varies from month to month),
calculate the monthly amounts by taking the annual amount and dividing
by 12.

Earnings. Your gross pay before any deductions are taken out.

Investment Income. The average monthly amounts you receive in
interest, dividends, etc. These amounts should be your best guess for the
next year.

Other Income. Include most kinds of income, including net income from
self-employment, rentals, alimony from a previous marriage, and job-
related reimbursements. Do not include SSI or any child support.

Step 1. Preliminary Information

Paying Parent

Name _____

Occupation _____

Employer _____

Address of employer _____

Tax filing status _____

Number of children _____

Number of dependents _____

Percentage of time with children _____

Receiving Parent

Name _____

Occupation _____

Employer _____

Address of employer _____

Tax filing status _____

Number of children _____

Number of dependents _____

Percentage of time with children _____

Taxes. This is the average monthly amount you pay, not the average monthly amount withheld. If you pay other taxes (such as Hospital Tax "MEDI"), include those under *Other deductions.*

Mandatory pension or retirement. This applies only if you are required to make a pension or retirement fund contribution. If your contributions are not mandatory, do not enter them.

Mandatory union dues. This only applies if union dues are required for all employees working under the same job classification for the same employer. If joining the union is not required, don't enter anything.

Children's health insurance premiums. Only enter the additional amount paid to insure the children. Do not include insurance costs for the parent.

Income. Subtract *Total Monthly Deductions* from *Total Gross Monthly Income.*

Step 3. Combined Income

In this step, you combine the net earnings of each parent.

Combined Income. Add *Paying Parent's Income* to *Receiving Parent's Income.*

Step 4. Minimum Child Support

This step uses the parents' combined income to calculate the minimum child support amount.

Minimum Child Support. Copy *Combined Income* from Step 3. Then, look up *Percent of Income* in the table below and copy it to the worksheet column. Now, multiply *Percent of Income* by *Combined Income.*

Number of Children	Percent of Income
1	.22
2	.34
3	.42
4	.47
5+	.50

Step 2a. Monthly Income (Paying Parent)

Gross Monthly Income

Earnings

Wages, salary $ _____

Bonuses $ _____

Commissions $ _____

Investment Income

Interest $ _____

Dividends $ _____

Capital Gains $ _____

Retirement plan distributions $ _____

Annuities $ _____

Other Income

Business net income $ _____

Rentals net income $ _____

Royalties $ _____

Pensions and Trusts $ _____

Social Security $ _____

Disability $ _____

Unemployment $ _____

Military basic allowance for quarters $ _____

Alimony $ _____

Other income $ _____

Total Gross Monthly Income $ _____

Monthly Deductions

Federal income tax $ _____

State and local income tax $ _____

Social Security (FICA) $ _____

State Disability Insurance (SDI) $ _____

Self-employment tax $ _____

Mandatory pension or retirement $ _____

Mandatory union dues $ _____

Children's health insurance $ _____

Other deductions $ _____

Minus (-)

Total Monthly Deductions $ _____

Equals (=)

Paying Parent's Income $ _____

Note: This is a general formula with an error factor of about ±2%. If you want to try to reduce the error to ±1%, do the following. If *Combined Income* is less than $1,500, add .1 to *Percent of Income.* If *Combined Income* is more than $2,500, subtract .1 from *Percent of Income.* If *Combined Income* is more than $3,500, subtract .2 from *Percent of Income.*

What does this mean? It means that the more you earn, the smaller the percentage of your total earnings you spend on your children.

Step 5. Paying Parent's Portion

Here, you determine the amount of child support attributable to the paying parent.

First, copy *Paying Parent's Income* from Step 2a and *Combined Income* from Step 3.

Then, divide *Paying Parent's Income* by *Combined Income.* This gives you *Paying Parent's Percentage.* This is the portion of the combined income the paying parent contributes.

Finally, multiply *Paying Parent's Percentage* by *Minimum Child Support* to get *Paying Parent's Portion.* This is the portion of the child support the paying parent should pay.

Step 6. Adjustments

In this step, you enter any adjustments for special circumstances. The list of possible adjustments is lengthy, but few may apply to you. Try to use known amounts whenever possible.

To make adjustments for special circumstances:

Add (+) for factors that *increase* child support
• Receiving parent suffers extreme hardship.
• Receiving parent pays travel costs for visitation.
• Receiving parent pays children's uninsured health care costs.
• Receiving parent pays for children's educational or other needs.
• Paying parent has income available from a new mate.
• Paying parent has less than 20% visitation.

Step 2b. Monthly Income (Receiving Parent)

Gross Monthly Income

Earnings

Wages, salary	$
Bonuses	$
Commissions	$

Investment Income

Interest	$
Dividends	$
Capital Gains	$
Retirement plan distributions	$
Annuities	$

Other Income

Business net income	$
Rentals net income	$
Royalties	$
Pensions and Trusts	$
Social Security	$
Disability	$
Unemployment	$
Military basic allowance for quarters	$
Alimony	$
Other income	$

Total Gross Monthly Income $

Monthly Deductions

Federal income tax	$
State and local income tax	$
Social Security (FICA)	$
State Disability Insurance (SDI)	$
Self-employment tax	$
Mandatory pension or retirement	$
Mandatory union dues	$
Children's health insurance	$
Other deductions	$

Minus (-)

Total Monthly Deductions $

Equals (=)

Receiving Parent's Income $

Subtract (-) for factors that *decrease* child support
- Paying parent suffers extreme hardship.
- Paying parent pays travel costs for visitation.
- Paying parent supports children from previous or subsequent relationships.
- Paying parent has an unusually high income, and the formula calculates an amount greater than what the children need.
- Paying parent would be left with an unreasonably low amount of money to live on.
- Paying parent has more than 20% visitation.
- Receiving parent has income available from a new mate.
- Receiving parent resides in the family residence and has a much lower mortgage payment compared to fair rent.

To make adjustments, you need to know which factors are relevant in your state. The factors most likely to affect support include: percentage of time with the children, support paid for children from previous relationships, child care costs, and possibly new mate income.

When adjusting support, keep in mind that the presumed correct figure is awarded an estimated 90% of the time.

Step 7. Child Support

In this step you add (or subtract) your adjustments to the minimum child support amount, and you've finished.

Compute *Child Support* by adding or subtracting *Total Adjustments* to *Paying Parent's Portion.*

Congratulations! You did it.

You now have an approximation of the support likely to be awarded. Remember, the estimate is based on a number of assumptions about both parents' future income and expenses. Don't assume it's absolute. Instead, use it as a guide for approximating your support order.

Step 3. Combined Income

Paying Parent's Income (*from 2a*) $ _____

Plus (+)

Receiving Parent's Income (*from 2b*) $ _____

Equals (=)

Combined Income $ _____

Step 4. Minimum Child Support

Combined Income (*from 3*) $ _____

Times (x)

Percent of Income (*see instructions*) $ _____

Equals (=)

Minimum Child Support $ _____

Step 5. Paying Parent's Portion

Paying Parent's Income (*from 2a*) $ _____

Divided (/)

Combined Income (*from 3*) $ _____

Equals (=)

Paying Parent's Percentage $ _____

Times (x)

Minimum Child Support (*from 4*) $ _____

Equals (=)

Paying Parent's Portion $ _____

Step 6. Adjustments

Adjustments

_____ $ _____   (+ or -)

_____ $ _____   (+ or -)

_____ $ _____   (+ or -)

Total Adjustments $ _____

Step 7. Child Support

Child Support $ _____

Chapter 25
Modifying Child Support

As children grow, their lives change. Perhaps a child takes up music, and now needs an instrument and lessons. Or maybe the child needs braces, and the costs aren't covered by insurance.

Or maybe it's not the children who change, but the parents. Suppose one parent gets a big raise, and now has a higher standard of living. Or the other parent remarries, and has another child.

Whatever the cause, child support can be modified anytime there is a *change of circumstances.*

However, what constitutes a change of circumstance varies from state to state. In some states, a 10% difference in payments justifies a return to court. But in others, the amount must be more.

If the parents can agree on their own, they may be able to draft a stipulated agreement and file it with the court. Otherwise, the parent who seeks the change will have to file a motion with the court and initiate a contested proceeding.

This chapter discusses how to modify your child support.

When You Can Modify Child Support

When you go to court, your lawyer will tell you that child support is "subject to modification at any time." That's true, but it's misleading. While child support can be modified at any time, that doesn't mean that it will be modified at any time.

You can only modify child support when there is a significant change in circumstances.

"Change in circumstances" means that something important enough has changed that justifies returning to court. More specifically, whatever has changed must either not have been considered originally, or must affect the child's standard of living.

The reason for this rule is to prevent a parent from making constant requests for modification.

In fact, if you file a motion to modify child support, you must prove there has been a significant change of circumstances. If you cannot prove it, the motion will be denied. Even worse, the court may order you to pay the other parent's lawyer.

Standards for Modification

While it varies from state to state, most states require that the new support being sought be at least 10% different from the old support. If the difference is less, there is no change of circumstances, and the modification may be denied.

Other states set the threshold even higher, such as 25% or 30%. And a few states simply ignore the amount and consider a modification after two years have passed since the prior order.

Timing is everything. It's a fine line between filing too quickly and waiting too long. If you file too early, you risk having the motion denied. But if you wait too long, you may be unfairly burdened with an inappropriate award. One rule of thumb is to wait until the new support being sought has changed by 15% for more than 30 days.

Types of Modifications

These are the various types of modifications:

Temporary Modification
Child support can be modified *temporarily*. This might make sense when a parent suddenly loses a job, or is injured, or when the child's needs change—but only for a definite period of time. The modification can be structured to last only for a specific period and then revert back to the prior terms.

Permanent Modification
Child support can be modified *permanently*. This happens when child support changes from a certain point forward for an indefinite period of time. Though nothing about child support is ever really permanent, the orders remain in place until the judge changes them or the support ends.

Retroactive Modification
As a general rule, child support is not modified *retroactively*. That's primarily to prevent a parent who owes a large amount of back support from going into court and arguing that the past-due payments were too large, and thus, the debt should be erased.

However, there are times when child support is modified from an earlier date. A judge may set support back to the date when the motion was filed, even if it was months—or years—earlier. And if a mother is establishing *paternity*, the court may order support back to the child's date of birth. Finally, support may be modified retroactively when the receiving parent is guilty of child snatching or child concealment, or when it is shown that a parent supplied fraudulent income and expense information.

Factors That May Modify Child Support

All kinds of events can trigger a modification. In fact, many of the same factors that cause child support to be adjusted initially can also cause it to be modified. For example:

Income
When either parent's ability to pay has changed, child support can be changed. That's because children are entitled to the same *standard of*

living as their parents. Thus, depending on which parent's income is affected and how it's affected, child support can either be raised or lowered. For example, support can be raised if the paying parent has more income, or if the receiving parent has less income. And the reverse is true too. Child support can go down if the paying parent experiences a drop in income or if the receiving parent has an increase in income.

Hardship

If either parent suffers an extreme financial *hardship,* support can be modified. A receiving parent who is suddenly burdened with huge financial losses can seek to have child support increased. Conversely, if the paying parent suffers a financial emergency, he or she can ask that support be decreased. By the way, if a hardship that was incorporated into a prior child support award has now ended, that constitutes a change of circumstance, and either parent can file a motion to modify.

 If you initially accept less than the guidelines, you can file for a modification at any time without having to prove a change of circumstances.

Health Care

If the children have a *medical emergency,* the parents will have to pay the bills. If the receiving parent has a health emergency and cannot work, the paying parent may have to pay additional support. If the paying parent has a medical crisis and cannot work, the receiving parent may have to accept less support. If the problem is temporary, the judge may grant a temporary change in support, but when a problem is permanent, such as a disability, support may be permanently modified.

School

If a child changes from private to public *school,* that may be a cost that justifies changing child support. However, if a child changes from public to private school, the parent insisting on the change may have to foot the entire bill. Other examples include the child needing a tutor, or the child joining a team and requiring money for uniforms and equipment.

New Children

If either parent gains a *new child,* that may be a reason to modify child support. In this case, however, the parent must be legally obligated to support the child. Because stepparents do not have the same legal obligations as biological parents, gaining a stepchild through remarriage may not be a change of circumstances. An adoption, on the other hand, is often considered a change of circumstance because it represents a genuine legal obligation.

New Mate
The *new mate* that comes along with a remarriage may well represent a change of circumstances. The new mate may represent additional available income, and in some states the judge can include that income in the calculations. If the receiving parent gets the new mate, child support can be decreased, and if the paying parent gains the new mate, child support may be raised.

Percentage of Time with the Child
One possible change of circumstances occurs if the parents change the *visitation schedule.* In states where percentage of time is included in child support calculations, whichever parent starts spending more time with the child will benefit. Thus, if the paying parent gets more time with the child, he or she will qualify for less child support. If the receiving parent gets more time, the opposite occurs.

Change in Law
Interestingly enough, there is one change of circumstance that has nothing to do with the parents—the laws change! When child support laws are *revised,* or new ones are passed, that's considered a change of circumstance all by itself. When that happens, parents can file without having to prove anything has changed.

Cost of Living
A final possible change of circumstance occurs when *inflation* has eroded the value of the child support. Either parent may seek to increase the support award.

Normally, *passage of time* is not considered a change of circumstances. However, passage of time combined with another reason—such as an increase in the cost of living—may be sufficient to modify child support.

How to Seek a Modification

Ask the other parent. That's the first thing to do if you want to modify the support. What happens determines what you do next.

If the other parent agrees with you, you can probably modify the support amount easily and cheaply. You can write up your own agreement and file it with the court, and if the judge has no objections, it will become the official order.

If the other parent does not agree, and you still feel a change is needed, you will have to prepare and file a motion. This is a lawsuit, and it will absorb your time, energy, and resources. Additionally, the burden will be on you to prove that a significant change of circumstance has occurred.

In either event, you will find yourself returning to the court that issued your current orders, because that court retains jurisdiction over you unless there is a reason to change.

 Periodic modification. Though federal laws require child support orders to be automatically reviewed every three years, very few states comply. Thus, if you want your support adjusted, you'll have to take the initiative and file a motion with the court.

If You Agree to the Modification

If you both agree—or *stipulate*—to the new amount, you can write up a *modification agreement* and present it to the judge for approval. The judge will review the agreement, and—unless there is something really unfair about it—put it into effect.

This may seem like a waste of time since you've already agreed, but there are good reasons why you should file your agreement with the court.

First, if the agreement is not signed by the judge, it cannot be enforced. If the paying parent violates the agreement, the receiving parent has no recourse except to file an independent lawsuit. This could cost more than the initial filing fee would have been.

Second, a change in payments agreed to by the parents—but not approved by the court—does not change the underlying legal obligation. Thus, if a paying parent is paying less than the amount specified in the original order, he or she may still be liable in the future for the entire amount that was never paid.

And third, if you include the reasons for the modification in the agreement, it becomes more difficult for one of the parents to subsequently claim they were coerced into making the agreement.

Four Tips for Writing Your Own Agreement

1. Have a lawyer draft the document in proper legal form.

2. State the specific reasons for the modification in the agreement.

3. Make sure the agreement is dated and signed by both parents.

4. File the agreement with the court.

What to Put In the Agreement

Basically, you can put anything you want into the agreement. Here are some basic items to include:

- The original case name and case number.
- The amount of child support to be paid.
- Whether a wage assignment will be served on the paying parent's employer.
- Whether the parents will notify each other if either one moves or changes employment.
- A statement indicating each parent agrees to the terms of the agreement.
- A statement indicating each parent knows his or her rights and obligations under the law.
- A statement indicating neither parent was subject to coercion or duress in making the agreement.
- That the support is in the best interests of the children and will meet their needs.

Additionally, you can add almost anything else. If you want to change who pays for the children's health insurance, or who pays travel costs for visitation, etc., that can be added as well.

The important thing to remember is that the agreement must spell out clearly and simply what your intentions are. That way, if either parent decides to contest it later, the agreement is more likely to withstand *judicial scrutiny.*

 If you don't know your original case number and can't find your original papers, call either your attorney or the other parent's attorney. If no one had an attorney, then go to the county clerk's office and ask to see your file.

If You Don't Agree to the Modification

If the other parent does not agree with your desire to change the support, and you believe you are right, you will have to go to court.

Here are the general steps involved in a *contested modification.*

Hire an Attorney (Optional)
You may decide to *hire an attorney*—or you may not. When the sought-after change is small, paying an attorney may simply not be cost-effective. In some states, procedures are in place for parents to represent themselves when they seek a change in child support.

File Papers with the Court
Though the procedures differ in different courts, you will have to *file a motion* requesting a modification. If you've hired an attorney, he or she will know what to do. Otherwise, you will have to go to the court that issued the original orders and buy the necessary forms. After filling them out, you must file them with the court clerk, and you must pay a fee. The court clerk will then give you a hearing date. If you are filing the forms yourself, you will have to serve a copy of the forms on the other parent, which may require that another adult deliver the papers.

Exchange Financial Information
In many states, prior to the hearing date, each parent has to complete a set of financial forms and send them to the other parent. If there is no reason to suspect that the other parent is engaging in financial misconduct, these forms will provide the information needed for calculating the guideline amount of child support.

Attend the Hearing
When it's time to go to court, you'll sit in the same courtroom with everyone else seeking a change in custody and support orders. Your attorney (if you have one), will meet you when the court clerk calls your name. The attorney will speak to the judge for you. If you don't have an attorney, you'll be asked questions by the judge.

Generally, the hearing will be short, often taking no more than five or ten minutes. If the judge makes a ruling that day, you or your lawyer will have to prepare an order for the judge's signature.

 It's not easy to modify child support. You have to submit detailed financial statements, elicit financial information from the other parent, and then sit though a lengthy court hearing. A better bet? Anticipate future reasons for a modification and bring them to the attention of the judge, who can add them to the original court order.

Appendix

Appendix

Now that you've seen what the laws of child custody and child support are, you may need answers to specific questions. Because custody laws are slightly different in each state, you'll need to do further research--such as talking to a lawyer or spending time in a law library.

This appendix contains information to help you get started. Keep in mind, though, that the laws are constantly changing, so you will need to verify the current laws in your state.

Child Custody

Here are some of the factors that can vary from state to state:

How is custody divided? In some states, a court can make different awards for legal and physical custody. In others, a custody award combines both legal and physical custody.

Is mediation authorized? Many states authorize or require their courts to order mediation. If the parents cannot reach an agreement in mediation, the court will try the case.

Will mediation be confidential? When parents use a mediator, generally the mediation session is considered confidential, and the mediator cannot testify in court about anything said during the session. This can only change if both parents expressly waive their right to confidentiality and let the mediator testify.

Is joint custody allowed? Some states allow joint custody only if both parents agree. Other states allow joint custody even if one parent objects. A few states require joint custody unless there is demonstrable harm to the parents, or the arrangement is proven to be not in the best interests of the children. And a few states have no statutes concerning joint custody at all.

Will a custody evaluation be required? A court can order a custody investigation or evaluation to help it make a decision.

Are the child's preferences considered? Many states include the preferences of the child when deciding custody or visitation.

Child Support

The information on child support guidelines was derived from *A Summary of Child Support Guidelines: February 1, 1990, National Center for State Courts.* Since the guidelines in your state may have changed, be especially sure to verify the information.

Guideline model. Different states have adopted different ways to calculate child support. The most common--called the Income Shares model-- assumes that the support amount should reflect the combined income of both parents. The Fixed Percent model assumes that the noncustodial parent's income should be the basis for support, because the custodial parent is already supporting the child. The Varying Percent of Income model is similar to the Fixed Percent, except that the percent varies based on the income of the noncustodial parent. Finally, the Melson Delaware model uses an older and more complicated formula that factors in the estimated cost of raising the child while prorating the support obligation between the parents.

Whose income is used? Depending on the guideline model, the income used to calculate support--or the income base--may be based on either the noncustodial parent's or both parents' income combined.

How is base income calculated? The guideline model also distinguishes the type of income included: gross income, adjusted gross, or net income.

Is income verification required? The level of documentation required by each state when setting child support varies. Some specify no formal requirement, while others insist upon pay stubs, tax returns, financial statements, and more.

Delinquencies: Parents (per thousand). Number of parents (per thousand residents) owing child support. Rank. The higher the ranking, the more parents who owe child support. The highest state, Indiana, has almost 100 delinquent parents per thousand residents. The lowest state, New Mexico, has less than 10.

Alabama

Child Custody

Age of majority:
19

How is custody divided?
Legal and physical combined.

Is mediation authorized?
Yes.

Will mediation be confidential?
Yes.

Is joint custody allowed?
Available if both parents agree.

Will a custody evaluation be required?
Not specified.

Are the child's preferences considered?
No.

Statutes:
Code of Alabama: Title 30, Chapter 3-1.

Child Support

Guideline model:
Income Shares.

Whose income is used?
Combined.

How is base income calculated?
Adjusted Gross.

Is income verification required?
Yes.

Delinquencies:
Parents (per thousand): 40
Rank: 12

Statutes:
Code of Alabama: Title 30, Chapter 3-1 and Alabama Rules of Judicial Administration: Rule 32.

Addresses

Alabama State Bar
P.O. Box 671 (36101)
415 Dexter St.
Montgomery, AL 36104
(205) 269-1515

Child Support Enforcement Division
Department of Human Resources
50 Ripley Street
Montgomery, AL 36130
(205) 242-9300

REGION IV
OCSE Regional Representative
101 Marietta Tower, Suite 821
Atlanta, GA 30323
(404) 331-5733

Alaska

Child Custody

Age of majority:
18

How is custody divided?
Legal and physical combined.

Is mediation authorized?
Yes.

Will mediation be confidential?
Yes.

Is joint custody allowed?
Permitted despite one parent objecting.

Will a custody evaluation be required?
Not specified.

Are the child's preferences considered?
Yes.

Statutes:
Alaska Statutes; Title 25, Chapter 24.150 and Chapter 20.090.

Child Support

Guideline model:
Fixed Percent.

Whose income is used?
Noncustodial.

How is base income calculated?
Net.

Is income verification required?
No.

Delinquencies:
Parents (per thousand): 51
Rank: 5

Statutes:
Alaska Statutes; Title 25, Chapter 24.160 and Title 47, Chapter 23.060 and Alaska Rules of Civil Procedure; Rule 67 and 90.3.

Addresses

Alaska Bar Association
P.O. Box 100279 (99510)
510 L St. #602
Anchorage, AK 99501
(907) 272-7469

Child Support Enforcement Division.
Department of Revenue
550 West 7th Avenue
4th Floor
Anchorage, AK
(907) 276-3441

REGION X
OCSE Regional Representative
2201 Sixth Avenue
Mail Stop RX-70
Seattle, WA 98121
(206) 553-2775

Arizona

Child Custody

Age of majority:
18

How is custody divided?
Legal and physical separate.

Is mediation authorized?
Yes.

Will mediation be confidential?
Yes.

Is joint custody allowed?
Permitted despite one parent objecting.

Will a custody evaluation be required?
Not specified.

Are the child's preferences considered?
Yes.

Statutes:
Arizona Revised Statutes Annotated; Title 25, Chapters 328, 331, and 332.

Child Support

Guideline model:
Income Shares.

Whose income is used?
Combined.

How is base income calculated?
Adjusted Gross.

Is income verification required?
Yes.

Delinquencies:
Parents (per thousand): 22
Rank: 25

Statutes:
Arizona Revised Statutes Annotated; Title 25, Chapters 320 and 322.

Addresses

State Bar of Arizona
111 W. Monroe St.
Phoenix, AZ 85003-1742
(602) 252-4804

Child Support Enforcement
Administration
Department of Economic Security
P.O. Box 40458
Site Code 776-A
2222 W. Encanto
Phoenix, AZ 85067
(602) 252-0236

REGION IX
OCSE Regional Representative
50 United Nations Plaza
Mail Stop 351
San Francisco, CA 94102
(415) 556-5176

Arkansas

Child Custody

Age of majority:
18

How is custody divided?
Legal and physical combined.

Is mediation authorized?
No.

Will mediation be confidential?
Not specified.

Is joint custody allowed?
No statutes.

Will a custody evaluation be required?
Not specified.

Are the child's preferences considered?
No.

Statutes:
Arkansas Code of 1987 Annotated; Title 9, Chapter 13-101.

Child Support

Guideline model:
Varying Percent.

Whose income is used?
Noncustodial.

How is base income calculated?
Net.

Is income verification required?
No.

Delinquencies:
Parents (per thousand): 29
Rank: 20

Statutes:
Arkansas Code of 1987 Annotated; Title 9, Chapter 12-312.

Addresses

Arkansas Bar Association
400 W. Markham
Little Rock, AR 72201
(501) 375-4605

Division of Child Support Enforcement
Arkansas Social Services
P.O. Box 3358
Little Rock, AR 72203
(501) 682-8398

REGION VI
OCSE Regional Representative
1200 Main Tower Building
Suite 1700
Dallas, TX 75202
(214) 767-9648

California

Child Custody

Age of majority:
18

How is custody divided?
Legal and physical separate.

Is mediation authorized?
Yes.

Will mediation be confidential?
Yes.

Is joint custody allowed?
Permitted despite one parent objecting.

Will a custody evaluation be required?
Court ordered.

Are the child's preferences considered?
Yes.

Statutes:
Annotated California Code; Sections 3011, 3024, 3040, 3042.

Child Support

Guideline model:
Varying Percent.

Whose income is used?
Combined.

How is base income calculated?
Net.

Is income verification required?
No.

Delinquencies:
Parents (per thousand): 26
Rank: 22

Statutes:
Annotated California Code; Sections 3024, 4040, 3622, 4001, and Judicial Council Forms; and California Rules of Court; Family Law Rule 1285.25.

Addresses

State Bar of California
555 Franklin St.
San Francisco, CA 94102
(415) 561-8200

Child Support Program Management Branch
Department of Social Services
744 P Street
Mail Stop 9-011
Sacramento, CA 95814
(916) 323-8994

REGION IX
OCSE Regional Representative
50 United Nations Plaza
Mail Stop 351
San Francisco, CA 94102
(415) 556-5176

Colorado

Child Custody

Age of majority:
21 (in certain situations, may be different)

How is custody divided?
Legal and physical separate.

Is mediation authorized?
Yes.

Will mediation be confidential?
Yes.

Is joint custody allowed?
Permitted despite one parent objecting.

Will a custody evaluation be required?
Not specified.

Are the child's preferences considered?
Yes.

Statutes:
Colorado Revised Statutes; Article 10, Sections 14-123, 14-124, and 14-129.

Child Support

Guideline model:
Income Shares.

Whose income is used?
Combined.

How is base income calculated?
Adjusted Gross.

Is income verification required?
Yes.

Delinquencies:
Parents (per thousand): 28
Rank: 21

Statutes:
Colorado Revised Statutes; Article 10, Sections 14-10-115 and 14-10-117.

Addresses

The Colorado Bar Association
1900 Grant St. #950
Denver, CO 80203
(303) 860-1115

Division of Child Support Enforcement
Department of Social Services
1575 Sherman St.
Denver, CO 80203-1714
(303) 866-5994

REGION VIII
OCSE Regional Representative
Federal Office Building, Room 1185
1961 Stout Street
Denver, CO 80294
(303) 844-5594

Connecticut

Child Custody

Age of majority:
18

How is custody divided?
Legal and physical separate.

Is mediation authorized?
Yes.

Will mediation be confidential?
Yes.

Is joint custody allowed?
Available if both parents agree.

Will a custody evaluation be required?
Not specified.

Are the child's preferences considered?
Yes.

Statutes:
Connecticut General Statutes Annotated; Title 46b, Chapters 56, 56a, and 84.

Child Support

Guideline model:
Income Shares.

Whose income is used?
Combined.

How is base income calculated?
Net.

Is income verification required?
No.

Delinquencies:
Parents (per thousand): 37
Rank: 15

Statutes:
Connecticut General Statutes Annotated; Title 46b, Chapters 84 and 215b.

Addresses

Connecticut State Bar Association
101 Corporate Place
Rocky Hill, CT 06067
(203) 721-0025

Bureau of Child Support Enforcement
Dept of Human Resources
1049 Asylum Avenue
Hartford, CT 06105
(203) 566-3053

REGION I
OCSE Regional Representative
John F. Kennedy Federal Building
23rd Floor, Room 2303
Boston, MA 02203
(617) 565-2463

Delaware

Child Custody

Age of majority:
18

How is custody divided?
Legal and physical combined.

Is mediation authorized?
Yes.

Will mediation be confidential?
Yes.

Is joint custody allowed?
Available if both parents agree.

Will a custody evaluation be required?
Court ordered.

Are the child's preferences considered?
Yes.

Statutes:
Delaware Code Annotated; Title 13, Chapters 722 and 1507.

Child Support

Guideline model:
Melson Delaware.

Whose income is used?
Combined.

How is base income calculated?
Net.

Is income verification required?
Yes.

Delinquencies:
Parents (per thousand): 44
Rank: 9

Statutes:
Delaware Code Annotated; Title 13, Chapters 501, 514, and 701.

Addresses

Delaware State Bar Association
1225 King Street
Wilmington, DE 19801
(302) 658-5279

Division of Child Support Enforcement
Department of Health & Social Services
P.O. Box 904
New Castle, DE 19720
(302) 421-8300

REGION III
OCSE Regional Representative
P.O. Box 8436
3535 Market Street, Room 4119 MS/15
Philadelphia, PA 19101
(215) 596-4365

District of Columbia

Child Custody

Age of majority:
18

How is custody divided?
Legal and physical combined.

Is mediation authorized?
No.

Will mediation be confidential?
Not specified.

Is joint custody allowed?
Available if both parents agree.

Will a custody evaluation be required?
Not specified.

Are the child's preferences considered?
Yes.

Statutes:
District of Columbia Code Annotated; Title 16, Chapter 9, Sections 911 and 914.

Child Support

Guideline model:
Varying Percent.

Whose income is used?
Noncustodial.

How is base income calculated?
Adjusted Gross.

Is income verification required?
No.

Delinquencies:
Parents (per thousand): 58
Rank: 4

Statutes:
District of Columbia Code Annotated; Title 16, Chapter 9, Sections 911 and 916.

Addresses

Bar Association of the District of Columbia
12th Floor
1819 H Street, NW
Washington, DC 20006-3690
(202) 223-6600

The District of Columbia Bar
6th Floor
1250 H Street, NW
Washington, DC 20005-3908
(202) 737-4700

Office of Paternity & Child Support
Department of Human Services
3rd Floor - Suite 3013
425 I Street, NW
Washington, D.C. 20001
(202) 724-5610

REGION III
OCSE Regional Representative
P.O. Box 8436
3535 Market Street, Room 4119 MS/15
Philadelphia, PA 19101
(215) 596-4365

Florida

Child Custody

Age of majority:
18

How is custody divided?
Legal and physical combined.

Is mediation authorized?
Yes.

Will mediation be confidential?
Yes.

Is joint custody allowed?
Permitted despite one parent
objecting.

**Will a custody evaluation be
required?**
Not specified.

**Are the child's preferences
considered?**
Yes.

Statutes:
Florida Statutes Annotated; Chapter
61.13.

Child Support

Guideline model:
Income Shares.

Whose income is used?
Combined.

How is base income calculated?
Net.

Is income verification required?
Yes.

Delinquencies:
Parents (per thousand): 64
Rank: 2

Statutes:
Florida Statutes Annotated; Chapters
61.13 and 61.30.

Addresses

The Florida Bar
650 Apalachee Parkway
Tallahassee, FL 32399-2300
(904) 561-5600

Office of Child Support Enforcement
Dept. of Health & Rehabilitative
Services
1317 Winewood Blvd. Bldg-3
Tallahassee, FL 32399-0700
(904) 488-9900

REGION IV
OCSE Regional Representative
101 Marietta Tower, Suite 821
Atlanta, GA 30323
(404) 331-5733

Georgia

Child Custody

Age of majority:
18

How is custody divided?
Legal and physical separate.

Is mediation authorized?
No.

Will mediation be confidential?
Not specified.

Is joint custody allowed?
Available if both parents agree.

Will a custody evaluation be required?
Court ordered.

Are the child's preferences considered?
Yes (age 14).

Statutes:
Code of Georgia Annotated; Title 30, Section 127.

Child Support

Guideline model:
Fixed Percent.

Whose income is used?
Noncustodial.

How is base income calculated?
Gross.

Is income verification required?
No.

Delinquencies:
Parents (per thousand): 34
Rank: 17

Statutes:
Code of Georgia Annotated;
Title 30, Section 207.

Addresses

State Bar of Georgia
800 The Hurt Bldg.
50 Hurt Plaza
Atlanta, GA 30303
(404) 527-8700

Office of Child Support Recovery
State Department of Human Resources
878 Peach Tree N.E., Room 529
Atlanta, GA 30309
(404) 894-4119

REGION IV
OCSE Regional Representative
101 Marietta Tower, Suite 821
Atlanta, GA 30323
(404) 331-5733

Hawaii

Child Custody

Age of majority:
18

How is custody divided?
Legal and physical combined.

Is mediation authorized?
No.

Will mediation be confidential?
Not specified.

Is joint custody allowed?
Available if both parents agree.

Will a custody evaluation be required?
Court ordered.

Are the child's preferences considered?
Yes.

Statutes:
Hawaii Revised Statutes; Title 571, Chapter 46.

Child Support

Guideline model:
Melson Delaware.

Whose income is used?
Combined.

How is base income calculated?
Net.

Is income verification required?
No.

Delinquencies:
Parents (per thousand): 37
Rank: 15

Statutes:
Hawaii Revised Statutes; Title 576D, Chapter 7, and Title 580, Chapter 47.

Addresses

Hawaii State Bar Association
Penthouse 1, 9th Floor
1136 Union Mall
Honolulu, HI 96813
(808) 537-1868

Child Support Enforcement Agency
Department of the Attorney General
680 Iwilei Rd., Suite 490
Honolulu, HI 96817
(808) 587-3712

REGION IX
OCSE Regional Representative
50 United Nations Plaza
Mail Stop 351
San Francisco, CA 94102
(415) 556-5176

Idaho

Child Custody

Age of majority:
18

How is custody divided?
Legal and physical separate.

Is mediation authorized?
Yes.

Will mediation be confidential?
Yes.

Is joint custody allowed?
Required unless health or safety compromised.

Will a custody evaluation be required?
Not specified.

Are the child's preferences considered?
No.

Statutes:
Idaho Code; Title 32, Chapters 717 and 717B, Title 39, Chapter 6303.

Child Support

Guideline model:
Income Shares.

Whose income is used?
Combined.

How is base income calculated?
Adjusted Gross.

Is income verification required?
Yes.

Delinquencies:
Parents (per thousand): 35
Rank: 16

Statutes:
Idaho Code; Title 32, Chapters 706, 706A, and 1205.

Addresses

Idaho State Bar
P.O. Box 895 (83701)
525 W Jefferson
Boise, ID 83701
(208) 334-4500

Bureau of Child Support Enforcement
Department of Health & Welfare
450 W. State Street
Towers Building
5th floor
Boise, ID 83720
(208) 334-5710

REGION X
OCSE Regional Representative
2201 Sixth Avenue
Mail Stop RX-70
Seattle, WA 98121
(206) 553-2775

Illinois

Child Custody

Age of majority:
18

How is custody divided?
Legal and physical combined.

Is mediation authorized?
Yes.

Will mediation be confidential?
Yes.

Is joint custody allowed?
Permitted despite one parent objecting.

Will a custody evaluation be required?
Court ordered.

Are the child's preferences considered?
Yes.

Statutes:
750 Illinois Compiled Statutes Annotated; Chapter 5, Sections 602, 602.1, 603.1, and 610.

Child Support

Guideline model:
Fixed Percent.

Whose income is used?
Noncustodial.

How is base income calculated?
Net.

Is income verification required?
No.

Delinquencies:
Parents (per thousand): 17
Rank: 29

Statutes:
750 Illinois Compiled Statutes Annotated; Chapter 5, Sections 505, 505.2 and 507.

Addresses

Illinois State Bar Association
424 S. Second St.
Springfield, IL 62701
(217) 525-1760

Bureau of Child Support Enforcement
Department of Public Aid
Prescott E. Bloom Building
201 South Grand Ave. East
P.O. Box 19405
Springfield, IL 62794-9405
(217) 782-1366

REGION V
OCSE Regional Representative
105 W. Adams St., 20th Floor
Chicago, IL 60606
(312) 353-4237

Indiana

Child Custody

Age of majority:
18

How is custody divided?
Legal and physical separate.

Is mediation authorized?
Yes.

Will mediation be confidential?
Yes.

Is joint custody allowed?
Permitted despite one parent
objecting.

**Will a custody evaluation be
required?**
Not specified.

**Are the child's preferences
considered?**
Yes (age 14).

Statutes:
Annotated Indiana Code; Titles 31,
Article 1, Chapter 11.5-21.

Child Support

Guideline model:
Income Shares.

Whose income is used?
Combined.

How is base income calculated?
Adjusted Gross.

Is income verification required?
Yes.

Delinquencies:
Parents (per thousand): 94
Rank: 1

Statutes:
Annotated Indiana Code; Title 31,
Article 1, Chapter 11.5-12.

Addresses

Indiana State Bar Association
230 E. Ohio Street, 4th Flr.
Indianapolis, IN 46204
(317) 639-5465

Child Support Enforcement Division
Department of Public Welfare
402 West Washington St., Rm. W360
Indianapolis, IN 46204
(317) 232-4885

REGION V
OCSE Regional Representative
105 W. Adams St., 20th Floor
Chicago, IL 60606
(312) 353-4237

Iowa

Child Custody

Age of majority:
18

How is custody divided?
Legal and physical separate.

Is mediation authorized?
Yes.

Will mediation be confidential?
Yes.

Is joint custody allowed?
Permitted despite one parent
objecting.

**Will a custody evaluation be
required?**
Not specified.

**Are the child's preferences
considered?**
Yes.

Statutes:
Iowa Code Annotated; Section 598.41.

Child Support

Guideline model:
Income Shares.

Whose income is used?
Combined.

How is base income calculated?
Net.

Is income verification required?
No.

Delinquencies:
Parents (per thousand): 41
Rank: 11

Statutes:
Iowa Code Annotated; Section 598.21.

Addresses

The Iowa State Bar Association
521 E. Locust
Des Moines, IA 50309
(515) 243-3179

Bureau of Collections
Iowa Department of Human Services
Hoover Building - 5th Floor
Des Moines, IA 50319
(515) 281-5580

REGION VII
OCSE Regional Representative
601 East 12th Street
Federal Building, Room 515
Kansas City, MO 64106
(816) 426-2806

Kansas

Child Custody

Age of majority:
18

How is custody divided?
Legal and physical combined.

Is mediation authorized?
Yes.

Will mediation be confidential?
Yes.

Is joint custody allowed?
Available if both parents agree.

Will a custody evaluation be required?
Court ordered.

Are the child's preferences considered?
Yes.

Statutes:
Kansas Statutes Annotated; Chapter 60, Article 16, Subject 1610.

Child Support

Guideline model:
Income Shares.

Whose income is used?
Combined.

How is base income calculated?
Adjusted Gross.

Is income verification required?
Yes.

Delinquencies:
Parents (per thousand): 24
Rank: 24

Statutes:
Kansas Statutes Annotated; Chapter 20, Subject 165 and Chapter 60, Article 16, Subject 1610.

Addresses

Kansas Bar Association
P.O. Box 1037 (66601-1037)
1200 Harrison Street
Topeka, KS 66612
(913) 234-5696

Division of Child Support Enforcement
Dept. of Social & Rehabilitation Services
Biddle Building
300 South West Oakley St.
P.O. Box 497
Topeka, KS 66603
(913) 296-3237

REGION VII
OCSE Regional Representative
601 East 12th Street
Federal Building, Room 515
Kansas City, MO 64106
(816) 426-2806

Kentucky

Child Custody

Age of majority:
18

How is custody divided?
Legal and physical combined.

Is mediation authorized?
Yes.

Will mediation be confidential?
Not specified.

Is joint custody allowed?
Available if both parents agree.

Will a custody evaluation be required?
Court ordered.

Are the child's preferences considered?
Yes.

Statutes:
Kentucky Revised Statutes; Title 35, Chapter 403.270.

Child Support

Guideline model:
Income Shares.

Whose income is used?
Combined.

How is base income calculated?
Adjusted Gross.

Is income verification required?
Yes.

Delinquencies:
Parents (per thousand): 39
Rank: 13

Statutes:
Kentucky Revised Statutes;
Title 35, Chapters 403.210, 403.211, and 403.212.

Addresses

Kentucky Bar Association
514 West Main
Frankfort, KY 40601-1883
(502) 564-3795

Division of Child Support Enforcement
Department of Social Insurance
Cabinet for Human Resources
275 East Main Street
6th Floor East
Frankfort, KY 40621
(502) 564-2285

REGION IV
OCSE Regional Representative
101 Marietta Tower, Suite 821
Atlanta, GA 30323
(404) 331-5733

Louisiana

Child Custody

Age of majority:
18

How is custody divided?
Legal and physical combined.

Is mediation authorized?
Yes.

Will mediation be confidential?
Yes.

Is joint custody allowed?
Available if both parents agree.

Will a custody evaluation be required?
Not specified.

Are the child's preferences considered?
Yes.

Statutes:
Louisiana Civil Code Annotated, Articles 131, 132, 133, and 134.

Child Support

Guideline model:
Income Shares.

Whose income is used?
Combined.

How is base income calculated?
Adjusted Gross.

Is income verification required?
Yes.

Delinquencies:
Parents (per thousand): 25
Rank: 23

Statutes:
Louisiana Revised Statutes Annotated, Article 9; Sections 302+.

Addresses

Louisiana State Bar Association
601 St. Charles Ave.
New Orleans, LA 70130
(504) 566-1600

Support Enforcement Services
Department of Social Services
P.O. Box 94065
Baton Rouge, LA 70804
(504) 342-4780

REGION VI
OCSE Regional Representative
1200 Main Tower Building
Suite 1700
Dallas, TX 75202
(214) 767-9648

Maine

Child Custody

Age of majority:
18

How is custody divided?
Legal and physical combined.

Is mediation authorized?
Yes.

Will mediation be confidential?
Not specified.

Is joint custody allowed?
Available if both parents agree.

Will a custody evaluation be required?
Not specified.

Are the child's preferences considered?
Yes.

Statutes:
Maine Revised Statutes Annotated: Title 19, Sections 751 and 752.

Child Support

Guideline model:
Income Shares.

Whose income is used?
Combined.

How is base income calculated?
Adjusted Gross.

Is income verification required?
Yes.

Delinquencies:
Parents (per thousand): 38
Rank: 14

Statutes:
Maine Revised Statutes Annotated: Title 19, Sections 311-319, and 752(10).

Addresses

Maine State Bar Association
PO. Box 788 (04332-0788)
124 State St.
Augusta, ME 04330
(207) 622-7523

Support Enforcement and Recovery
Department of Human Services
State House, Station 11
Augusta, ME 04333
(207) 289-2886

REGION I
OCSE Regional Representative
John F. Kennedy Federal Building
23rd Floor, Room 2303
Boston, MA 02203
(617) 565-2463

Maryland

Child Custody

Age of majority:
18

How is custody divided?
Legal and physical combined.

Is mediation authorized?
Yes.

Will mediation be confidential?
Yes.

Is joint custody allowed?
Available if both parents agree.

Will a custody evaluation be required?
Court ordered.

Are the child's preferences considered?
No.

Statutes:
Annotated Code of Maryland; Family Law, Title 7, Sections 5-203, 8-207, 8-208, and 9-101.

Child Support

Guideline model:
Income Shares.

Whose income is used?
Combined.

How is base income calculated?
Adjusted Gross.

Is income verification required?
No.

Delinquencies:
Parents (per thousand): 48
Rank: 7

Statutes:
Annotated Code of Maryland; Family Law, Title 7, Sections 12-101, 12-201, 12-202, 12-203, 12-204 and 8-206.

Addresses

Maryland State Bar Association
520 W. Fayette St.
Baltimore, MD 21201
(410) 685-7878

Child Support Enforcement
Administration
Department of Human Resources
311 W. Saratoga St.
Baltimore, MD 21201
(401) 333-3979

REGION III
OCSE Regional Representative
P.O. Box 8436
3535 Market Street
Room 4119 MS/15
Philadelphia, PA 19101
(215) 596-4365

Massachusetts

Child Custody

Age of majority:
18

How is custody divided?
Legal and physical combined.

Is mediation authorized?
No.

Will mediation be confidential?
Not specified.

Is joint custody allowed?
Permitted despite one parent
objecting.

**Will a custody evaluation be
required?**
Not specified.

**Are the child's preferences
considered?**
No.

Statutes:
Massachusetts General Laws
Annotated; Chapter 208, Sections 28
and 31.

Child Support

Guideline model:
Varying Percent.

Whose income is used?
Noncustodial.

How is base income calculated?
Adjusted Gross.

Is income verification required?
No.

Delinquencies:
Parents (per thousand): 24
Rank: 24

Statutes:
Massachusetts General Laws Annotated;
Chapter 208,
Section 28.

Addresses

Massachusetts Bar Association
20 West St.
Boston, MA 02111-1218
(617) 542-3602

Child Support Enforcement Division
Department of Revenue
141 Portland St.
Cambridge, MA 02139
(617) 621-4200

REGION I
OCSE Regional Representative
John F. Kennedy Federal Building
23rd Floor, Room 2303
Boston, MA 02203
(617) 565-2463

Michigan

Child Custody

Age of majority:
18

How is custody divided?
Legal and physical combined.

Is mediation authorized?
Yes.

Will mediation be confidential?
Yes.

Is joint custody allowed?
Permitted despite one parent
objecting.

**Will a custody evaluation be
required?**
Court ordered.

**Are the child's preferences
considered?**
Yes.

Statutes:
Michigan Compiled Laws Annotated;
Sections 552.16, 722.23 and 722.26a.

Child Support

Guideline model:
Income Shares.

Whose income is used?
Combined.

How is base income calculated?
Net.

Is income verification required?
Yes.

Delinquencies:
Parents (per thousand): 61
Rank: 3

Statutes:
Michigan Compiled Laws Annotated;
Sections 552.1 5, 552.16, 552.452, and
552.519.

Addresses

State Bar of Michigan
306 Townsend St.
Lansing, MI 48933-2083
(517) 372-9030

Office of Child Support
Department of Social Services
235 Grand Avenue, Suite 1046
P.O. Box 30037
Lansing, MI 48909
(517) 373-7570

REGION V
OCSE Regional Representative
105 W. Adams St., 20th Floor
Chicago, IL 60606
(312) 353-4237

Minnesota

Child Custody

Age of majority:
18

How is custody divided?
Legal and physical separate.

Is mediation authorized?
Yes.

Will mediation be confidential?
Yes.

Is joint custody allowed?
Permitted despite one parent
objecting.

**Will a custody evaluation be
required?**
Court ordered.

**Are the child's preferences
considered?**
Yes.

Statutes:
Minnesota Statutes Annotated; Chapter
518.17.

Child Support

Guideline model:
Varying Percent.

Whose income is used?
Noncustodial.

How is base income calculated?
Net.

Is income verification required?
No.

Delinquencies:
Parents (per thousand): 33
Rank: 18

Statutes:
Minnesota Statutes Annotated; Chapters
518.551 and 518.552.

Addresses

Minnesota State Bar
Association
514 Nicollet Mall
Suite 300
Minneapolis, MN 55402
(612) 333-1183

Office of Child Support Enforcement
Department of Human Services
444 Lafayette
4th Floor
St. Paul, MN 55155-3846
(612) 296-2499

REGION V
OCSE Regional Representative
105 W. Adams St., 20th Floor
Chicago, IL 60606
(312) 353-4237

Mississippi

Child Custody

Age of majority:
21

How is custody divided?
Legal and physical separate.

Is mediation authorized?
Yes.

Will mediation be confidential?
Yes.

Is joint custody allowed?
Permitted despite one parent objecting.

Will a custody evaluation be required?
Not specified.

Are the child's preferences considered?
No.

Statutes:
Mississippi Code Annotated; Section 93, Chapters 5-23, 5-24, and 11-65.

Child Support

Guideline model:
Fixed Percent.

Whose income is used?
Noncustodial.

How is base income calculated?
Adjusted Gross.

Is income verification required?
No.

Delinquencies:
Parents (per thousand): 37
Rank: 15

Statutes:
Mississippi Code Annotated; Section 93, Chapters 5-23, and 11-65.

Addresses

Mississippi State Bar
P.O. Box 2168 (39225-2168)
643 N State Street
Jackson, MS 39202
(601) 948-4471

Child Support Division
Department of Human Services
515 E. Amite Street
P.O. Box 352
Jackson, MS 39205
(601) 354-0341

REGION IV
OCSE Regional Representative
101 Marietta Tower, Suite 821
Atlanta, GA 30323
(404) 331-5733

Missouri

Child Custody

Age of majority:
18

How is custody divided?
Legal and physical separate.

Is mediation authorized?
Yes.

Will mediation be confidential?
Yes.

Is joint custody allowed?
Permitted despite one parent objecting.

Will a custody evaluation be required?
Court ordered.

Are the child's preferences considered?
Yes.

Statutes:
Annotated Missouri Statutes; Title 30, Chapter 452, Sections 375 and 400.

Child Support

Guideline model:
Income Shares.

Whose income is used?
Combined.

How is base income calculated?
Adjusted Gross.

Is income verification required?
No.

Delinquencies:
Parents (per thousand): 43
Rank: 10

Statutes:
Annotated Missouri Statutes; Title 30, Chapter 452, Sections 340, 345, and 353.

Addresses

The Missouri Bar
P.O. Box 119 (65102)
326 Monroe
Jefferson City, MO 65102
(314) 635-4128

Division of Child Support Enforcement
Department of Social Services
P.O. Box 1527
Jefferson City, MO 65102-1527
(314) 751-4301

REGION VII
OCSE Regional Representative
601 East 12th Street
Federal Building, Room 515
Kansas City, MO 64106
(816) 426-2806

Montana

Child Custody

Age of majority:
18

How is custody divided?
Legal and physical combined.

Is mediation authorized?
Yes.

Will mediation be confidential?
Yes.

Is joint custody allowed?
Permitted despite one parent objecting.

Will a custody evaluation be required?
Not specified.

Are the child's preferences considered?
Yes.

Statutes:
Montana Code Annotated; Section 40, Titles 4-212, and 4-223.

Child Support

Guideline model:
Income Shares.

Whose income is used?
Combined.

How is base income calculated?
Net.

Is income verification required?
Yes.

Delinquencies:
Parents (per thousand): 18
Rank: 28

Statutes:
Montana Code Annotated; Section 40, Title 4-204.

Addresses

State Bar of Montana
P.O. Box 577 (59624)
46 North Last Chance Gulch
Helena, MT 59624
(406) 442-7660

Child Support Enforcement Program
Department of Social & Rehabilitation Services
P.O. Box 5955
Helena, MT 59604
(406) 444-4614

REGION VIII
OCSE Regional Representative
Federal Office Building, Room 1185
1961 Stout Street
Denver, CO 80294
(303) 844-5594

Nebraska

Child Custody

Age of majority:
19

How is custody divided?
Legal and physical combined.

Is mediation authorized?
No.

Will mediation be confidential?
Not specified.

Is joint custody allowed?
Permitted despite one parent objecting.

Will a custody evaluation be required?
Court ordered.

Are the child's preferences considered?
Yes.

Statutes:
Revised Statutes of Nebraska; Chapter 42, Section 364.

Child Support

Guideline model:
Income Shares.

Whose income is used?
Combined.

How is base income calculated?
Net.

Is income verification required?
Yes.

Delinquencies:
Parents (per thousand): 40
Rank: 12

Statutes:
Revised Statutes of Nebraska; Chapter 42, Section 364.

Addresses

Nebraska State Bar Association
P.O. Box 81809 (68501)
635 S. 14th Street, 2nd Floor
Lincoln, NE 68508
(402) 475-7091

Child Support Enforcement Office
Department of Social Services
P.O. Box 95026
Lincoln, NE 68509
(402) 471-9125

REGION VII
OCSE Regional Representative
601 East 12th Street
Federal Building, Room 515
Kansas City, MO 64106
(816) 426-2806

Nevada

Child Custody

Age of majority:
18

How is custody divided?
Legal and physical combined.

Is mediation authorized?
Yes.

Will mediation be confidential?
Yes.

Is joint custody allowed?
Available if both parents agree.

Will a custody evaluation be required?
Court ordered.

Are the child's preferences considered?
Yes.

Statutes:
Nevada Revised Statutes; Chapter 125; Sections 480 and 490.

Child Support

Guideline model:
Fixed Percent.

Whose income is used?
Noncustodial.

How is base income calculated?
Gross.

Is income verification required?
Yes.

Delinquencies:
Parents (per thousand): 29
Rank: 20

Statutes:
Nevada Revised Statutes; Chapter 125; Section 230 and Chapter 125B, Section 070, 080, and 090.

Addresses

State Bar of Nevada
201 Las Vegas Blvd. Suite 200
Las Vegas, NV 89101
(702) 382-2200

Child Support Enforcement Program
Department of Human Resources
2527 N. Carson Street
Capital Complex
Carson City, NV 89710
(702) 885-4744

REGION IX
OCSE Regional Representative
50 United Nations Plaza
Mail Stop 351
San Francisco, CA 94102
(415) 556-5176

New Hampshire

Child Custody

Age of majority:
18

How is custody divided?
Legal and physical separate.

Is mediation authorized?
No.

Will mediation be confidential?
Not specified.

Is joint custody allowed?
Required unless health or safety compromised.

Will a custody evaluation be required?
Not specified.

Are the child's preferences considered?
Yes.

Statutes:
New Hampshire Revised Statutes Annotated; Chapter 458:17.

Child Support

Guideline model:
Income Shares.

Whose income is used?
Combined.

How is base income calculated?
Net.

Is income verification required?
No.

Delinquencies:
Parents (per thousand): 25
Rank: 23

Statutes:
New Hampshire Revised Statutes Annotated; Chapters 458:17, 458:18, 458-C:1-5.

Addresses

New Hampshire Bar Association
112 Pleasant St.
Concord, NH 03301
(603) 224-6942

Child Support Enforcement Services
Division of Human Services
Health & Welfare Building
6 Hazen Drive
Concord, NH 03301
(603) 271-4426

REGION I
OCSE Regional Representative
John F. Kennedy Federal Building
23rd Floor, Room 2303
Boston, MA 02203
(617) 565-2463

New Jersey

Child Custody

Age of majority:
18

How is custody divided?
Legal and physical separate.

Is mediation authorized?
Yes.

Will mediation be confidential?
Yes.

Is joint custody allowed?
Permitted despite one parent objecting.

Will a custody evaluation be required?
Court ordered.

Are the child's preferences considered?
No.

Statutes:
New Jersey Statutes Annotated; Title 2A, Chapter 34-23.

Child Support

Guideline model:
Income Shares.

Whose income is used?
Combined.

How is base income calculated?
Net.

Is income verification required?
Yes.

Delinquencies:
Parents (per thousand): 43
Rank: 10

Statutes:
New Jersey Statutes Annotated; Title 2A, Chapter 34-23.

Addresses

New Jersey State Bar Association
One Constitution Square
New Brunswick, NJ 08901-1500
(908) 249-5000

Division of Economic Assistance
Department of Human Services
Bureau of Child Support and Paternity Programs
CN 716
Trenton, NJ 08625
(609) 588-2361

REGION II
OCSE Regional Representative
Federal Building, Room 4048
26 Federal Plaza
New York, NY 10278
(212) 264-2890

New Mexico

Child Custody

Age of majority:
18

How is custody divided?
Legal and physical combined.

Is mediation authorized?
Yes.

Will mediation be confidential?
Not specified.

Is joint custody allowed?
Required unless health or safety compromised.

Will a custody evaluation be required?
Court ordered.

Are the child's preferences considered?
Yes.

Statutes:
New Mexico Statutes Annotated; Article 4, Section 40-4-9-9.1.

Child Support

Guideline model:
Income Shares.

Whose income is used?
Combined.

How is base income calculated?
Gross.

Is income verification required?
No.

Delinquencies:
Parents (per thousand): 9
Rank: 31

Statutes:
New Mexico Statutes Annotated; Article 4, Sections Section 27-2-27, 40-4-7, 40-4-11 and 40-4-11.1.

Addresses

State Bar of New Mexico
P.O. Box 25883
Albuquerque, NM 87125
(505) 842-6132

Child Support Enforcement Division
Department of Human Services
P.O. Box 25109
Santa Fe, NM 87504
(505) 827-7200

REGION VI
OCSE Regional Representative
1200 Main Tower Building
Suite 1700
Dallas, TX 75202
(214) 767-9648

New York

Child Custody

Age of majority:
18

How is custody divided?
Legal and physical combined.

Is mediation authorized?
No.

Will mediation be confidential?
Not specified.

Is joint custody allowed?
Available if both parents agree.

Will a custody evaluation be required?
Not specified.

Are the child's preferences considered?
No.

Statutes:
Consolidated Laws of New York Annotated; Domestic Relations Law, Volume 8, Section 240.

Child Support

Guideline model:
Income Shares.

Whose income is used?
Combined.

How is base income calculated?
Net.

Is income verification required?
Yes.

Delinquencies:
Parents (per thousand): 35
Rank: 16

Statutes:
Consolidated Laws of New York Annotated; Domestic Relations Law, Volume 8, Sections 32, 33, 236-Part B, 240, and 243.

Addresses

New York State Bar Association
One Elk St.
Albany, NY 12207
(518) 463-3200

Office of Child Support Enforcement
New York State Dept. of Social Services
P.O. Box 14
1 Commerce Plaza
Albany, NY 12260
(518) 474-9081

REGION II
OCSE Regional Representative
Federal Building, Room 4048
26 Federal Plaza
New York, NY 10278
(212) 264-2890

North Carolina

Child Custody

Age of majority:
18

How is custody divided?
Legal and physical combined.

Is mediation authorized?
Yes.

Will mediation be confidential?
Yes.

Is joint custody allowed?
Available if both parents agree.

Will a custody evaluation be required?
Not specified.

Are the child's preferences considered?
No.

Statutes:
General Statutes of North Carolina; Chapter 50, Section 50-13.2.

Child Support

Guideline model:
Fixed Percent.

Whose income is used?
Noncustodial.

How is base income calculated?
Gross.

Is income verification required?
No.

Delinquencies:
Parents (per thousand): 25
Rank: 23

Statutes:
General Statutes of North Carolina; Chapter 50, Section 50-13.4.

Addresses

North Carolina State Bar
P.O. Box 25908 (27611)
208 Fayetteville Street Mall
Raleigh, NC 27611
(919) 828-4620

North Carolina Bar Association
P.O. Box 12806 (27605)
1312 Annapolis Drive
Raleigh, NC 27608
(919) 828-0561

Child Support Enforcement Section
Division of Social Services
Dept. of Human Resources
Anderson Plaza
100 East Six Forks Rd.
Raleigh, NC 27609-7750
(919) 571-4120

REGION IV
OCSE Regional Representative
101 Marietta Tower, Suite 821
Atlanta, GA 30323
(404) 331-5733

North Dakota

Child Custody

Age of majority:
18

How is custody divided?
Legal and physical combined.

Is mediation authorized?
Yes.

Will mediation be confidential?
Yes.

Is joint custody allowed?
No statutes.s

Will a custody evaluation be required?
Court ordered.

Are the child's preferences considered?
Yes.

Statutes:
North Dakota Century Code; Volume 3A, Chapters 14-05-22, 14-09-06, 14-09-06.1 and 14-09-06.2.

Child Support

Guideline model:
Varying Percent.

Whose income is used?
Noncustodial.

How is base income calculated?
Net.

Is income verification required?
Yes.

Delinquencies:
Parents (per thousand): 41
Rank: 11

Statutes:
North Dakota Century Code; Volume 3A, Chapters 14-08-07, 14-09-08, 14-09-08.1, 14-09-08.4, 14-09-09.1, 14-09-09.2, and 14-09-09.7.

Addresses

State Bar Association of North Dakota
515-1/2 E. Broadway
Suite 101
Bismarck, ND 58502
(701) 255-1404

Child Support Enforcement Agency
Department of Human Services
P.O. Box 7190
Bismarck, ND 58507
(701) 224-3582

REGION VIII
OCSE Regional Representative
Federal Office Building, Room 1185
1961 Stout Street
Denver, CO 80294
(303) 844-5594

Ohio

Child Custody

Age of majority:
18

How is custody divided?
Legal and physical separate.

Is mediation authorized?
Yes.

Will mediation be confidential?
Yes.

Is joint custody allowed?
Permitted despite one parent objecting.

Will a custody evaluation be required?
Court ordered.

Are the child's preferences considered?
Yes.

Statutes:
Ohio Revised Code Annotated; Sections 3105.21, 3109.03, 3109.04, and 3109.051.

Child Support

Guideline model:
Income Shares.

Whose income is used?
Combined.

How is base income calculated?
Adjusted Gross.

Is income verification required?
Yes.

Delinquencies:
Parents (per thousand): 51
Rank: 5

Statutes:
Ohio Revised Code Annotated; Sections 3105.71, 3113.215, and 3113.217.

Addresses

Ohio State Bar Association
P.O. Box 6562 (43216-6562)
1700 Lake Shore Drive
Columbus, OH 43216-6562
(614) 487-2050

Bureau of Child Support
Ohio Dept. of Human Services
State Office Tower - 27th Floor
30 East Broad Street
Columbus, OH 43266-0423
(614) 752-6561

REGION V
OCSE Regional Representative
105 W. Adams St., 20th Floor
Chicago, IL 60606
(312) 353-4237

Oklahoma

Child Custody

Age of majority:
18

How is custody divided?
Legal and physical combined.

Is mediation authorized?
No.

Will mediation be confidential?
Not specified.

Is joint custody allowed?
Permitted despite one parent objecting.

Will a custody evaluation be required?
Not specified.

Are the child's preferences considered?
Yes.

Statutes:
Oklahoma Statutes Annotated; Title 10, Section 21.1 and Title 43, Section 109.

Child Support

Guideline model:
Income Shares.

Whose income is used?
Combined.

How is base income calculated?
Adjusted Gross.

Is income verification required?
No.

Delinquencies:
Parents (per thousand): 17
Rank: 29

Statutes:
Oklahoma Statutes Annotated; Title 43, Sections 110, 112, 118, 119, 121, and 136; and Title 56, Sections 235+.

Addresses

Oklahoma Bar Association
P.O. Box 53036 (73152)
1901 N. Lincoln
Oklahoma City, OK 73105
(405) 524-2365

Child Support Enforcement Division
Department of Human Services
P.O. Box 25352
Oklahoma City, OK 73125
(405) 424-5871

REGION VI
OCSE Regional Representative
1200 Main Tower Building
Suite 1700
Dallas, TX 75202
(214) 767-9648

Oregon

Child Custody

Age of majority:
18

How is custody divided?
Legal and physical combined.

Is mediation authorized?
Yes.

Will mediation be confidential?
Yes.

Is joint custody allowed?
Available if both parents agree.

Will a custody evaluation be required?
Not specified.

Are the child's preferences considered?
No.

Statutes:
Oregon Revised Statutes; Volume 2, Sections 107.105, 107.137, and 107.169.

Child Support

Guideline model:
Income Shares.

Whose income is used?
Combined.

How is base income calculated?
Adjusted Gross.

Is income verification required?
Yes.

Delinquencies:
Parents (per thousand): 40
Rank: 12

Statutes:
Oregon Revised Statutes; Volume 2, Sections 25.275, 107.105, and 107.820.

Addresses

Oregon State Bar
P.O. Box 1689
Lake Oswego, OR 97035
(503) 620-0222

Recovery Services Section
Adult and Family Services Division
Department of Human Resources
P.O. Box 14506
Salem, OR 97309
(503) 378-5439

REGION X
OCSE Regional Representative
2201 Sixth Avenue
Mail Stop RX-70
Seattle, WA 98121
(206) 553-2775

Pennsylvania

Child Custody

Age of majority:
21

How is custody divided?
Legal and physical separate.

Is mediation authorized?
Yes.

Will mediation be confidential?
Not specified.

Is joint custody allowed?
Available if both parents agree.

Will a custody evaluation be required?
Court ordered.

Are the child's preferences considered?
No.

Statutes:
Pennsylvania Consolidated Statutes Annotated, Title 23, Sections 5302, 5303, 5304, and 5305.

Child Support

Guideline model:
Income Shares.

Whose income is used?
Combined.

How is base income calculated?
Net.

Is income verification required?
No.

Delinquencies:
Parents (per thousand): 44
Rank: 9

Statutes:
Pennsylvania Consolidated Statutes Annotated, Title 23, Sections 4322.

Addresses

Pennsylvania Bar Association
P.O. Box 186 (17108)
100 South Street
Harrisburg, PA 17108
(717) 238-6715

Bureau of Child Support Enforcement
Department of Public Welfare
P.O. Box 8018
Harrisburg, PA 17105
(717) 783-3672

REGION III
OCSE Regional Representative
P.O. Box 8436
3535 Market Street, Room 4119 MS/15
Philadelphia, PA 19101
(215) 596-4365

Rhode Island

Child Custody

Age of majority:
18

How is custody divided?
Legal and physical combined.

Is mediation authorized?
Yes.

Will mediation be confidential?
Yes.

Is joint custody allowed?
No statutes.

Will a custody evaluation be required?
Not specified.

Are the child's preferences considered?
No.

Statutes:
General Laws of Rhode Island; Title 15, Chapter 15-5-16.

Child Support

Guideline model:
Income Shares.

Whose income is used?
Combined.

How is base income calculated?
Adjusted Gross.

Is income verification required?
No.

Delinquencies:
Parents (per thousand): 34
Rank: 17

Statutes:
General Laws of Rhode Island; Title 15, Chapters 15-5-16.1, 15-5-16.2, 15-5-16.6, 15-5-22, and 15-9-1

Addresses

Rhode Island Bar Association
115 Cedar Street
Providence, RI 02903
(401) 421-5740

Bureau of Family Support
Department of Human Services
77 Dorance Street
Providence, RI 02903
(401) 277-2409

REGION I
OCSE Regional Representative
John F. Kennedy Federal Building
23rd Floor, Room 2303
Boston, MA 02203
(617) 565-2463

South Carolina

Child Custody

Age of majority:
18

How is custody divided?
Legal and physical combined.

Is mediation authorized?
Yes.

Will mediation be confidential?
Not specified.

Is joint custody allowed?
Available if both parents agree.

Will a custody evaluation be required?
Not specified.

Are the child's preferences considered?
No.

Statutes:
Code of Laws of South Carolina; Chapter 3, Sections 20-3-160, 20-7-100 and 20-7-1520.

Child Support

Guideline model:
Income Shares.

Whose income is used?
Combined.

How is base income calculated?
Adjusted Gross.

Is income verification required?
Yes.

Delinquencies:
Parents (per thousand): 20
Rank: 27

Statutes:
Code of Laws of South Carolina; Chapter 3, Sections 20-3-160, 20-7-40, 20-7-100, 20-7-852, 20-7-1315, and 43-5-580.

Addresses

South Carolina Bar Association
P.O. Box 608 (29202)
950 Taylor Street
Columbia, SC 29202
(803) 799-6653

Child Support Enforcement Division
Department of Social Services
P.O. Box 1520
Columbia, SC 29202-9988
(803) 737-9938

REGION IV
OCSE Regional Representative
101 Marietta Tower, Suite 821
Atlanta, GA 30323
(404) 331-5733

South Dakota

Child Custody

Age of majority:
18

How is custody divided?
Legal and physical combined.

Is mediation authorized?
Yes.

Will mediation be confidential?
Not specified.

Is joint custody allowed?
Permitted despite one parent
objecting.

**Will a custody evaluation be
required?**
Court ordered.

**Are the child's preferences
considered?**
Yes.

Statutes:
South Dakota Codified Laws; Title 25,
Chapters 25-3-11, 25-4-25, 25-4-45.1,
and 25-5-7.1-7.3.

Child Support

Guideline model:
Income Shares.

Whose income is used?
Combined.

How is base income calculated?
Net.

Is income verification required?
No.

Delinquencies:
Parents (per thousand): 31
Rank: 19

Statutes:
South Dakota Codified Laws; Title 25,
Chapters 25-3-11, 25-4-38, 25-4-45, 25-
7-6.2 to 25-7-6.12, and 25-7A-9.

Addresses

State Bar of South Dakota
222 E. Capitol
Pierre, SD 57501
(605) 224-7554

Office of Child Support Enforcement
Dept. of Social Services
700 Governors Drive
Pierre, SD 57501-2291
(605) 773-3641

REGION VIII
OCSE Regional Representative
Federal Office Building, Room 1185
1961 Stout Street
Denver, CO 80294
(303) 844-5594

Tennessee

Child Custody

Age of majority:
18

How is custody divided?
Legal and physical combined.

Is mediation authorized?
No.

Will mediation be confidential?
Not specified.

Is joint custody allowed?
Available if both parents agree.

Will a custody evaluation be required?
Not specified.

Are the child's preferences considered?
No.

Statutes:
Tennessee Code Annotated; Volume 6A, Title 36, Sections 36-6-101 and 36-6-102.

Child Support

Guideline model:
Fixed Percent.

Whose income is used?
Noncustodial.

How is base income calculated?
Net.

Is income verification required?
No.

Delinquencies:
Parents (per thousand): 50
Rank: 6

Statutes:
Tennessee Code Annotated; Volume 6A, Title 36, Sections 36-5-101, 36-5-501, 36-5-604.

Addresses

Tennessee Bar Association
3622 West End Avenue
Nashville, TN 37205
(615) 383-7421

Child Support Services
Department of Human Services
Citizens Plaza Bldg. - 12th Floor
400 Deadrick Street
Nashville, TN 37219
(615) 741-1820

REGION IV
OCSE Regional Representative
101 Marietta Tower, Suite 821
Atlanta, GA 30323
(404) 331-5733

Texas

Child Custody

Age of majority:
18

How is custody divided?
Legal and physical separate.

Is mediation authorized?
Yes.

Will mediation be confidential?
Not specified.

Is joint custody allowed?
Available if both parents agree.

Will a custody evaluation be required?
Not specified.

Are the child's preferences considered?
Yes (age 12).

Statutes:
Texas Codes Annotated; Family Code, Chapters 3.55, 14.01, 14.03, 14.021, 14.032, 14.033, 14.034, and 36.02.

Child Support

Guideline model:
Fixed Percent.

Whose income is used?
Noncustodial.

How is base income calculated?
Net.

Is income verification required?
Yes.

Delinquencies:
Parents (per thousand): 15
Rank: 30

Statutes:
Texas Codes Annotated;
Family Code, Chapters 14.05, 14.051-14.058, and 14.061.

Addresses

State Bar of Texas
P.O. Box 12487 (78711)
1414 Colorado
Austin, TX 78701
(512)463-1463
(800) 204-2222

Child Support Enforcement Division
Office of the Attorney General
P.O. Box 12017
Austin, TX 78711-2017
(512) 463-2181

REGION VI
OCSE Regional Representative
1200 Main Tower Building
Suite 1700
Dallas, TX 75202
(214) 767-9648

Utah

Child Custody

Age of majority:
18

How is custody divided?
Legal and physical separate.

Is mediation authorized?
Yes.

Will mediation be confidential?
Yes.

Is joint custody allowed?
Permitted despite one parent objecting.

Will a custody evaluation be required?
Court ordered.

Are the child's preferences considered?
Yes.

Statutes:
Utah Code Annotated; Sections 30-2-10, 30-3-5, 30-3-5.2, 30-3-10.1, 30-3-10.2, and 30-3-10.3.

Child Support

Guideline model:
Income Shares.

Whose income is used?
Combined.

How is base income calculated?
Adjusted Gross.

Is income verification required?
Yes.

Delinquencies:
Parents (per thousand): 29
Rank: 20

Statutes:
Utah Code Annotated; Sections 30-3-5, 30-3-5.1, 78-45-7 to 78-45-7.5.

Addresses

Utah State Bar
645 S. 200 East, #310
Salt Lake City, UT 84111
(801) 531-9077

Office of Recovery Services
Department of Social Services
120 North 200 West
P.O. Box 45011
Salt Lake City, UT 84145-0011
(801) 538-4400

REGION VIII
OCSE Regional Representative
Federal Office Building
Room 1185
1961 Stout Street
Denver, CO 80294
(303) 844-5594

Vermont

Child Custody

Age of majority:
18

How is custody divided?
Legal and physical combined.

Is mediation authorized?
No.

Will mediation be confidential?
Not specified.

Is joint custody allowed?
Available if both parents agree.

Will a custody evaluation be required?
Not specified.

Are the child's preferences considered?
No.

Statutes:
Vermont Statutes Annotated; Title 15, Section 664.

Child Support

Guideline model:
Income Shares.

Whose income is used?
Combined.

How is base income calculated?
Adjusted Gross.

Is income verification required?
Yes.

Delinquencies:
Parents (per thousand): 28
Rank: 21

Statutes:
Vermont Statutes Annotated; Title 15, Sections 653-669, 757, and 781-783, Title 33, Section 4103.

Addresses

Vermont Bar Association
RO. Box 100 (05601)
35-37 Court Street
Montpelier, VT 05602
(802) 223-2020

Child Support Division
Agency of Human Services
103 South Main Street
Waterbury, VT 05676
(802) 241-2319

REGION I
OCSE Regional Representative
John F. Kennedy Federal Building
23rd Floor, Room 2303
Boston, MA 02203
(617) 565-2463

Virginia

Child Custody

Age of majority:
18

How is custody divided?
Legal and physical separate.

Is mediation authorized?
Yes.

Will mediation be confidential?
Yes.

Is joint custody allowed?
No statutes.

Will a custody evaluation be required?
Court ordered.

Are the child's preferences considered?
No.

Statutes:
Code of Virginia; Title 20, Section 20-107.2.

Child Support

Guideline model:
Income Shares.

Whose income is used?
Combined.

How is base income calculated?
Adjusted Gross.

Is income verification required?
No.

Delinquencies:
Parents (per thousand): 31
Rank: 19

Statutes:
Code of Virginia; Title 20, Sections 20-107.2, 20-108.1, and 20-108.2.

Addresses

Virginia State Bar
707 E. Main Street
Suite 1500
Richmond, VA 23219-2803
(804) 775-0500

Virginia Bar Association
7th & Franklin Bldg.
701 E. Franklin St., #1515
Richmond, VA 23219
(804) 644-0041

Division of Support Enforcement
Department of Social Services
8007 Discovery Drive
Richmond, VA 23288
(804) 662-9629

REGION III
OCSE Regional Representative
P.O. Box 8436
3535 Market Street
Room 4119 MS/15
Philadelphia, PA 19101
(215) 596-4365

Washington

Child Custody

Age of majority:
18

How is custody divided?
Legal and physical combined.

Is mediation authorized?
Yes.

Will mediation be confidential?
Yes.

Is joint custody allowed?
Available if both parents agree.

Will a custody evaluation be required?
Court ordered.

Are the child's preferences considered?
No.

Statutes:
Revised Code of Washington Annotated; Title 26, Chapters 26.09.050, and 26.09.181-26.09.220.

Child Support

Guideline model:
Income Shares.

Whose income is used?
Combined.

How is base income calculated?
Net.

Is income verification required?
Yes.

Delinquencies:
Parents (per thousand): 45
Rank: 8

Statutes:
Revised Code of Washington Annotated; Title 26, Chapters 26.09.050, 26.09.100, 26.09.120, 26.18.070, 26.19.040, 26.23.050, and 26.23.135.

Addresses

Washington State Bar Association
500 Westin Bldg.
2001 6th Ave.
Seattle, WA 98121-2599
(206) 727-8200

Revenue Division
Department of Social & Health Services
P.O. Box 9162
Mailstop HJ-31
Olympia, WA 98507
(206) 459-6481

REGION X
OCSE Regional Representative
2201 Sixth Avenue
Mail Stop RX-70
Seattle, WA 98121
(206) 553-2775

West Virginia

Child Custody

Age of majority:
21

How is custody divided?
Legal and physical separate.

Is mediation authorized?
Yes.

Will mediation be confidential?
Not specified.

Is joint custody allowed?
Available if both parents agree.

Will a custody evaluation be required?
Not specified.

Are the child's preferences considered?
No.

Statutes:
West Virginia Code; Section 48-2-15.

Child Support

Guideline model:
Melson Delaware.

Whose income is used?
Combined.

How is base income calculated?
Net.

Is income verification required?
No.

Delinquencies:
Parents (per thousand): 29
Rank: 20

Statutes:
West Virginia Code; Sections 48-2-13, 48-2-15, 48-2-15a, 48-2-16, and 48A-2-8.

Addresses

West Virginia Bar Association
P.O. Box 346 (25322)
904 Security Bldg.
100 Capitol Street
Charleston, WV 25301
(304) 342-1474

West Virginia State Bar
2006 Kanawha Blvd. E
Charleston, WV 25311
(304) 558-2456

Child Advocate Office
Department of Human Services
State Capitol Complex
Building 6, Room 812
Charleston, WV 25305
(304) 348-3780

REGION III
OCSE Regional Representative
P.O. Box 8436
3535 Market Street
Room 4119 MS/15
Philadelphia, PA 19101
(215) 596-4365

Wisconsin

Child Custody

Age of majority:
18

How is custody divided?
Legal and physical separate.

Is mediation authorized?
Yes.

Will mediation be confidential?
Yes.

Is joint custody allowed?
Permitted despite one parent objecting.

Will a custody evaluation be required?
Court ordered.

Are the child's preferences considered?
Yes.

Statutes:
Wisconsin Statutes Annotated; Section 767.24.

Child Support

Guideline model:
Fixed Percent.

Whose income is used?
Noncustodial.

How is base income calculated?
Adjusted Gross.

Is income verification required?
No.

Delinquencies:
Parents (per thousand): 45
Rank: 8

Statutes:
Wisconsin Statutes Annotated; Sections 767.10, 767.25, 767.261, 767.265, 767.27, and 767.29.

Addresses

State Bar of Wisconsin
402 W. Wilson
Madison, WI 53703
(608) 257-3838

Division of Economic Support
Bureau of Child Support
1 West Wilson Street
Room 382
P.O. Box 7935
Madison, WI 53707-7935
(608) 266-1175

REGION V
OCSE Regional Representative
105 W. Adams St.
20th Floor
Chicago, IL 60606
312) 353-4237

Wyoming

Child Custody

Age of majority:
19

How is custody divided?
Legal and physical combined.

Is mediation authorized?
No.

Will mediation be confidential?
Not specified.

Is joint custody allowed?
Available if both parents agree.

Will a custody evaluation be required?
Not specified.

Are the child's preferences considered?
No.

Statutes:
Wyoming Statutes Annotated: Title 20, Chapters 20-2-112 and 20-2-113.

Child Support

Guideline model:
Varying Percent.

Whose income is used?
Noncustodial.

How is base income calculated?
Net.

Is income verification required?
No.

Delinquencies:
Parents (per thousand): 21
Rank: 26

Statutes:
Wyoming Statutes Annotated; Title 20, Chapters 20-2-112, 20-2-113, 20-6-221, 20-6-302, and 20-6-304.

Addresses

Wyoming State Bar
P.O. Box 109 (82003-0109)
500 Randall Avenue
Cheyenne, WY 82001
(307) 632-9061

Child Support Enforcement Section
Department of Health & Social Services
Hathaway Building
Cheyenne, WY 82002
(307) 777-7892

REGION VIII
OCSE Regional Representative
Federal Office Building
Room 1185
1961 Stout Street
Denver, CO 80294
(303) 844-5594

Glossary

A

Ability to earn. What a parent is capable of earning.

Ability to pay. What a parent actually earns.

Abuse. Behavior that causes physical, mental, or emotional harm.

Acknowledged father. A biological father who has admitted paternity.

Action. A legal proceeding in a court of law.

Adjudication. The act of pronouncing a judgment after evidence has been submitted.

Adjusted gross income. Gross income after making certain adjustments (such as IRA contributions).

Admissible. Evidence that may be introduced.

Adulterine bastard. A child born to a married woman when she is not married to the father.

Adversary system. The system of resolving disputes where the two sides compete instead of cooperate.

Affidavit. A written statement made under oath and filed with the court.

Allegations. The claims made by one side in a lawsuit.

Alternative Dispute Resolution (ADR). A collection of techniques that settle a dispute without a trial.

Answer. A response to allegations made in a complaint.

Appeal. A request to a higher court to review a decision made by a lower court.

Appellant. The person initiating the appeal.

Appellate court. A court that can review the decisions of another court.

Appellee. The person against whom the appeal is filed.

Arbitration. A form of alternative dispute resolution where the two sides submit the dispute to a third party, who makes the decision.

Arrearage. A past due debt.

Attorney. A person who can represent you.

Award. Compensation given by the court.

B

Bailiff. A person who keeps order in the courtroom

Bench trial. A trial conducted by a judge without a jury.

Best interests of the child. The legal standard used to guide decisions about child custody and child support.

Bias. An inability of the judge to make an impartial decision.

Brief. A written statement containing facts and law that support an argument in a case.

Burden of proof. The standard by which a case is decided. The duty to prove a fact in dispute.

C

Calendar. The list of cases with the day and time to be heard.

Caption. The heading on a court paper. The caption contains the names of the parties, the name of the court, the case number, and the title of the document.

Case law. Law based on prior decisions.

Case-in-chief. The main body of evidence presented during a trial.

Case. A legal dispute.

Cause of action. The facts or legal theories that form the basis for the lawsuit.

Certiorari. An order allowing an appeal.

Chambers. The judge's office.

Change of venue. The act of moving a lawsuit to another court in the same county or district.

Child care credit. A credit for parents who pay someone to care for their child so they can work or look for work.

Child custody. The right to raise the child and/or to decide how the child is raised.

Child support. The money one parent pays the other for the care and welfare of the children.

Child support guidelines. A mathematical formula used to calculate how much money one parent should pay the other.

Citation. A reference to a legal source, such as a case, statute, or treatise.

Claim. An assertion made by the person who is suing.

Complainant. The person who initiates the lawsuit. Also, petitioner or plaintiff.

Complaint. The first document in a lawsuit that states what the plaintiff is suing for.

Conciliation. A form of alternative dispute resolution where a neutral person helps the parties settle their dispute.

Contempt of court. Behavior intended to obstruct a court order.

Contingency fee. A legal fee based on the outcome of the case.

Continuance. The act of postponing a legal proceeding to a later date.

Counsel. An attorney.

Counterclaim. A complaint made by the defendant against the plaintiff.

Count. A statement in a complaint or petition claiming a specific legal violation or injury.

Clerk. A court employee who may maintain the record of court proceedings, file documents, or assist the judge.

Court costs. Additional expenses in a lawsuit beyond those charged by a lawyer.

Court papers. Papers filed with the court related to the lawsuit.

Court reporter. An official who records the discussions and proceedings in a hearing, deposition, or trial.

Court rule. Rules created by the court to handle administrative details.

Cross-examination. The questioning of a witness by the opposing side.

Custodial parent. The parent who is primarily responsible for raising the children.

D

Decision. A judgment made by the court.

Decree. A decision or order of the court.

Deductions. Expenses that are subtracted from gross income.

Default judgment. The judgment made when the defendant fails to respond.

Defendant. A person being sued.

Dependent. A person supported by someone else.

Dependent exemption. A tax deduction for a dependent.

Deposed. The act of being questioned under oath.

Deposition. An oral statement made under oath.

Direct examination. The questioning of a witness by the party who called the witness.

Discovery. The process of gathering information to present at a hearing or trial.

Dispute. The conflict that the court is being asked to resolve.

Divorce. A legal decision that ends a marriage

Docket. A record containing the list of the court proceedings.

Due process. The administration of law through the court system.

E

Earned income. All the income you get from working.

Emancipation. When a minor child demonstrates freedom from parental control, and the parents have no more obligations to the child.

Equitable parent. A parent who is not the biological or adoptive parent, but who nevertheless may be granted custody or visitation.

Equitable relief. A remedy meant to make amends for an injury.

Evidence. Proof presented to the court that supports allegations.

Ex parte. A procedure that allows only one side in a dispute to address the court.

Exemptions. A tax deduction for a person.

Exhibit. Physical evidence used to prove a point.

Expert. A person who is a recognized authority. An expert witness is allowed to give his or her opinion in court.

F

Fact finder. In a bench trial, the role of the judge to decide what evidence will be accepted.

Family law. The body of law involving marriage, separation, custody, support, and so on.

Family support. A taxable form of support combining child support and spousal support into one payment.

Federal Parent Locator Service (FPLS). A service run by the Office of Child Service Support Enforcement (OCSE) to help locate parents who owe child support.

Filing status. The category of tax filer you are.

Financial statement. A court paper containing a parent's income and expense information.

Finding. A decision made by a judge.

Full faith and credit. The legal principle requiring a judge in one state to enforce a decision made by a judge in another state.

G

Garnishment. A proceeding in which a debtor's money or property is seized to pay a debt.

Gross income. Generally, all the money you receive.

Guardian. A person appointed by the court to be responsible for a child.

Guardian ad litem. A person appointed by the court to represent a child in a legal matter.

Guideline. A standard method for determining child support.

H

Hardship. When a person suffers extreme losses.

Head of household. The filing status of a person who maintains a home for a dependent and is not married.

Hearing. Any court proceeding where testimony is given or arguments are heard.

Hearsay. An out-of-court statement offered to prove something.

Hostile witness. A witness who is antagonistic to the party who called him.

I

Illegitimate child. A child born to parents who are not married.

Impeachment. The act of undermining the credibility of a witness.

In camera. A private discussion in the judge's office.

Inadmissible. Evidence that is not allowed to be introduced.

Injunction. An order requiring someone to do something, or preventing someone from doing something.

Interlocutory. Temporary orders.

Interrogatories. Written questions one side asks the other.

Issue. The items being disputed.

IV-D agency. A government agency that handles child support enforcement.

J

Joint custody. An arrangement allowing for mutual sharing of the children. Joint legal custody involves shared decision making, and joint physical custody allows for equal time with the children.

Judge. The official who presides over a courtroom.

Judgment. The official decision of a court.

Jurisdiction. A court's authority to hear a case.

L

Lawsuit. A legal proceeding that settles a private dispute between two people.

Leading question. A question that suggests how a witness should answer.

Legal custody. The right to make major decisions for the child.

Legal father. A man recognized by law as the father.

Lien. A claim against property designed to stop a sale of transfer until the debt is paid.

Litigant. A person involved in a lawsuit.

Litigation. The process of pursuing a lawsuit.

M

Material evidence. Evidence that is relevant to the dispute.

Mediation. A form of alternative dispute resolution where the two sides meet with a third person who tries to help them resolve the dispute.

Memoranda of law. A written argument that supports a motion.

Memorandum of understanding. A document that identifies the decisions reached in negotiation.

Mental health professional. A psychiatrist, psychologist, marriage counselor, or licensed social worker.

Merits. The essential issues in a case.

Modification. When a court revises an existing order.

Motion. A formal request to a court for an order or ruling.

N

Neglect. Ignoring a child's needs.

Negotiation. The attempt to resolve a dispute through discussion.

Net income. Gross income minus allowable expenses.

New mate. A new spouse or partner.

Noncustodial parent. A parent who is not responsible for raising the children.

Notice. The official notification that a lawsuit has been filed.

Notice of appeal. A court document that indicates a party is appealing the decision.

Notice to produce. A court document that requires the other party to deliver evidence.

O

Objection. The act of protesting a statement made in court. Objections are sustained or overruled.

Obligation. A requirement to pay money.

Obligee. The person who is owed the money.

Obligor. The person who must pay the money.

Office of Child Support Enforcement (OCSE). A government agency that helps locate absent parents, establishes paternity, and establishes and enforces child support obligations.

Officer of the court. A court official. Judges, court clerks, and lawyers are all officers of the court.

Offset. Money deducted from a person's income tax refund to pay a court judgment.

Opinion. The written explanation of a court decision.

Oral argument. The time when a party can verbally summarize the dispute to the judge.

Order. Instructions from the court.

Order of protection. An order forbidding one person from harming another.

P

Paralegal. Someone other than an attorney with legal skills.

Parties. The people in a lawsuit.

Paternity action. A lawsuit designed to identify the father.

Perjury. A false statement made under oath.

Personal exemption. A tax deduction you may claim for yourself.

Personal jurisdiction. The authority of the court to make orders involving someone.

Petition. A court document requesting something.

Petitioner. The person who files a lawsuit. Also, plaintiff.

Physical custody. The right to have the children live with you.

Plaintiff. The person who files a lawsuit. Also, petitioner.

Pleading. A court document that outlines the issues in a dispute.

Prayer. The part of a petition that describes what the person wants the court to do.

Precedent. The decision in a case that influences future cases that are similar.

Prejudice. When a judgment is made with prejudice, the issues cannot be relitigated. When a judgment is made without prejudice, the issues may be retried.

Prejudicial error. A mistake made in a decision that by a court that justifies a reversal by an appellate court.

Preponderance of the evidence. The standard used to decide civil disputes.

Presumed correct. The guideline amount of child support assumed to be correct.

Presumed father. A man assumed to be the father unless he proves otherwise.

Pretrial conference. A meeting before trial between the judge and the attorneys.

Primary caretaker. The parent who provides most of the daily care for the child.

Propria persona. Pro per and pro se are Latin terms that describe individuals who represent themselves.

Q

Quash. A decision to void or cancel a court order or judgment.

R

Rebuttal. Arguments or evidence used to disprove.

Record. All papers filed with the court, including documents, evidence, and transcripts.

Recusal. When a judge removes himself from a case.

Redirect examination. The questioning that follows cross-examination.

Relevant. Evidence which directly addresses an issue.

Remand. When a higher court returns a case back to a lower court.

Remedy. The way a court can make amends for an injury.

Rent-a-judge. A private judge hired by the parties to resolve the dispute.

Reply. The response to a pleading.

Res judicata. A question that has already been settled and cannot be relitigated.

Residence. Where someone lives.

Respondent. The person being sued.

Response. A court document that answers the allegations made in a complaint.

Retainer. Money paid to a lawyer for future work.

Reverse. When a higher court cancels a lower court's decision.

Revised Uniform Reciprocal Enforcement of Support Act (RURESA). A revised version of URESA that makes it easier to establish and enforce child support obligations across state lines.

Rules of evidence. Legal standards that establish what type of evidence can be heard.

S

Sanction. A penalty for violating a court order.

Service. The official delivery of a legal document.

Settlement. When the two sides come to an agreement without a trial.

Settlement agreement. A written agreement between the two sides.

Show cause. An order requiring someone to appear in court.

Significant change of circumstance. The minimum requirement for changing an existing court order.

Single. The filing status of a person who is not married and has no dependents.

Sole custody. An arrangement where the children are raised by only one of their parents.

Split custody. An arrangement where the time with the children is divided between the two parents.

Standard of living. The relative comfort the children were accustomed to before the parents separated.

Standing. The right to sue or join a lawsuit.

Statute. A law created by the legislature.

Stay. A court order that stops the enforcement of a court order.

Stipulation. An agreement between the two sides in a lawsuit.

Strike. An order to remove improper evidence from the court record.

Subject-matter jurisdiction. The authority of the court to decide a particular type of case.

Subpoena. A court order requiring someone to appear and give testimony.

Subpoena Duces Tecum. A court order requiring someone to provide documents or evidence.

Summary judgment. An order that decides a case before the trial begins.

Summons. The notice informing someone that he or she is being sued, the location of the court, and when the matter will be heard.

T

Taxable income. Your income after reducing it by claiming various exemptions, credits, and deductions.

Temporary restraining order (TRO). An order that prohibits someone from doing something until a hearing can be held.

Testimony. A statement made under oath.

Transcript. A written record of court proceedings.

Trial. A court hearing when a judge listens to evidence and decides issues in dispute.

Trial memorandum. A document that presents the facts and arguments in a case.

U

Uniform Interstate Family Support Act (UIFSA). A uniform law that strengthens child support enforcement across state lines by preventing the second state from altering the amount of support ordered by the home state.

Uniform Reciprocal Enforcement of Support Act (URESA). A uniform law that makes it easier to collect child support from a parent who lives in a different state.

Unwed father. A father who is not married to the mother.

V

Venue. A place where a trial can be held.

Visitation. The time a noncustodial parent spends with the children.

W

Wage assignment. An automatic deduction from wages to pay a debt, such as child support. Also wage withholding.

Weight of evidence. The preponderance of credible evidence.

Witness. A person who testifies under oath.

Writ. A court order requiring someone to do something.

Index

About the Author

Webster Watnik is a writer living in southern California. After earning a Master's degree at USC, he began a career writing interactive multimedia for personal computers. Soon after, he was drawn into a custody battle over his son. During the course of the litigation, he decided to write a book to help other single parents understand the issues involved in sharing their children.

The author is available for speaking engagements. Please contact him at:

Single Parent Press
P.O. Box 1298
Claremont, CA 91711
(909) 624-6058 phone
(909) 624-2208 fax

Single Parent Press

Name
_____

Address
_____

City _____ State _____ Zip _____

Phone / Fax _____ Email _____

I Would Like to Order

Quantity	Title	Price	Total
	Child Custody Made Simple	$21.95	
		Subtotal	
		Tax (CA add 8.25%)	
		Shipping	
		TOTAL	

Payment Method

☐ Check   ☐ Visa   ☐ MasterCard   ☐ American Express

Card Number _____ Expiration Date _____

Signature _____

Make checks payable to *Single Parent Press*. Please do not send cash.

Shipping

$3.50 One item
+$1.00 Each additional item

To Order

Phone   (909) 624-6058
Fax   (909) 624-2208
Email   Order@divorcebookstore.com

Single Parent Press, P.O. Box 1298, Claremont, CA 91711